Workshop of the World

Workshop of the World

Essays in People's History

Raphael Samuel

Edited by John Merrick

VERSO

London • New York

First published by Verso 2024
© Raphael Samuel 2024
Introduction © John Merrick 2024

1 3 5 7 9 10 8 6 4 2

Verso
UK: 6 Meard Street, London W1F 0EG
US: 388 Atlantic Avenue, Brooklyn, NY 11217
versobooks.com

Verso is the imprint of New Left Books

ISBN-13: 978-1-80429-280-8
ISBN-13: 978-1-80429-283-9 (US EBK)
ISBN-13: 978-1-80429-282-2 (UK EBK)

British Library Cataloguing in Publication Data
A catalogue record for this book is available from the British Library

Library of Congress Cataloging-in-Publication Data

Names: Samuel, Raphael, author. | Merrick, John (Writer), editor.
Title: Workshop of the world : essays in people's history / Raphael Samuel
 ; edited by John Merrick.
Description: London ; New York : Verso, 2024. | Includes bibliographical
 references. | Summary: "Workshop of the World brings the full range and
 depth of Samuel's historical writing on nineteenth-century Britain to
 the fore"-- Provided by publisher.
Identifiers: LCCN 2023024982 (print) | LCCN 2023024983 (ebook) | ISBN
 9781804292808 (paperback) | ISBN 9781804292839 (US ebook) | ISBN
 9781804292822 (UK ebook)
Subjects: LCSH: Great Britain--History--19th century. | Great
 Britain--History--19th century--Historiography.
Classification: LCC DA530 .S26 2024 (print) | LCC DA530 (ebook) | DDC
 941.0072/2--dc23/eng/20230613
LC record available at https://lccn.loc.gov/2023024982
LC ebook record available at https://lccn.loc.gov/2023024983

Typeset in Sabon by MJ & N Gavan, Truro, Cornwall
Printed and bound by CPI Group (UK) Ltd, Croydon, CR0 4YY

Contents

Introduction

The Making of a People's Historian

John Merrick

There is a video of Raphael Samuel, one of the most original of that remarkable generation of historians within the British left in the late twentieth century, sitting in a characteristically book-filled room, his unruly mop of thick black hair pushed across the crown of his head, discussing the drama of British history. The recording, short at only a minute and a half, is now on YouTube and is one of only a handful of surviving recordings of that famously captivating lecturer.

'If you want to understand Britain between the two wars', he says, his eyes bright with the enthusiasm and attentiveness that marked the 'rare capacity to listen' that his widow Alison Light has suggested made him so charismatic, then 'something like the ballroom dancing craze of the 1920s ... or the rambling craze, or the cycling craze' is equally as important as the major political shifts of those decisive decades. By taking seriously and understanding such fleeting national enthusiasms – everything from sunbathing to cycling – as the raw material of history, not only can we understand the changing relationship between people and nature or work, but perhaps we can also see something new in the drama of history. History from below, he says, is 'at least as dramatic ... as history from above'. 'I absolutely refuse the idea that the Treaty of Utrecht, interesting though it is, ... represents as it were the high point of national drama.'

Such was his thoroughly democratic historical vision. More than that, history, according to Samuel, was far too important to be left to professional historians alone. *Theatres of Memory*, the only sole-authored book he published in his lifetime, is a thrilling and often labyrinthine text that evokes the occult Renaissance memory theatres of its title. It explores those sources of unofficial memory that for most people constitute their historical consciousness. Historians, who spend their lives writing specialised texts, often read by none but the accredited few, have at best a walk-on part; the book's joy comes as much from its following unexpected detours and new connections as from its central argument.

It is also, as Bill Schwarz remarks in his preface to the second edition, a self-consciously open text. Samuel, Schwarz writes, 'works to minimize, at every point, the gap between the author and the printed word and between the printed word and the reader'.[1] His vast erudition and the depth of his historical understanding was not used to build new professionalised historical structures, but to tear them down. If there was an animating spirit of his work it was a deep faith in the ability, and necessity, of ordinary people to become the custodians of their own histories. His mission was nothing less than the democratisation of historical knowledge.

'History,' Samuel writes, 'in the hands of the professional historian, is apt to present itself as an esoteric form of knowledge.' It is a discipline that, with all its Rankean claims to scientific specialism, and in the hands of its ensconced elite, forgets as much as it remembers. It serves to enclose knowledge behind thick walls of academic apparatus. The professional's view of knowledge is a hierarchical one. Knowledge flows downward from its practitioners to, if they are lucky, the inert public at large. And what counts as history, and who counts as a historian, is radically curtailed.

Samuel's aim in *Theatres of Memory* is to disrupt this hierarchy, and to take seriously such disparaged cultural forms as historical re-enactment societies, the boom in period productions on stage and screen, and such miscellany of the heritage industry as Crabtree & Evelyn. What, he asks, can the late-1980s mania for bare brickwork interiors tell us about how contemporary society sees its own past? How can we read popular culture – David

Lynch's *Elephant Man*; Christine Edzard's *Little Dorrit* – as a crucible of popular memory? And just what does each say about the popular articulations of the past in the present?

There is, however, an obvious tension here. History may be in thrall to all manner of arcane questions and occult knowledges – the 'cabbala of acronyms, abbreviations and signs' that typify the discipline's professionalisation and signal to the lay reader its off-putting specialism, along with its 'dense thickets of footnotage' and fetishisation of archive-based research – but these are occult methods at which Samuel himself was adept.[2] Samuel may have sought to democratise and de-professionalise the production of historical knowledge, but as the essays collected in this volume demonstrate, the depth and breadth of his own historical writing should not be forgotten either.

Born towards the end of 1934 in London and brought up first in Hampstead Garden Suburb, and later in nearby Parliament Hill, Raphael Samuel was a committed member of the Communist Party of Great Britain from a young age. His mother, Minna Nerenstein, later Keal, joined the Party (as it was universally known to its activists) in 1939, the same year that Samuel's progressive north London school was evacuated to Bedfordshire. Minna was one of twelve of Raphael's close relatives who were in the Party, and many of his weekends away from school were spent with his mother in Slough, where she worked in an aircraft factory, or assisting with Party work. Otherwise, he could be found in Belsize Park with his aunt and uncle, Miriam and Chimen Abramsky, the latter a renowned Judaic scholar and historian of socialism with an encyclopaedic knowledge of Marxism.

His early life was, he later reflected, 'an intensely Communist one'.[3] 'To be a Communist', he wrote in a series of essays posthumously gathered together into the book *The Lost World of British Communism*, 'was to have a complete social identity, one which transcended the limits of class, gender and nationality.'[4] It was a 'crusading order' as much as a political grouping; 'the way, the truth, the light', in which members like Samuel were 'waging temporal warfare for the sake of a spiritual end'.[5] If this sounds more like an ecclesiastical order than a political party, then that's partly due to the healthy dose of the religious mixed in, albeit in stridently atheistic tones. As he writes in the essay 'A Spiritual Elect? Robert Tressell and the Early Socialists' collected in this volume, socialists had long seen themselves as a 'people apart' and a 'peculiar people' – a phrase resonant with the echoes of Christian Dissent.[6] It was, Samuel writes, often a 'kind of displaced religious longing' that drew Communists into the fold, and 'those who came to socialism in these years embraced it with the rapture of a new-found faith.'[7]

If Communism provided a faith, as well as a powerful sense of belonging, it was also an apprenticeship in learning. As Samuel evocatively recalls, Party members and fellow travellers alike were a deeply learned bunch, and the Party itself placed great emphasis on intellectual self-improvement. The work required of Party membership was met by the young Ralph (as he was then known, due to the inability of his comrades to pronounce the name Raphael) with such seriousness that, during the war years, he become 'a kind of juvenile commissar of the family', maintaining the orthodoxy of their commitment, and even giving a copy of Plekhanov's *In Defence of Materialism* to his mother for Christmas 1950. And if Party work gave him a form of belief that stretched beyond the immediate and out into the world at large, it also provided a sense of mission and an intense suspicion of the merely individual. One of the great 'folk devils' of the Party was the 'careerist', 'a species being' he writes 'of whom I am, to this day, wary'; its hero, the committed and selfless organiser.[8]

The essays in *The Lost World*, blending memoir and historical analysis with a literary skill that few other historians have managed, contain many such richly suggestive details. The focus is as much on the passing remark as the flow of narrative. As Alison Light remarks, even the essays' footnotes speak volumes, bringing together the more conventional historical source material with the quixotic: autobiographies, both published and unpublished, from Party leaders and ordinary members; the amateur poetry of cadre; posters, handbills and other pieces of ephemera; and a plethora of original interviews conducted by Samuel himself with Party veterans.[9] We hear of Iris Kingston, the unlucky comrade from St Pancras, who in 1926 was reprimanded by London District for questioning the materialist conception of history. Elsewhere, a young and eager Raphael impishly whistles the tune of 'The Internationale' on the London Underground to see which passengers might respond. There is, here, a wonderful eye for the telling detail. His essays seem to delight in piling information together into great mounds that could easily, in the hands of a less gifted storyteller, collapse, taking all with it. But Samuel seems to conjure forth whole historical worlds from the mere gathering of information.

At the age of seventeen, Samuel left King Alfred's School in Hampstead, another progressive institution, to attend Balliol College, Oxford, on a scholarship. Here he read history with Christopher Hill, the historian of the seventeenth century and fellow member of the Communist Party Historians' Group, which Raphael had joined as a precocious sixteen-year-old under the influence of his uncle. Yet, despite Hill's mentorship, the atmosphere for the young Communist at Oxford was hostile, and Samuel found the intellectual climate of the college cold. As he told Brian Harrison in an interview conducted in the late 1970s, the majority of his time at Oxford was spent, at least initially, 'as a political activist, as a Communist', helping to revive the moribund Oxford Labour Club as well as organising with the university branch of the CPGB.[10]

After a year's break in order to do Party work in London, Samuel graduated in the summer of 1956 with a first-class degree, and immediately set his sights on becoming a full-time Communist organiser. Events in Eastern Europe were, however, to intervene. Nikita Khrushchev's 'secret speech' given to the Twentieth Congress of the Communist Party of the Soviet Union took place in late February of that year, and by mid-March the news had begun to trickle through to the British press. By November, the crisis in the Party became more acute again as Soviet tanks rolled into Budapest to crush the Hungarian uprising. These events threw the Party into turmoil, and nearly ten thousand people, Samuel included, left in protest by the end of 1958.[11]

That the events that have come to stand in the annals of the left under the heading '1956' – and which included the Anglo-French imperial debacle in Suez as well as events beyond the Iron Curtain – occasioned no retreat from the political would have surprised those who lived through previous such crises. Rather, a great outpouring of political enthusiasm ensued, a result of which was the birth of the New Left, one of the more creative and consequential political and intellectual movements to emerge in post-war Britain. Barely a month after the events in Hungary reached their tragic nadir, Samuel, along with his friends and comrades from Oxford, Gabriel Pearson, Stuart Hall, and Charles Taylor, founded the magazine *Universities and Left Review*. Its first issue emerged in spring of 1957, and contained essays by Pearson, Hall, and Taylor, as well as contributions from the artist Peter de Francia, the noted British New Wave filmmaker Lindsay Anderson, the economist Joan Robinson, the historians E. P. Thompson, Eric Hobsbawm, and Isaac Deutscher, and the town planner Graeme Shankland. This heterogeneous mix of contributors, blending more conventional socialist essays with cultural criticism, would mark it out from many of the left periodicals that had come before. And, while only running for seven issues, with the last sent to the printers in late 1959, its deep intellectual and political commitment, alongside its engagement with the burgeoning youth culture of the late 1950s and its pioneering design work from future Penguin design director Germano Facetti among others, would mean that its influence stretched far beyond its limited run.

Driven by an 'activist zeal', Raphael was the organising force behind much of what the magazine achieved.[12] He was also – despite the initial misgivings of his fellow editors – the primary architect of both the New Left Clubs, whose aim was to create spaces for the discussion of contemporary politics across the country, and the Partisan Coffee House, the left-wing 'anti-espresso bar' in Soho that first opened its doors in October 1958.

In late 1959, *ULR* merged with fellow socialist magazine *New Reasoner* to produce *New Left Review*. This was edited from Yorkshire by John Saville and E. P. Thompson, both former CP members. Politically, they were a generation older than the editors of *ULR*, and exponents of a kindred form of socialist humanism. By 1963, however, under severe financial constraint and amid mounting internal pressure, the original *NLR* editorial board, then led by Stuart Hall, was replaced by a new collective under

Perry Anderson, a young historian fresh from Oxford. Samuel was to edit one transitional issue of the journal in early 1962, published characteristically late and over-length, in the brief hiatus between Hall's resignation and Anderson's appointment.

The early 1960s were something of a political caesura. Into this, many expected, or hoped, to see a new political generation emerge. Yet the cumulative effects of the political and personal crises that began in 1956 were starting to take their toll. Samuel experienced a deep crisis of confidence and, later, a near break-down. By 1963, following a bout of political disenchantment, Samuel left Britain for Ireland where he hoped to find refuge and the freedom to write history and poetry – even hoping, he later suggested, to become Irish.[13]

Samuel's stay in Ireland was a significant one. Although he found little work in Dublin, and often went hungry for lack of money, it was not a stay without reward. The research rekindled his passion for history and set the tone for much of his later work. These years also saw the germination of his particular historical and educational philosophy. This can be seen in a letter Samuel wrote to his mother at some point in 1964, not long after he returned to London from Dublin. 'When we were students', Samuel writes, 'we were terribly underground and polite, and traditional learning seemed absolutely dominant.' What was needed, he wrote, was for this 'academic cast of learning' to be broken with:

> Whether one looks at it in history or sociology or (astonishingly) in English literature, it shows the same ineffable signs. Always one is presented with a great screen of obfuscation, subjects approached so indirectly that it's the critical mind at work that matters rather than the experience, or the text, itself.[14]

So much of his writing and his teaching was aimed at removing such a screen and approaching the material directly. His work is an attempt to uncover something of the quality of life and experience as it was lived. In the often acrimonious and painful aftermath of the first New Left was the making of Raphael Samuel the historian.

It was also around this time that the historian Sheila Rowbotham first encountered Samuel at a lecture he delivered on the famine in Ireland of the 1840s, given either shortly before he left London for Ireland or soon after this return. Rowbotham, at the time a student at St Hilda's College, Oxford, writes that the lecture was 'revelatory':

> The small, skinny, dark figure with a lock of black hair falling persistently over his nose had a hypnotic aspect. Raphael kept shifting papers from one great pile to another across the table and, like spectators at Wimbledon, we watched them go faster and faster as his time ran out. His talk was a devastating *tour de force* in which he described how belief in free trade and opportunism had combined.[15]

The Irish working class, particularly those who made the move across the Irish Sea in the years after that devastating act of colonial violence, were to become the paradigmatic outsider for Samuel: a key figure, along with Gypsies, travellers, and other plebeian 'comers and goers', in his historical imagination.

Some two decades later, in 1985, Samuel published an essay on 'The Roman Catholic Church and the Irish Poor'. Based on extensive archival research conducted during the mid-1960s, the essay is a brilliant piece of historical reconstruction that takes as its object the 'moral atmosphere characteristic of the congregations of the Irish poor in England during the second half of the nineteenth century'.[16] The Catholic Church in England during these years was, Samuel writes, a 'plural church'. At one end of the social spectrum the church served the 'well-born and the rich', particularly with the addition of those newly recruited to the church via Edward Pusey's Anglo-Catholic Oxford Movement. At the other, and constituting the vast bulk of the growing number of Catholics in England, were the Irish migrant poor, attracted to the towns and cities of England by the rising demand for labour as well as the economic and political ravaging of their homeland.[17]

The essay is as much an attempt to grasp a qualitive shift in Roman Catholicism during these years, produced by the successive waves of Irish Catholic immigration and the reaction of local

Protestants, as it is to track the quantitative shift in congregations they produced. What is at stake is a social history, drawn from a diverse range of sources, whose aim is to show what a 'merely ecclesiastical history of religion is likely to neglect': namely, the social and moral tenor of the life of the Irish Catholic poor in Britain. Usually housed in the poorest districts, the Catholic congregations were crammed into small chapels, often little more than dilapidated rooms or jerry-built huts set amid the dense network of lodgings that made up the new Irish quarters of towns and cities. Their schools, founded in great numbers by the Church in the latter part of the century for the education of the Catholic children, were in many instances worse: one in Liverpool merely a room above a cowshed, another in Barnsley 'only a cellar'. Nor were the clergy hidden away in more respectable and salubrious surroundings. Priests in poor neighbourhoods lived in modest dwellings in close proximity to their congregations, and their houses often served as a focal point for the community. At St Peter's, Birmingham, in the winter of 1862–3, the priest was twice taken to remind his flock that sick calls were not to come later than 10 p.m., 'except in very urgent cases which seldom happen as those which are *called* urgent are nearly always nothing of the kind'.[18]

Many of the laity were a tough and riotous lot, ready to defend their faith with 'something of that primitive violence which made it dangerous, in the more inflammatory parts of rural Ireland, for a bailiff to serve his writ or for a landlord to reside'.[19] To this, the Catholic priests attempted to introduce some Victorian respectability, often with little success. One notable figure was Father Theobald Mathew, the Capuchin friar and temperance campaigner who became the leader of the Cork Teetotal Society in 1838. He toured Ireland, making the bombastic claim in 1842 of having delivered the pledge to some five million of his countrymen, before transferring the crusade to England.[20] Of those who made the pledge to Father Mathew that year, many soon fell off the wagon, it being 'less a decision for life ... than an interlude of remorse between compulsive bouts of drink'.[21]

Surprisingly, the essay ends with something akin to a methodological and historiographical coda. It was, Samuel writes, 'in the summer of 1966' that he first began to conduct the research for the essay, 'travelling the parishes and record offices of northern England' in search of material. The old Irish quarters of towns and cities that he encountered in those years had 'not yet succumbed to the bulldozer and the depredations of comprehensive clearance and re-development'. The Irish Catholic churches he visited 'often seemed to stand in half-deserted urban wastelands', and in taking tea with the local priests (including one who sat down to dinner 'in his tobacco-stained waistcoat') he was able to gain access to long-forgotten documents, those scraps of paper that in the hands of a skilled historian can open new historical vistas. There is, in this essay, a palpable sense of Samuel's passion for historical inquiry as well as his devotion to telling the stories of those outcast from respectable society.

The cast of characters it conjures forth includes Tom Barclay, recalling his Irish Catholic childhood in Leicester, and whose mother, brought up 'in the wilds of County Mayo', takes consolation from her difficult life in an 'old Irish lamentation or love song and the contemplation of the sufferings of "Our Blessed Lord" and his virgin mother'. Father Vere, a Soho priest, is described chasing after the truant children from the local Catholic schools – or 'child hunting', as he called it in his memoirs. There is also the group of Irishmen in Ancoats, Manchester, who in 1871 filled in their census returns in the local pub, or 'the House of Commons for Ireland' as the local newspaper called it. We even read of the oft-remembered figure of the 'turbulent Irishwoman, with her sleeves tucked up, and her apron full of stones', ready to defend her patch from the sectarian attacks of the local Protestant working class.

It is this attention to the details of life that makes Samuel's writing so thrilling to read. Yet there is a broader point as well. As Samuel wrote in a letter to his mother from a Cheshire record office:

It is often the most ordinary things which are the most difficult to rescue from oblivion, and that's one reason why history sometimes seems to be a thing quite on its own, with its own kinds of subject and reality – revolutions, constitutions, epic heroes – which have little connection with everyday life, and therefore can't be used as part of the evidence on which we try to work out a philosophy of life and of society. You have to work against the grain and bias of the documents to find the material. So simple a thing, I find in my work, as for example a man crossing himself, or keeping sacred pictures in his parlour – or meeting his fellows, or quarrelling, in a pub is infinitely more difficult to find than the exquisite points of political controversy and alignment; yet obviously for an understanding of the way in which people lived – of what people are – vastly more important.[22]

Contained here, in condensed form, are the principles that drove Samuel's work for the rest of his life.

Samuel's most comprehensive survey of the Victorian outsider comes in an earlier essay, 'Comers and Goers', originally published in the superb 1973 H. J. Dyos and Michael Wolff volume *The Victorian City*, and republished here for the first time. The essay charts the 'migrating classes' of the late nineteenth century, a capacious group that stretches from Gypsies and travellers, trailing their caravans across the back roads of rural England, to itinerant labourers, circus folk, navvies and boatmen, country hop-pickers, urban craftsmen, and the sailors of all nations who cruised the harbours and night-time pleasure strips of great Victorian ports such as London and Cardiff. This was a group who, in nineteenth-century England, 'played a much greater part in industrial and social life than they do today'.[23] Yet it was also a people who, by their very nature, left few traces in the historical record. Often their world was erased almost as soon as it was built. Their workplaces and lodging houses left behind no records, existing as they did on the fringes of legality where every written report was a potential threat, and few wrote of their own exploits. It was thus often left to the middle-class social reformers and philanthropists to document the urban and rural poor. And these sources were to be used with caution.

That Samuel recreates with such skill the world of the itinerant poor is a remarkable achievement. There were, Samuel writes, four distinct classes of comers and goers in Victorian Britain. The first were the 'habitual wanderers', often tramps who spent the great majority of the year sleeping rough, whether in town or country. The second were those who spent much of the year labouring in the countryside, but who kept regular winter lodgings in town. The third were 'fair weather' travellers who wandered during the summer season but stayed in one place the rest of the time; and fourth were those who remained in urban areas, but who made frequent trips into the country for work. These types, though, in themselves constituted no cohesive groups. Such wanderers were internally variegated, and examples of each of the four types could be found in all of the 'wandering tribes', as the contemporary journalist Henry Mayhew called them, of Victorian England. Each of them followed distinct rhythms, often determined by the nature of their work as well as the changing patterns of the weather. March and April saw the first movements out of the cities, with the travelling showmen leaving for the great country fairs and meets of the spring and summer, later followed by the first waves of agricultural workers and Gypsies. Summer saw a large exodus from towns and cities to the country, where 'there was big money to be earned in the fields, for the man who was prepared to rough it, and to try his luck on tramp' – a group that often included unemployed industrial labourers and those out on strike looking for extra income.

Also heading off 'on the tramp' during the summer season were navvies, nomads, hawkers, and dealers, as well as a yearly influx of Irish labourers and Italian organ-grinders and ice-cream sellers. August was the off-season for many industrial occupations, owing to the heat and the slackening of trade, which pushed many urban labourers out of the towns to try their luck elsewhere, and this was soon followed by the harvest months, work for which the nimble fingers of women and children gave them an advantage. The winter, on the other hand, saw the movement reverse, and with it the great wandering tribes returned to the city once again.

Samuel makes wonderful use of Mayhew's reports on the lives of the poor for the *Morning Chronicle* and his four-volume compendium of interviews and reports, *London Labour and the London Poor*, as well as the work of the social researcher and reformer Charles Booth and his multi-volume study, *Life and Labour of the People in London*. But Samuel also draws on news stories, official reports and a vast quantity of memoirs and autobiographies by labouring men and women. The picture of Victorian England in the essay is one in which 'distinction between the nomadic life and the settled one was by no means hard and fast'; rather than being the 'prerogative of the social outcast it is today', itinerance was 'a normal phase in the life of entirely respectable classes of working men'.

The end of this period, therefore, as the nineteenth century turned into the twentieth, was determined more by economic change than moral reform. The growth of labour that did not fluctuate with the seasons and the increasing mechanisation of agriculture played their part, as did the growth of trades unions. Writing from the mid-twentieth century, when the life of the wandering tribes could be imagined a distant one, Samuel wrote of his fear that such research appeared anachronistic. 'It is not easy to imagine a time', he writes, 'when men slept rough in the shadows of the gas-works, the warmth of the brick-kilns, and the dark recesses of places like London Bridge; or lined up their hundreds with tin cans or basins at Ham Yard, Soho, or the midnight soup-kitchens of Whitechapel and Drury Lane.'

During the period, roughly from the mid-1960s to the end of the 1970s, Samuel's work bore the strong and obvious influence of the discipline of social anthropology. The essay on the Catholic poor opens with a reflection on 'the changing balance of intimacy and unease' shared between a Soho Catholic congregation and its priest, Father Sheridan, who at the weekly meeting of St Bridget's Confraternity recites comic stories of Irish life, designed, he admits, to excite the 'risible qualities' of the women. This relationship between clergy and congregation, Samuel writes, 'social anthropology may explain', but the historian, lacking evidence, 'can do little more than record'. An earlier essay on the village of Headington Quarry, on the outskirts of Oxford, of which a version is published here, pushed the anthropological approach further, drawing on living memory and oral testimony to show the village community as a whole way of life.

Samuel was by no means the only historian to turn to the discipline of anthropology for inspiration. In 1963, Keith Thomas published his influential essay for *Past and Present* on the conjuncture of the two subjects, and in it he remarks that even thirty years earlier R. H. Tawney was calling for historians to acquaint themselves with the work of anthropologists.[24] Published that same year was E. P. Thompson's groundbreaking *The Making of the English Working Class*, another work hugely indebted to the field of anthropology, followed two years later by Peter Laslett's similarly ethnographic *The World We Have Lost*. Each placed culture at the centre of their historical analysis, but not culture as traditionally defined to mean the great works of a civilisation. Instead, this was culture as a whole way of life encompassing everything from folklore to trades unions, rough music to sports.

Samuel's engagement with anthropology can perhaps be traced back to an earlier period still. While editing and organising at *New Left Review* in the late 1950s, he worked as a researcher for sociologist Michael Young's Institute of Community Studies, the research institute formed in 1953 to investigate post-war social change. Much of the work conducted by Young and others at the Institute had a strong ethnographic feel, an influence that can be seen clearly in Young and Peter Wilmott's now classic study *Family and Kinship in East London*, first published in 1957 and based on research conducted by the Institute.[25] Samuel's work for the Institute came later, and made up the basis of two studies: the first on life in the new town of Stevenage in Hertfordshire, and a later one on adolescent boys in the working-class East London area of Bethnal Green that began in 1959.[26]

Both studies involved hundreds of hours of interviews with participants that aimed to get a picture of the social attitudes of those who lived in each location. Samuel initially met the work with enthusiasm. There was a humanism to this form of research that appealed to him politically and it seemed to match his vision of how society both is and should be run: the face-to-face contact with people, and the probing of personal experience from which general arguments develop. But he soon became disillusioned by the limitations of the Institute's abstract sociological vision and the orientation of its work towards public policy. To this, anthropology, along with his own burgeoning historical research, was to prove something of an antidote.[27]

In later interviews with Harrison, Samuel mentions that Erving Goffman's study of 'total institutions' in *Asylums* had made an impression on him; and Samuel's continuing focus on the concrete and particular, or (to summon a perhaps unhelpful abstraction) the human over the system, shows a clear line of influence from such works of social and historical anthropology. A 1966 letter written to his father, Barnett Samuel, testifies to the kind of effect that the infusion of anthropology had on his work, but also to the genesis of the History Workshops from the work he was doing with his students during the same period.

> Both the First and the Second Year History people are turning in first class material which they've dug up in their local reference libraries [over the holiday period], and this makes the History seminars really creative work; certainly it's encouraging the first year people to see that history isn't something you dig out of textbooks and secondary work (however scholarly) but is something which you can make for yourself if you're ready to do the work. It is marvellous the confidence with which people read papers on what they really know and are familiar with – the historical and social character of their own community: and it serves as a very natural basis for many of the most important themes of nineteenth-century history. The sociology is also quite radically improved from the injection of anthropology and folk culture. I've got one excellent folk singer, a miner, who's been admirably fusing his own interests with some of the anthropological stuff: and the seminar discussions and tutorial essays are always about real things – family, community, popular religion, social solidarity, aggression, prejudice. It also puts up lots of valuable questions to the historian.[28]

The letter gives a sense of not only Samuel as a teacher, but also of his work more generally. In the words of the historian Sally Alexander, an early student of Samuel's at Ruskin, his teaching was life-changing: 'I learnt everything from Raphael', she writes, 'though he scarcely "taught" so much as encouraged, engaged in conversation, led us to the libraries and archives.'[29]

Although never mentioned by name, another possible influence during the mid- to late 1960s was Clifford Geertz and his method of 'thick description'. As Robin Blackburn, his long-time editor at *New Left Review*, remembers, Samuel often submitted his essays with comments about how a particular paragraph 'needs further thickening'.[30] Thickening here meant the addition of further layers of reference to an already rich text, giving his writing its characteristic density of material as well as its depth and range. This approach may also have been the result of his own particular, and slightly peculiar, research method – inspired by the work of the Fabian social investigators Sidney and Beatrice Webb – in which copious notes were made on loose sheets of paper, which were then sorted, shuffled, and reshuffled to create new historical constellations.[31]

While reading Samuel's work, it often feels as though (in his own, perhaps playful, misquotation of Blake against that most Blakean of historians, E. P. Thompson) you really can 'hold eternity in a grain of sand'; that a close and detailed explication of the concrete can in itself yield the most culturally rich work of historical analysis.[32] Occasionally, an argument seems to spring forth unexpectedly from the thicket of references and archival material, resulting in sudden moments of illumination and clarity. At others, the argument remains elusive, hinted at beyond the wealth of information, and carried through by Samuel's immensely lucid prose. There are often hints of that other great miniaturist, Walter Benjamin, another writer whose guide through the pathways of modernity was the outsider – the ragpicker – sifting through capitalism's waste for the fragments of a universal otherwise hidden.

All of these influences can be seen clearly in Samuel's work on Headington Quarry, a formerly plebeian village now mostly engulfed by Oxford's outward expansion. The research on the village had its origins in a pedagogical exercise he developed with his students at Ruskin in the late 1960s. Long chafing at the restrictions of the history curriculum at the college, particularly its emphasis on the teaching of secondary material in the classroom at the expense of an engagement with primary documents and archival work, Samuel designed a series of short research projects for students, one of which focused on the Quarry – a site with easily accessible documents relating to a common rights struggle between the community and the local authorities, as well as being on the students' doorstep.

The work on the village began in 1969 with Samuel working alongside the first group of history diploma students at the college, including Sally Alexander, whose work concentrated on the local St Giles fair, and Alun Howkins, whose father was an Oxfordshire labourer and who introduced him to labourers, poachers, and travelling showmen from the village.[33]

At the start of the nineteenth century, Headington Quarry was a small, open squatters' village on the outskirts of the city. The 1841 census records a population of just 264, which was to increase to nearly 1,500 by the turn of the twentieth century. Yet even then, Samuel writes, the village had something of the feel of a squatters' settlement.[34] Even the topography of the village signalled its contested history. Centuries of quarrying for the Headington stone that provided building materials for the grand colleges had left the village a warren of ditches, pits, and declivities. As one local described it to Samuel, in one of the many oral history interviews that make up the vast material for the two essays he wrote on Headington Quarry, the village is 'all 'oles and alleys and 'ills, that's what the Quarry is, all up and down'.[35] Nor was there anything like the bucolic village green with its picturesque church spire rising above the surrounding cottages. This was, and remained long into the twentieth century, a thoroughly plebeian settlement: 'a village, a rare case', Samuel writes, 'where enclosure may be said never to have taken place'.[36]

The inhabitants of the Quarry were notoriously rowdy, prone to fighting and causing havoc at the feasts and fairs of neighbouring villages. The 'Headington Quarry Roughs', as they were known to the local newspapers, also had a reputation as poachers. 'We used to get some saucy buggers come out of different places', one former resident told Samuel; 'there was some handy blokes in this village at one time.'[37] What these people must have thought of Samuel with his shock of black hair hanging across his forehead, his accent clearly signifying his place as across the Magdalen Bridge in Oxford proper, as he sat among the drinkers in the Mason's Arms, we can only guess – but it must surely have been a strange sight.

The first fruits of this research, written up from the numerous tapes recorded with Quarry locals, many of whom Samuel found in and around the pub, came in 1972. Published in the fourth issue of the journal *Oral History*, 'Headington Quarry: Recording a Labouring Community' – included in this volume – is an engaging portrait of the village and its people.[38] It was also one of the first pieces of historical research that Samuel published.

Between the end of the first New Left in 1962 and the early 1970s, Samuel published little. Yet from then until the end of his life, a steady stream (later a vast flood) of writing was to see the light of day. From the 1970s, Samuel increasingly began to focus on nineteenth-century social history and the history of labour, culminating in one of the great pieces of historical research and writing of the decade: 'Workshop of the World'. Published in *History Workshop* in 1977, the essay showcases to the full Raphael's wealth of historical knowledge, backed by a huge array of footnotes – over three hundred in total, many pertaining to the most unexpected material, what Samuel calls 'more fugitive sources': autobiographies of working people; trade journals such as *The Trade Associations of Birmingham Brick Masters* and *The British Clayworker*; obscure historical works including the fascinating-sounding volume on *The History of Chairmaking in High Wycombe*; plus a few characteristic references 'temporarily mislaid'.

Written in his habitual supple and open style, the essay has an iconoclastic intent, taking aim at the conventional view of the Industrial Revolution as represented by David Landes's *The Unbound Prometheus*. According to this view, by the mid-eighteenth century the factory system with its infernal machines pumping out cartloads of commodities had come definitively to replace the old system of craft production. One of the key cross-over points in marking this transition was Luddism, with the plight of the handloom weavers of the 1830s written in either a heroic or a tragic key: the defiant resistance against a new and inhuman order, or the forlorn hope of a world predestined to expire.

Against this, Samuel gathers a huge quantity of both empirical data and richly sourced qualitative material to demonstrate that the advance of capitalism in the nineteenth century was not the triumphal march of progress so often imagined, but an uneven process, internally variegated and beset throughout by the kind of workplace resistance to the imposition of technology which as often as not sets the pace of change. 'In mid-Victorian England', Samuel writes, 'there were few parts of the economy which steam power and machinery had left untouched, but fewer still where it ruled unchallenged.'[39]

If the standard narrative of the Industrial Revolution, in which the juggernaut of 'machinofacture' rapidly tramples all before it, is incorrect, then what kinds of work did people actually do during this period? What we're left with is a complex and nuanced picture of labour during these decades. In describing this, Samuel guides us through the mid-Victorian economy, taking in industries as diverse as agriculture and cheesemaking, the building trades and glassmaking, and from puddlers and shinglers in the great ironworks that produced the steam engines powering industry to the cabinet-makers whose work barely moved beyond the kind of handicraft labour that had long been dominant.

Just below the surface of this historical detail is a partly concealed methodological argument. 'The materials for an inquiry into nineteenth-century work', Samuel writes with evident excitement, 'are inexhaustible', and much of them were as yet untouched. One of the principal sources for the essay was the technical literature of individual trades, then as now little used by historians, 'and it is hoped that this article may indicate something of its potentiality'. We're also told in several places, in typical Samuel style, that the essay is merely the first in a series, with the next instalment imminent. We're even promised that the essay is based on an 'unwritten chapter of a half-finished book'. This wasn't to be, and keen readers of Samuel's work will be familiar with such promises.

What we got instead was a deeper engagement with historiography, and a renewed interest in theoretical questions. Far from being merely a narrow empiricist or antiquarian, Samuel was long interested in questions of method. Never as philosophically minded as many of those who came later and who made up the second New Left, he was nevertheless a writer for whom the abstract was always present, pressed up alongside and mingling with the particular. 'Theory-building', he wrote, 'cannot be an alternative to the attempt to explain real phenomena'; but neither can historical scholarship avoid contact with abstractions, no matter how deep the historians' 'hostility to theory' may go, if it is to avoid the fragmentation of its discipline.[40] Raphael Samuel was thus a 'people's historian', but one with a very specific vision of what that could, and should, mean.

If, as he writes in his essay that traces the long arc of the term, writing people's history often meant studies of a local and specific kind – 'taking as its subject the region, the township or the parish' – then that was not always so. Its roots, Samuel writes, lay in the liberal-democratic school of history that emerged in France during the Bourbon restoration, and its practitioners included François Guizot, Augustin Thierry, and François Mignet, as well as (later and in a more romantic mode) Jules Michelet. In Britain, just a few years later, similar historiographical moves began to take place. Its antecedents lay in writers such as William Cobbett and Thomas Carlyle, as well as the myriad folk ballads and myths of popular memory, but it was not until the 1860s and 1870s, with the publication of J. R. Green's *Short History of the English People*, that people's history as a self-conscious genre in Britain fully emerged.

In this sense, the roots of people's history lie in a pre-Marxist form of writing, one that exalted the long-gone days of 'Merrie England' and the virtues of the common people. It is also one that in the hands of the political and intellectual right, such as in G. M. Trevelyan's *English Social History*, becomes 'devoid of struggle, devoid of ideas, but with a very strong sense of religion and of values': 'history with the politics left out'. In this, there is, as Samuel admits, an 'uncomfortable' overlap at times between its right- and left-wing variants. Each shares a yearning for the vanished solidarities of the past, which modern society has destroyed, and both celebrate 'the natural, the naïve and the spontaneous'.[41] If this is something that Marxists may feel uncomfortable with – and many of them have – it need not be so. People's history, Samuel writes, 'always represents some sort of attempt to broaden the basis of history'. It is, by definition, oppositional, even if it is conducted by those on the intellectual right, and to reject it is to reject 'the major heritage of socialist historical work' in Britain.[42]

To simply give up people's history and exalt in the abstract is no answer to the difficult questions that Samuel's essay raises. It served as an editorial preface to the collected proceedings of the History Workshop conference of 1979, which saw one of the more public and antagonistic clashes of the intellectual left. There, on a Saturday evening in December, gathered a crowd of hundreds packed tight in a dilapidated neoclassical church in Oxford to witness a discussion between the historian E. P. Thompson and the cultural theorists Stuart Hall and Richard Johnson over the status of theory and structuralism. Following initial remarks by the chair Stephen Yeo, Hall and Johnson presented papers that reiterated their critique of Thompson's work, notably his earlier fierce assault on Louis Althusser published as *The Poverty of Theory*. There followed a blistering riposte from Thompson that shaded into personal insult. As the historian Dennis Dworkin has noted, after E. P. Thompson's bad-tempered intervention, 'what had begun as a debate about Althusser was transformed into a debate about Thompson'.[43] It is in this context that Samuel's essay must be read, not least his concluding remark about the need for *both* theory *and* historical work in conjunction. 'British Marxism', he writes, with the figures of Thompson, Hall and others looming behind him, 'is certainly in need of the kind of nourishment – or dialectical tension – which an encounter with people's history could provide.'

What people's history has always sought to do, and Samuel's work is no exception, is to 'broaden the basis of history, to enlarge its subject matter, make use of new raw materials and offer new maps of knowledge'.[44] What that broadening means in practice is as varied as its practitioners.

The essays gathered here show what the outlines of such an encounter could be. The writer and thinker contained in these essays is at his most historically acute. The work offers no escape from the theoretical into the empirical, but rather shows his immense gift for holding the two in dialectical tension. To read the essays collected in this volume is to be reminded of the depth of Raphael Samuel's historical understanding and his contribution to history and historical thinking. More than that, it is to understand the value of living memory and oral testimony. It is to see that capitalism's rise was not the triumphal march of progress, but a bloody combined and uneven process whose messiness and meanings were shaped by the marginal, the migrant and the fugitive. It is to feel the depth of the socialist tradition in English life, rooted so often in a particularly Christian philosophy, but one which has reached out to international radical movements since the English and French revolutions and beyond; and to understand the legacies of empire entrenched in people's minds and everyday lives everywhere. From this, I hope, both students of history and the contemporary left have much to learn.

The initial idea for this collection came from Sally Alexander and the late Alun Howkins, who proposed it to Verso a decade or more ago. Sadly, I wasn't able to meet Alun in person before his death in 2018, but his work on the social history of the British countryside has been an inspiration to me over many years. Similarly, to be able to work with a historian like Sally has been an immense privilege. That my name is here, along with Raph's, is down to Sally's encouragement over the past few years. I also owe an immense debt of gratitude to Alison Light, whose enthusiasm and assistance made this collection possible. Thanks to her also for generously allowing me to quote from several previously unpublished letters. It is from Sally and Alison that the idea of my introduction came: without the two of them, I would have had neither the confidence nor the resources to do it.

In a book like this it would be remiss of me to not thank those who kindled my passion for history. I was lucky to have a teacher in the subject at school without whose passion and encouragement I would not be writing these words today. He taught me more than anyone else, bar perhaps Raphael Samuel himself, about the power of ordinary people to make and remake the world. If, by some quirk of fate, you end up reading this, Mr Turner: thank you!

Sophie Scott-Brown shared with me her immense knowledge of Samuel's work, her enthusiasm for this project, and several pieces of archival material that have proved invaluable, all of which I remain deeply grateful for. Others who have helped in the preparation of this volume are too numerous to mention, but my thanks in particular must go to Leo Hollis, Ellen Greig, Andrew Whitehead, Robin Blackburn, Gareth Stedman Jones, Tariq Ali, Mike Watson, Ken Worpole, the librarians at the London Library, the archivists at the Bishopsgate Institute, and my colleagues at Verso – along with everyone who has been kind enough to let me ramble on about my love of Raphael's writing over the years.

The essays in this collection, bar the occasional slight editorial intervention to regularise the grammar or correct the odd spelling mistake, appear here as they were first published. There are two exceptions to this. First, the essay 'Headington Quarry: Recording a Labouring Community', originally published in the journal *Oral History* in 1972, omits the opening paragraph that introduces the project from which it grew, and slightly alters the first sentence for readability. The second is the essay 'A Spiritual Elect? Robert Tressell and the Early Socialists', originally given as the annual Robert Tressell Lecture, on 16 March 1985 in Falaise Hall, Hastings, and later published by the Workers' Education Association South Eastern District in the volume *The Robert Tressell Lectures 1981–88*. This essay incorporates several small changes and revisions made by Raphael Samuel to his edition of the published text. For help with this, my thanks go to Alison Light.

Pimlico, January 2023

People's History

The term 'people's history' has had a long career and covers an ensemble of different writings.[1] Some of them have been informed by the idea of progress, some by cultural pessimism, some by technological humanism, as in those histories of 'everyday things' which were so popular in 1930s Britain. The subject matter of 'people's history' varies too, even if the effort is always that of 'bringing the boundaries of history closer to those of people's lives'. In some cases the focus is on tools and technology, in others on social movements, in yet others on family life. 'People's history' has gone under a variety of different names – 'industrial history' in the 1900s and the years of the Plebs League, 'natural history' in those comparative ethnologies which arose in the wake of Darwin (Marx called Volume 1 of *Capital* a 'natural history' of capitalist production); *'Kulturgeschichte'* (cultural history) in those late-nineteenth-century studies of folkways to whose themes the 'new' social history has recently been returning. Today 'people's history' usually entails a subordination of the political to the cultural and the social. But in one of its earliest versions, splendidly represented in this country by John Baxter's *New and Impartial History of England* (1796) – the 830-page work of a radical Shoreditch artisan, dedicated to his friends in jail – it was concerned rather with the struggle for constitutional rights.[2]

The term 'people's history' is one which could be applied, in the present day, to a whole series of cultural initiatives which are to be found mainly, though not exclusively, outside the institutions of higher education, or on their extra-mural fringes. It has been enthusiastically adopted by such community-based publishing projects as the 'People's autobiography of Hackney', whose work is discussed in these pages by Ken Worpole, Jerry White, and Stephen Yeo. Here the emphasis – as in the History Workshop – has been on democratising the act of historical production, enlarging the constituency of historical writers, and bringing the experience of the present to bear upon the interpretation of the past. A good deal of oral history work falls within the same ambit. 'People's history' is also a term which might be retrospectively applied to those various attempts to write an archive-based 'history from below' which have played such a large part in the recent revival of English social history. As a movement, this began outside the universities. One of the key texts – *The Making of the English Working Class* (1963) – was generated in the WEA classes of the West Riding. 'History on the ground', the movement immediately preceding 'history from below' – represented by such fine books as Maurice Beresford's *Lost Villages of England* (1954) and W. G. Hoskin's *Making of the English Landscape* (1955) – found its natural constituency among those who were termed, in the 1950s, 'amateur historians'; much the same is true of that kindred recent enthusiasm, industrial archaeology. Nevertheless 'history from below' has found an increasing resonance in the research seminars, and one may note a gravitational shift in scholarly interest from the national to the local or regional study, from public institutions to domestic life, from the study of statecraft to that of popular culture. Parallel shifts of attention appear to be occurring in other countries in Europe, as a number of papers in the present volume suggest.[3] In France, where there is a long-standing reading public for '*vie privée*' and '*vie quotidienne*' (i.e. the history of everyday things), and where social history has long enjoyed a far greater intellectual prestige than it does in England, the change is less apparent. Yet one may note, in the wake of the student revolt of 1968, a shift in the Annales school from a 'history without people' – a history built on the impersonal determinants of climate, soil, and centuries-long cycles of change – to the kind of ethno-history, dealing with individual experience at a particular time and place, represented by Le Roy Ladurie's *Montaillou* and *Carnival*; a new attention to outcast social groups (the 'marginal' and 'deviant'); and latterly a strong, if somewhat belated, recognition of the claims of oral history.

People's history always represents some sort of attempt to broaden the basis of history, to enlarge its subject matter, make use of new raw materials and offer new maps of knowledge. Implicitly or explicitly it is oppositional, an alternative to 'dry as dust' scholarship, and history as taught in the schools. But the terms of that opposition are necessarily different in different epochs and for different modes of work. For J. R. Green, writing in the 1870s, the main enemy was what he called 'drum and trumpet' history – i.e. the preoccupation with wars and conquest.[4] Against these his *Short History of the English People* (1877) opposed the history of English civilisations, a history of society rather than of the state. As he wrote in his famous preface:

> The aim of the following work is defined by its title; it is a history not of English kings or English conquest but of the English People ... I have preferred to pass lightly and briefly over the details of foreign wars and diplomacies, the personal adventures of kings and nobles, the pomp of courts, or the intrigues of favourites, and to dwell at length on the incidents of that constitutional intellectual, and social advance, in which we read the history of the nation itself. It is with this purpose that I have devoted more space to Chaucer than to Cressy, to Caxton than to the petty strife of Yorkist and Lancastrian, to the Poor Law of Elizabeth than to her victory at Cadiz, to the Methodist revival than to the escape of the Young Pretender.

For Paul Lacombe (1839–1919), one of the intellectual forefathers of the Annales school, the chief enemy was the notion of historical contingency, and the preoccupation of historians with individual personalities and events. As against this – '*histoire evenementielle*' as the Annales historians were to call it – he wanted history to be placed on a scientific footing and to occupy itself with causal uniformities; even when studying a particular subject – as in his own work on the family in ancient Rome – the historian had to devote the major effort to showing its place in an overall scheme of development. Thierry, writing in the 1820s, was no less opposed to the ruling historical orthodoxies of his day, but it was their abstract reasoning which he reproached them with, the 'calculated dryness' of their philosophy.[5] The alternative which he pursued (much influenced by the novels and poems of Sir Walter Scott) was that of immersing himself in medieval ballads and ransacking the documents for concrete, pictorial detail. He was, in fact, an early practitioner of what a recent writer, in another context, has witheringly labelled 'resurrectionism': i.e. attempting to bring the past to life again by listening to the voices of the dead.

People's history today is characteristically used to denote a history which is local in scale, taking as its subject the region, the township or the parish: in the case of the city, the morphology of the individual quarter or suburb, or even of the individual house and street. In the past, however, it was more concerned with the broad lines of national development. 'Whatever value this book may have', writes A. L. Morton in his preface to *The People's History of England* – a Marxist work, first published by the Left Book Club in 1938 – 'must be rather in the interpretation than in the novelty of the facts it presents ... It sets out to give the reader a general idea of the main lines of the movement of our history.' Much the same might be said of J. R. Green's *Short History* which takes its start from the 'peasant commonwealths' of Anglo-Saxon times, and moves in measured sweep across the centuries. Similarly Michelet, in his populist histories as in the profiles he wrote of his time (*Tableau de France* and *Le Peuple*), was concerned with the great collective forces shaping the destiny of the French nation.[6] He was interested in events as illustrations of underlying social processes, in individuals as representatives of movements and groups. His whole notion of society was that of an organic historically derived unity, and he saw the task of people's history as that of covering all departments of human activity, following (as he wrote) industry and religion, law and art, as interrelated threads.

The practitioners of what was called in Germany '*Kulturgeschichte*' (cultural history), and in other countries historical anthropology, cultural sociology, or the history of 'civilisation', worked on an even longer timespan. Their subject matter was nothing less than universal history, whether in the sphere of material culture, mass psychology, or popular religion. They were concerned to seek out a linear path of development, delving into

the recesses of pre-history, and tracing the evolution of humanity through savagery and barbarism to civilisation. This was
the version of people's history that was most highly regarded
in the Plebs League, as can be seen from the Ruskin student
paper on 'Worker-historians in the 1920s'. It offered a captivating sense of totality – 'not a partial history of facts ... but an
attempt ... to understand how history worked'. Müller-Lyer's
History of Social Development (translated into English in 1920)
was a favourite text, the work of a disciple of Lamprecht.[7] He
believed that everything, from the evolution of tools to the rise
of romantic love, could be reduced to world-wide uniformities:
divergences were largely accidental or of a purely local character. The worker-historians of the 1910s and 1920s followed
suit, and their histories – 'outline' histories such as Mark Starr's
A Worker Looks at History – were global in scale and universal
in their timespan, following the trajectory indicated by Engels,
and exploring the origins of family, class, and state.[8]

The main thrust of people's history in recent years has been
towards the recovery of subjective experience. One might note,
in oral history, the overwhelming interest in reconstituting the
small details of everyday life; in local history, the shift from
'places' to 'faces', from topographical peculiarities to the quality
of life; in labour history, the preoccupation with the more spontaneous forms of resistance. More generally one could note the
enormous research ingenuity which has gone into attempting
to capture the voice of the past – the cadences of vernacular
speech, the tell-tale turns of phrase which can be gleaned from
court records or anonymous letters. As in hermeneutics, the
major effort is to present historical issues as they appeared to the
actors at the time; to personalise the workings of large historical
forces; to draw on contemporary vocabularies; to identify the
faces in the crowd. Seventy or eighty years ago, by contrast the
whole attention of people's history was turned on the working
of *impersonal* historical forces, located by some in climate and
geography, others in tools and technology, by yet others in bio-
logical necessity. Its leading feature was a kind of multi-layered
determinism in which contingency could be disregarded while
necessity ruled in its stead. History was conceived as an orderly,

logical development, an inevitable passage from lower to higher stages. In a conspectus like this, there was little patience for the small details of everyday life. As a Welsh miner told the Ruskin students: 'we weren't interested in whether so-and-so had sugar in his coffee or not. What interested us was how and why societies change.' This version of people's history invoked the authority of Marx, but it borrowed freely from the positivist sociology of Spencer and Comte as also, in another direction, from Darwinian biology. Folk-life studies in this period were conducted in the same spirit using the comparative method to situate myths in an evolutionary grid. The deterministic vision is no less apparent in the 'folk psychology' of Wundt – a kind of historical ethnography of mental characteristics and in those various theories of mass behaviour which make the individual a compulsive creature of instinct.[9] The most deterministic history of all was that of human geography, which explained the character of peoples by reference to geography, climate, and soil. In France it was influentially represented by Vidal de la Blache, in Britain by H. T. Buckle, whose *Civilisation in England* figures alongside the works of Marx, Engels, Darwin, and Dietzgen in the standard book-lists of the Plebs League.[10]

As a literary mode, people's history bears the enduring marks of both the aesthetic of realism and the romantic movement in literature. The 'discovery of the people' in late-eighteenth-century Europe – i.e. the discovery of popular ballads, and the use of folk-life materials to reconstitute the ancient past – was in the first place, as Peter Burke has argued in *Popular Culture in Early Modern Europe*, the work of literary scholars and poets, seeking in peasant culture an escape from the artificialities of the salons and the courts. Later, the emergence of people's history in France is part of a very much wider movement of literary sensibility to which the label of 'social romanticism' has been attached. Many of the early writers of people's history were self-conscious literary artists. Some wrote their history as epics, like Motley in his *Rise of the Dutch Republic*.[11] Others found their poetry in the symbolical use of circumstantial detail, as Thierry put it, 'constantly filling the senses with the sharp detail of sight and sound'. E. P. Thompson's work shares both these characteristics, and his philippics against the abstractions of structuralism echo Thierry's thunderbolts against the 'calculated dryness' of the philosophers. Above all, the conceptual importance which Thompson and others give to experience – the central point at issue in the debates around *The Poverty of Theory* – is clearly derived from the fundamental opposition which the Romantics made between reason and passion, imagination and mechanical science. The social realism of people's history may also be derived from the Romantic movement in poetry and art, especially from the ways in which it was developed in 1830s and 1840s France. Michelet's *Le Peuple* (1846) – radical and democratic in its purposes, realistic in its mode – is, on this view, absolutely at one with the social realism of Victor Hugo's novels, or the peasant paintings of Gustave Courbet: a tireless search for authenticity. In today's people's history it is not difficult to see affinities to the documentary realism of the cinema, or the social realism of television drama; while in a more symbolic mode – what Isaac Deutscher has called 'Marxist realism' – an aesthetic of the socially typical, and symbolic, is no less apparent in such classics of socialist history as Marx's *Capital*, Trotsky's *History of the Russian Revolution*, or the work of Deutscher himself.

In a very different lineage, people's history may be seen as one of the oldest forms of social science. It traces one of its origins to the eighteenth-century Enlightenment, and in particular to Vico, whose *Scienza Nuova* (1725) introduced the whole notion of stages of historical development which was to be so central for Michelet and for Marx. It was Vico, too, who, in his portrait of the 'heroic states' of antiquity, first set out a paradigm of class struggle:

> The whole life of these heroic states centres in the conflict between patricians and plebeians ... the plebeians wishing always to change the state, the nobles to preserve it as it was. The patricians were better organized; they owned the land; they had the arms and the military discipline; they had a monopoly of public office and knowledge of law; they alone knew how to ascertain the will and win the favour of the gods; the solemn rites of marriage and burial were theirs alone; and they were bound by oath to keep the plebs

in subjection. But it was inevitable that the plebs should press successively for land tenure, legal marriage, legitimate children, testamentary succession, citizenship, eligibility to office, and the sharing of the auspices, the key to all the rest. And it was inevitable that the ruling class should be compelled to admit the plebs to one after another of the rights which it had at first so jealously guarded.

People's history, whatever its particular subject matter, is shaped in the crucible of politics, and penetrated by the influence of ideology on all sides. In one version it is allied with Marxism, in another with democratic liberalism, in yet another with cultural nationalism, and it is difficult to dismiss these couplings as illegitimate even where they may be mutually exclusive. The main thrust of people's history has usually been radical, yet the Left can make no proprietorial claim to it. In our own time one might note the almost simultaneous appearance of E. P. Thompson's *Making of the English Working Class* and Peter Laslett's *World We Have Lost* (1965), the one a celebration of popular insurrection, the other a Betjamanesque lament for the vanished patriarchal family of old. Each in its own way represents a revolt from 'dry as dust' scholarship, an attempt to return history to its roots, yet the implicit politics in them could hardly be more opposed.

The 'people' of people's history have as many different shades of meaning as the term has usages. They are always majoritarian, but the connotations vary according to whether the pole of comparison is that of kings and commons (as it is in J. R. Green), rich and poor; or the 'educated' and those whom Michelet called the 'simples'. In one version of people's history – radical-democratic or Marxist – the people are constituted by relations of exploitation, in another (that of the folklorists) by cultural antinomies, in a third by political rule. The term also takes on quite different meanings within particular national traditions. In France, the nineteenth-century idea of the people was indelibly marked by the rhetoric of the Revolution, the term was inescapably associated with notions of class power. In England, with its long inheritance of popular constitutionalism, it was rather associated with the defence of political and social rights. In Germany, where folk-life studies ('*Volkskunde*') provided the chief idiom for people's history, in both its radical and conservative versions, the people were defined in terms of externality, as a folk community subject to alien influences and rule. For the folklorists 'the people' is fundamentally a peasantry, for sociologists it is the working class, while in democratic or cultural nationalism, it is coextensive with an ethnic stock.

The right-wing version of people's history is characteristically a history with the politics left out – as in Trevelyan's *English Social History* – a history devoid of struggle, devoid of ideas, but with a very strong sense of religion and of values. It is apt to idealise the family – 'a circle of loved, familiar faces' – and to interpret social relationships as reciprocal rather than exploitative. Class antagonisms may be admitted, but they are contained within a larger whole, and softened by cross-cutting ties. The characteristic location of right-wing people's history is in the 'organic' community of the past – the recent past in the case of Ronald Blythe's *Akenfield*, early modern England in Laslett's *World We Have Lost*, the free German peasants before the Carolingian conquest in Riehl's *Natural History of German Life*. The ideology is determinedly anti-modern, with urban life and capitalism as alien intrusions on the body politic, splintering the age-old solidarities of 'traditional' life. In the case of Riehl, the father of German ethnology, and the founder of '*Volkskunde*' as an empirical science, the conservative implications are quite explicit. Writing in the aftermath of the failed revolution of 1848, he advocated decentralisation, a return to the system of feudal estates, and a revival of the traditional family 'in which the key virtues were authority, piety and simplicity'. G. K. Chesterton – a liberal populist turned Catholic – is more ambiguous: he had a keen sense of the dignity of the poor, and his *Short History of England* (1917) retains an anti-plutocratic edge: medieval England 'possessed many democratic ideals ... it ... was moving towards a more really democratic progress'. But there is no doubt that he regarded 'Protestantism', 'Rationalism', and the 'Modern World' as enemies; he yearned for a return to the 'lovable localisms' of the past, and in his enthusiasm for it he was apt to idealise medieval Kingship – Edward I 'was never more truly representative ... than in the fact that he expelled the Jews'; Richard II championed the cause of the peasants.

Despite their obvious differences, the left and right-wing versions of people's history overlap at an uncomfortable number of points. Both may be said to share a common heritage of romantic primitivism, celebrating the natural, the naïve, and the spontaneous. Both share a common yearning for the vanished solidarities of the past, and a belief that modern life is inimical to them; but whereas for socialists the alienating force is capitalism, in the right-wing version of people's history it is characteristically such asocial forces as 'individualism', 'industrialism', or 'mass society'. There is a certain traffic of ideas between the right and left-wing views. G. K. Chesterton's interpretation of medieval England leans heavily on Cobbett's *History of the Reformation* (1827), a proclaimedly radical work which anticipates some of the leading themes later developed, in a more socialist direction, by R. H. Tawney and Christopher Hill. Conversely, one could point to the indebtedness of contemporary Marxist and left-wing studies of 'mentalities collectives', to the anti-class sociology of Durkheim, the right-wing crowd theories of Le Bon, and even to such sinister inventions of turn-of-the-century social theory as the notion of the racial soul.

The liberal version of people's history is characteristically much more optimistic than either the socialist or the conservative, treating material progress as fundamentally benevolent in its effects. Capitalism, whether in the form of the growth of towns, the extension of commerce, or the rise of individualism, is very far from being a destructive force, but appears rather as the harbinger of moral and social advance, 'laying the foundations of that glorious and growing system which is destined, ere long, to sweep from the face of the land the last vestiges of feudal tyranny'. Modernisation is synonymous with the march of mind, the progress of civil liberty, and the extension of religious toleration. The people, far from representing the forces of traditionalism, may rather be seen as the subterranean source of change, 'a slow but always progressive influence upon the social life of the country'. Medievalism, by contrast, is equated with superstition and warfare. One of the major themes of liberal nineteenth-century history is the struggle of the medieval municipalities to achieve self-government (the subject of a massive appendix in Thierry's *Rise of the Third Estate*). Another is the emancipation of the peasantry from serfdom. While in the battle of ideas between science and religion, liberal history places itself firmly on the side of heresy and experimentalism against the sacerdotal authority of the church. The idea of nationality is pursued in a similar spirit – as a progressive assertion of liberty on the part of subject peoples.

These were some of the grand themes taken up by the French liberal historians of the Restoration – Guizot, Mignet, and Thierry – using the platform of history to vindicate the principles of 1789, and combat the mystifications of a resurgent Bourbon monarchy. Guizot and Mignet were moderate constitutionalists, championing the cause of the Third Estate by showing the inevitability of the bourgeois triumph. Thierry went a good deal further. He had started life as a disciple of Rousseau, and served as a secretary to the socialist Saint-Simon before becoming a historian. He was distinctly an innovator, using ballad literature and folk tradition to give him access to the mental world of the past, and insisting that the study of history should be based exclusively on the use of primary sources. Thierry regarded the common people – he calls them 'the masses' – as both the victims of history and its ultimate arbiters. He had a keenly developed sense of pathos (a childhood reading of Chateaubriand's *Les Martyrs* seems to have converted him to the study of history), and in the most radical and productive period of his life – the 1820s – his whole sympathy was engaged by the historically defeated and oppressed. In his *Conquête d'Angleterre* (1826) he adopted the theory of the Norman Yoke, starting from the free Anglo-Saxons and then mapping the contours of their subsequent degradation. In his *Histoire de Jacques Bonhomme* (1820) – a typification of the Third Estate through the medium of an imaginary peasant – he tells the story of a relentless series of travails.

Victim of Romans, Franks, the absolute rule of republicans and then the Empire, and finally five years of laws of exception under the Charter, Jacques Bonhomme had led a long life of servitude. In recounting these trials, Thierry made Jacques's feelings strikingly vivid; his overwhelming sadness on experiencing the Frankish invasion; his resigned fatigue as he toiled for his master; his shame as he was himself confounded with real property; his furious outrage in the fourteenth-century rebellion. Always he loved liberty; and always he suffered under conquerors.

This was a note which was to be powerfully amplified in the 'romantic realism' of the 1830s and 1840s. It was a leitmotif in Michelet's work, and it was to be given powerful fictional representation in the novels of Victor Hugo and Eugene Sue (Sue's *Mysteries of the People*, subtitled 'the history of a proletarian family across the ages', starts as an exact imitation of Jacques Bonhomme, but carries the story up to the revolution of 1848). The people's history of the 1830s and 1840s moved far beyond the moderate constitutionalism of Guizot and Mignet. It was definitely republican in its sympathies, anti-clerical, or even – in the case of Michelet – anti-Christian, and by no means uncritical of the bourgeoisie. Buchez and Roux set about the rehabilitation of Robespierre in their *Histoire Parlementaire de la Revolution Francaise*; Buonarroti that of Babeuf, while works such as Michelet's *The People* (1846), Louis Blanc's *Histoire des Dix Ans* (1841–4), and Lamartine's *Girondins* are widely credited with having prepared the way for the outbreak of revolution in February 1848. In short, the liberal history of these years moved as far in the democratic direction as the Jacobinism which it celebrated. These were the years which saw the republican Left making full use of the so-called 'Celtic' myth (i.e. the notion of Free Gaul, subjugated by Roman and Frankish invaders), and they also saw the rather belated French 'discovery' of folklore. Above all there was the work of Michelet, who combined scholarly audacity with lifelong loyalty to his plebeian childhood, growing up, 'like a blade of grass' between the Paris cobblestones. His work prefigures some of the favoured subjects of social history today – as in his writings on language, on sexuality, and on witchcraft; and the human geography and regionalist themes which his *Tableau de France* explored may be said to have determined some of the main lines of subsequent French social history. Michelet translated his democratic sympathies into a populist methodology, using folk ballads as his access to the categories of ancient law, studying folk magic for the origins of science, and using oral history as his faithful companion when exploring the recent past.

The remote origins of people's history in England are lost in that no-man's land of ballad tradition where myth and historicity cross, though it is clear from such studies as that of Rosamund Faith printed in this volume that the notion of 'lost rights' figured prominently among them.[12] Better documented, in a fine early study by Christopher Hill, is the notion of the Norman Yoke, a kind of plebeian equivalent to that idea of the 'ancient constitution' which has recently been preoccupying the historian of ideas. Hill calls it an 'elementary class theory of politics' and traces its influence first in the writings of the seventeenth-century constitutional lawyers, then in the pamphlets and addresses of the Levellers and Diggers; finally – and perhaps most influentially – in the reborn radicalism of the 1780s. The notion of the free Anglo-Saxons, with their democratic forms of self-government and people's militia, was one which sustained the English Jacobins of the 1790s, when they went on trial for their ideas. It was largely elaborated in the pamphlet literature of the time, proving the historicity of democracy and showing that it was a birth-right of which the English people had been robbed. (It appears in the lengthy passages on tythings and shire moots in Baxter's *New and Impartial History*.) The English Civil War was another great touchstone for popular radicals yielding encouraging examples of how tyrants met their doom, while in another kind of discourse, pioneered by Cobbett in his *History of the Reformation* and taken up by English socialists of the 1880s, a second age of self-government was discovered in the Middle Ages.

People's history surfaces, as a self-conscious literary and intellectual practice, in the 1860s and 1870s, when it is represented by Goldwin Smith, J. R. Green, and Thorold Rogers. Politically it was associated with the Liberal Party, especially its more advanced and radical wing. These were the years which saw the passage of the Second Reform Bill, and the first hesitant alliance between the Liberal Party and the trade unions; they were also marked, on the Liberal side, by a growing attack on the landed interest and a deliberate appeal to the 'masses' against the 'classes (i.e. the common people versus aristocratic vested interests). These were also, educationally, the first years of 'extension' classes, i.e. of university-based adult education; of the popular publications of the classics (Stopford Brooke's Primers; Sir John Lubbock's Hundred Best Books; Morley's Universal Library); and of the coming of universal elementary education. Amongst the Liberal intelligentsia one sees a very mild (and very English) version of Russian populism, with liberal academics 'going to the people' (as extra-mural lecturers), appearing on public platforms with such unorthodox figures as Cobden and Bright, and in one famous case – that of the historian Thorold Rogers – allegedly taking part in a riot. Goldwin Smith, Regius Professor of History at Oxford, took up the cause of the artisan 'against the united phalanx of employers'; C. G. Brodrick in *The Domesday of Enclosures* exposed the cupidity of the landowners. J. R. Green was the most widely read of the liberal-radical historians of this epoch, and his *Short History* came to enjoy the same kind of esteem which an earlier generation of readers had bestowed on Macaulay.

The liberal-democratic impulse can also be seen in the local newspapers of these years. They devoted a vast amount of space to local history, both in the form of regular 'Notes and Queries', and also, if more occasionally, by serialising autobiographies of local life (Joseph Lawson's recently reprinted *Progress in Pudsey*, a celebration of nineteenth-century social change, looking back to the hard times of the 1830s and 1840s, is a representative example). Another symptomatic publication of the period is the civic histories of the manufacturing towns of the Midlands and the North. In the large towns these histories are apt to be taken up with the story of municipal progress, and they may be said to reflect, in some sort, the newly formed civic consciousness of the local bourgeoisie. But in the smaller industrial towns one finds a species of what might be called 'democratic antiquarianism': books, often written by liberal worthies or radical journalists, which leaned on oral tradition, and placed a high valuation on the more plebeian elements in local life (Frank Peel's *Spen Valley, Past and Present* is a fine example). Democratic antiquarianism can also be seen in two uncharacteristic developments of the time: the publication of county and regional glossaries (the English Dialect Society was founded in 1873); and the starting of the Folklore Record in 1878. (The Folklore Society, which was led by enthusiastic Darwinians, represents another important strand in the advanced liberalism of the day: militant free-thought agnosticism).

The grand theme of this liberal version of people's history is that of democratic self-government. It is this which accounts for the utterly arbitrary but brilliantly chosen starting point for J. R. Green's *Short History* – the lyrical evocation of a 'Merry England' when three-fourths of the population were landowners and unemployed beggars were unknown; and it also provided him with a uniting thread for his subsequent chapters: the 'real life' of the English people lay in their 'ceaseless, sober struggle with oppression, their steady, unwearied battle for self-government'. This is also the focal point of his widow, Alice Stopford Green in her splendid *Town Life in Fifteenth Century England* – a 'picture', as she wrote in the preface, 'inspired by ardent sympathy' which showed a time when the English boroughs lived in a republican spirit of independence, 'a free self-governing community, a state within a state, boasting of rights derived from immemorial customs'. A similar inspiration may occasionally be encountered among the folklorists. Laurence Gomme, one of the founding fathers of the Folklore Society, editor of the *Archaeological Review*, and in his professional life, a clerk at the London County Council, found his democratic ideals realised by the open-air assemblies of the ancient Britons. His *Primitive Folk Moots* (1880) leaves little doubt about where his sympathies lay: 'These researches tell us that Englishmen of the nineteenth century are connected by innumerable ties to Englishmen of preceding centuries, before Cromwell had broken ... the fetters of feudal monarchy, before William had fastened these fetters, before Alfred ...'

A more controversial contribution to 'people's history' in this period is that of Thorold Rogers. Rogers was a thoroughgoing radical, who stood with Joseph Arch, the farm-workers' leader, during the strikes of 1872, and whose anti-Tory opinions were so pronounced that in 1868 he was run out of his professorship at Oxford. Rogers set out a programme for 'people's history' in the preface to his monumental *History of Agriculture and Prices* published in seven volumes between 1864 and 1902. Here, rejecting a history of 'constitutional antiquities', he turns instead to what he calls sometimes 'social' and sometimes 'economical' history. Despite its daunting title, Rogers's book is in fact an immense treatise on social and domestic economy. He tells us that he began work by collecting prices, 'but soon widened my research and included ... everything which would inform me as to the social condition of England six centuries ago and onwards'. Rogers was a tireless scholar who worked with zest in the archives, and brought a splendid wealth of documentation to his cause (he seems to have been the first English historian to appreciate the value of the Domesday book). He was incapable of touching a document – even the remotest statistic in a medieval building account – without it coming alive; and he also engaged in various types of 'action' research – tramping through Hampshire to track the ancient distribution of land, measuring, by his own walks, the medieval cost of transporting a sack of flour from Oxford to Eynsham. Doctrinally, Rogers never moved beyond advanced liberalism. Temperamentally, though, he was more intransigent, and his book, like Marx's *Capital*, is a tremendous historic indictment of the British ruling class. It breathes a spirit of indignation against oppression, and it is perhaps this – the felt and sustained sense of injustice – which explains why, in its abridged version as *Six Centuries of Work and Wages*, it was regarded as a fundamental text in the education classes of the early socialist movement.

The early socialists took up a different class standpoint from that of the advanced liberals, proclaiming capitalists rather than landlords as the main enemy, and identifying the people, first and foremost, with the industrial working class. But they took over the liberal-radical version of 'people's history' almost intact. Land served them – as it did the liberal-radicals – as the chief idiom for class oppression, and in their historical work they devoted far more attention to peasant risings than they did to industrial strikes. Enclosure rather than the factory system served them as the historical symbol of injustice – the great act which had robbed the English people of their birth-right; while the fifteenth century is the 'Golden Age' of the artisan and peasant – for H. M. Hyndman, Belfort Bax, and William Morris, as for Thorold Rogers and Mrs J. R. Green. Another common link was the historical taking of sides in the English Civil War, while in Belfort Bax's three-volume *Social Side of the German Reformation* (1894–1903) it is not difficult to discern an unarticulated Protestant view of history very much akin to that of the liberal-radicals. There was also a shared commitment to the cause of Ireland, and it is no accident that James Connolly in his *Labour in Irish History* (1910) pays especial tribute to Mrs Green's *Making of Ireland and its Undoing*. In France, the indebtedness of the early socialists to their liberal-radical forbears is even more apparent, both in the centrality accorded to the French Revolution, and in a common loyalty to Jacobinism which has continued to mark the 'Marxist' interpretation of the Revolution down to the present day. Jaures declared that he owed as much to the mysticism of Michelet as he did to the materialism of Marx, and in compiling his *Histoire Socialiste de la Revolution Francaise* (1890) he displayed some of Michelet's finer qualities – the appetite for new archives, the strong sense of region, the belief in the creative power of the masses, the importance attached to popular art.

The notion of 'people's history' is not one which Marxists find themselves at ease with, even though in Britain they make up a large part of its present-day practitioners. As the previous pages have indicated, it has in the past been appropriated by the Right as well as by the Left, while its philosophic roots are pre-Marxist. People's history is very often backward-looking while socialism, in principle, is futurist, seeking – in the spirit of Tom Paine – to throw off the dead hand of tradition and to make the world anew. Again, the spirit of Marxism is critical, while that of people's history is characteristically affirmative, celebrating the creative power of the masses while ignoring (so it is alleged) the imperatives under which they labour. Marxism is concerned with the totality of social experience whereas 'people's history' (so its critics argue) takes as its optics only one point of view, 'privileging' the people as the bearers of change, while ignoring the wider determinations at work. The term 'people' is also one which many present-day British Marxists view with discomfort. It belongs, they feel, to an alien vocabulary – at its best, that of bourgeois democracy, at its worst that of the capitalist press. It is a unifying notion whereas Marxists (so the argument runs) should be concerned with identifying points of division. When applied to history it is mystificatory, lumping together artisans and tradesmen, proletarians and peasants. It can show the people as a community, but hardly as a class. People's history is also suspected of 'naïve' realism, and it is certainly true, as I have tried to indicate, that its fortunes have often been tied to a realist movement in literature, and the documentary movement in the arts. This realism, it is argued, subverts the Marxist enterprise, substituting description for explanation and privileging the visible at the expense of the invisible forces at work. The gain in immediacy is purchased by the loss of that necessary moment of abstraction which is the essence of a Marxian analysis. These strictures are sometimes amplified by derogatory references to 'populism' which in the contemporary Marxian Dunciad seems to occupy a place of dishonour somewhat akin to that of the 'labour fakirs' of old.

These difficulties are not, on the face of it, easily surmountable, but they rest in part on a false opposition between Marxism and the bourgeois-democratic currents of thought which preceded it. Marx himself was less frightened of contamination than some of his latter-day followers, and many of his political concepts are borrowed or transposed from his bourgeois-democratic predecessors. Lenin – notwithstanding his polemics in that field – was positively insistent in acknowledging the populist heritage and in 1917, on the eve of revolution, he acclaimed Jacobinism as 'the greatest expression of an oppressed class in its struggle for liberation'. It is true that Marx spoke not of 'the people' but of 'the proletariat', but in his writing the term is used in a convertible sense, and its specifically industrial component is apt to be subsumed in a wider and more indeterminate constituency, that of the propertyless and the poor. Marx may not have used 'a populist vocabulary', but the working class, as it appears in his thought, is always, by definition, *majoritarian*, and in embryo indeed a universal class – one that in abolishing its own conditions of existence will emancipate humanity as a whole. Socialism, for Marx as for his followers, was a realisation of the democratic idea. The populist strain in Marxist thought became far more pronounced when – in the twentieth century – socialists and communists found themselves at the head of mass movements. In Europe, in the epoch of the October Revolution and the Third International, Communist appeals were characteristically directed at 'the broad masses' or 'the toiling millions'; while in the more moderate years which have followed the turn to the Popular Front (1935-6), Communists (in common with Social Democrats) have preferred the term 'working people' to the stricter terminology of *The Communist Manifesto*; often, as in present-day campaigns of 'the people' against 'the monopolists', they have taken on a populist vocabulary unchanged. In Italy Gramsci's notion of the national-popular is one of the historic bases of Italian communism. In Chinese communism and the Third World Liberation movements of recent years, Marxists have necessarily adopted the idiom of nationalism, in which the people are addressed as a whole.

The relationship of Marxism to people's history may be an uneasy one, but they are tied to one another as by an umbilical cord. It should be evident that Marxist historians, whether they are aware of it or not, have drawn heavily on the work of their radical-democratic forbears, as one can see from the shaping influence of the Hammonds on the work of E. P. Thompson, of Tawney on Christopher Hill, of Frazer and Jane Harrison on George Thomson, of Riegel on Antal and Klingender. Marx himself certainly practised a species of people's history, and the debt to his predecessors in this respect – Vico, the Scottish historical school of the eighteenth century, the French liberal historians of the Restoration, the German folklorists and peasant historians – has hardly been explored. His whole account of *Capital* might be described, under one optic, as a history of below – the history of a development seen through the eyes of its victims; and his chapters on 'Primitive Accumulation' in that book are very far from displaying that Olympian spirit of detachment which some of his latter-day epigones seem to regard as the quintessence of 'method'. Marx derives his concept of the 'bourgeois revolution' from Thierry and Guizot, who applied it both to the English Revolution of 1640 and to the French Revolution of 1789; and it is arguable that the 'two great camps' which confront each other in the opening passages of *The Communist Manifesto* – bourgeois and proletarians – are modelled on, or transposed from, those which confronted each other at the States-General in 1789: the privileged on one side, productive on the other. Certainly Marx's notion of proletarian revolution – that day of reckoning for which generations socialists were to look – seems to come less from his study of capitalist industry than from the Jacqueries of the medieval peasantry, and the plebeian uprisings in ancient Rome, while the universalist claim for the proletariat, at a time when, in every country but Britain, the industrial working class was comparatively insignificant in numbers, surely takes its paradigm from that age-old contrast of patricians and plebians which provided people's history – and the 'discovery of the people' generally – with its very groundwork.

For Marxists, to reject people's history would be, in Britain, to reject the major heritage of socialist historical work. The whole movement of 'history from below', and therefore if only indirectly, the present flourishing state of English social history, was incubated in the Communist Party Historians' Group of the late 1940s and early 1950s, during the dark days of the Cold War. It was there – as Hans Medick indicates in his paper – that some of its major themes were rehearsed; that its most creative practitioners – Christopher Hill, Eric Hobsbawm, and E. P. Thompson – did their early work; and that its most prestigious journal, *Past and Present*, was conceived, as also, if more obliquely, the Society for the Study of Labour History. In the case of the second folk song revival, and the 'discovery' of industrial song, the whole movement, from the Hootenannies of the early 1950s to the folk clubs of today, owes its inspiration (and much of its historical scholarship) to two Communist scholar-singers, A. L. Lloyd and Ewan Maccoll. Socialists have also been very much to the fore in the recovery of popular art: one need only mention the pioneering role of the Marxist art critic Francis Klingender, whose *Art and the Industrial Revolution* (1947) was undertaken in collaboration with the Amalgamated Engineering Union, of John Gorman's *Banner Bright*, the work of a printer-historian who was making banners for the labour movement before he came to research them, or of Victor Neuburg and Louis James in the 'discovery' of popular literature. Community-based publications projects – such as

Centerprise in Hackney, Queenspark in Brighton, Strong Words in Durham – usually turn out to have a nucleus of strongly committed socialists among both the writers and the co-ordinators. Women's history in Britain is to a striking extent in the hands of, or strongly influenced by, Marxist-feminists, and Sheila Rowbotham's work has given some of its themes a mass readership. It is right that such work should be submitted to theoretical interrogation, but to reject it on the grounds that it was tainted with populism or epistemologically impure, would leave us with little but such *histoire raisonnée* as Hindess and Hirst's *Pre-Capitalist Modes of Production* – a thin fare to offer the labour movement, and hardly the brightest ornament of either literary art or Marxist historical scholarship.

The notion of 'real life experience' is certainly in need of critical scrutiny but whatever its ambiguities it is certainly not one which Marxists can afford to despise at a time when questions of subjectivity are so insistently on the socialist agenda. The attempt to recover the texture of everyday life may be associated with a 'neo-Romantic intellectual enterprise' – one of the charges levelled against it; but it is perfectly compatible – if that is to be the test of scientificity – with elaborate day-charts and passionless prose.[13] Among Marxist and feminist historians it has arisen from a radical discontent with the use of categories which remain wholly external to the object they purport to account for. For the women's movement it is plainly a political decision; not a question of investigating trivia, but a way of challenging centuries of silence. It is unclear why a preoccupation with the material practices of everyday life or for that matter the structure of popular belief – is either Utopian or undesirable from a Marxist point of view. Nor is there any reason to counterpose the personal and the familial with global, overall views. In most of the periods with which historians deal, the home has been the principal site of production, the family the vector of property and inheritance, the locality a universe of class. Hans Medick, in his work on 'proto-capitalism', has shown that it is only by reconstructing the life cycle of domestic workers, and the material deprivations under which they worked, that one can understand the base, in production, of primitive capitalist accumulation; and it seems possible that the work of Marxist-feminist historians, centring on the interrelationship of family, work, and home, will have a comparably radical effect on our understanding of class formation and class consciousness. It is of course possible for a preoccupation with the everyday to degenerate into a catalogue of inanimate objects. But work such as Ronald Fraser's *Blood of Spain*, or Luisa Passerini's article on Turin workers under fascism shows that, ambitiously handled, an understanding of subjective experience and everyday social relationships can be used to pose major questions in theory.

British Marxism is certainly in need of the kind of nourishment – or dialectical tension – which an encounter with people's history could provide. Too often, in theory as in political practice, its propositions have been impoverished by the fact that they have remained locked in their own conceptual world, as though designed to keep reality at bay rather than to engage with it. A history of capitalism 'from the bottom up' might give us many more clues as to the sources of its continuing vitality than debates on the law of value, necessary and illuminating though these may be; a discussion of lordship or chivalry in the Middle Ages or of, say, the peasant roots of individualism might do more for our theoretical understanding of ideology and consciousness than any number of further 'interpellations' on the theme of 'relative autonomy'; and indeed it is unlikely that we shall ever be able effectively to combat bourgeois ideology until we can see how it arises in ourselves, until we explore the needs and desires it satisfies, and the whole substratum of fears on which it draws. Our understanding of socialism too might be less abstract, if we were to explore it historically 'from the bottom up', looking at its secret languages, its unarticulated passions, its cognitive unconscious and dissonances. Above all, the questions posed by feminism leave no category of Marxist historical analysis unscathed, and it is one of the strengths of people's history that it provides a far more hospitable terrain for asking them than more abstract analytic planes. People's history also has the merit of raising a crucial question for both theoretical and political works – that of the production of knowledge, both the sources and its ultimate point of address. It questions the existing intellectual division of labour and implicitly challenges the professionalised monopolies of knowledge. It makes democratic practice one of the yardsticks by which socialist thought is judged, and thus might encourage us not only to interpret the world, but to see how our work could change it.

On the other side of the coin, it is also true that people's history needs, or at any rate would benefit from, a more sustained encounter with Marxism. If it is to achieve the aim implicit in its title – that of creating an alternative, or oppositional history – then it has to link the particular to the general, the part to the whole, the individual moment to the *longue durée*. To write a history of the oppressed – one of its abiding inspirations – needs an understanding of the totality of social relations, while that of marginal social groups, one of its more recent preoccupations (e.g. bandits, outcasts, heretics), can only be understood in terms of centre–periphery relationships. Working lives – one of the major subjects of community-based people's history – need to be situated within the wider social and sexual division of labour and the ideologies clustering around the notions of (say) skill and masculinity; family reconstitution, if it is to do more than computerise nuclear households, must address itself to those questions of power, patriarchy, and property relationships which Marxist feminists have so insistently raised. Popular culture, if it is not to be cut up by students of 'leisure' and 'recreation', needs to be discussed in relation to those questions of symbolic order and non-verbal communication which structural linguistics have raised, as well as to that changing balance of the 'public' and the 'private' spheres which, in this volume, Catherine Hall discusses in relation to notions of femininity.[14] Again, if we are to learn from life histories, whether in the form of oral history or written autobiography, we need a theoretically informed discussion of both language and oral tradition if we are to avoid misconstruing the words that we record. That is, that we have to ask ourselves theoretical questions about popular memory and historical consciousness, to take into account the double character of the spoken word – what it conceals as well as what it represses – and to build our understanding from such dualities.

Left to itself, people's history can enclose itself in a locally defined totality where no alien forces intrude. It can serve as a kind of escapism, a flight from the uncertainties of the present to the apparent stabilities of the past. But it can also suggest a strenuous programme of work, an attempt to change our understanding of history as a whole.

Headington Quarry

Recording a Labouring Community

I want to start by quoting Ronald Blythe's *Akenfield*.[1] 'Evidence of the good life', he says, 'is there for all to see.' He goes on to characterise the village: 'a tall church on the hillside, a pub selling the local brew, a pretty stream, a football pitch, a handsome square vicarage with a cedar of Lebanon shading it, a school with a jar of tadpoles in the window, three shops with doorbells, a Tudor mansion, half a dozen farms and a lot of quaint cottages'. Akenfield, on the face of it, is the kind of place in which an Englishman has always felt it his right and duty to live. It is, he says 'patently the real country, untouched and genuine'. Here we have note of the national village cult which is constantly sounded in country books.

Headington Quarry had none of these Arcadian regularities celebrated by Blythe. The whole setting was make-shift and extempory. The village had grown up higgledy-piggledy, with no ivied church or village green to serve it as a focus; no regular pattern of lanes, such as can be seen fairly clearly on the Ordnance Survey maps, but a maze-like multitude of alleyways and paths, whose obscurity contributed to the legendary difficulties faced by the County Police when they ventured into the village. Sand pits, working or abandoned, twisted and turned the physiognomy of the village into ups and downs and waste, and indeed it seems to have been known in the mid-nineteenth century under the expressive name of Headington Quarries. Development of the brick-making industry during the second half of the nineteenth century, with its attendant trail of diggings, added a fresh perimeter of waste. No pretty stream coursed through the village, though abandoned clay pits filling up with water provided the village horse keepers and donkey owners with a liberal supply of ponds. The approach to the village was marked neither by meadow land nor leafy lanes, but by the smoking brick kilns of Titup on one side, sand pits and the Union Work Castle on the other. The vicarage, though handsome enough, was invisible to villagers by reason of its trees, which nevertheless barely separated it from the village pit on the other side of Quarry Road, a sand pit where blasting and explosives went on until 1914. On the other side were the clay hills, where the lime pits were said to be burning day and night. There were no shops in Quarry, with or without doorbells, down to a very late date. A pork butcher was the first to come. As for the village school, no tadpoles were displayed in its windows because in 1897, according to the school log book, they had to be blocked up to protect the classroom from the epidemic of stonethrowing by the more unruly Quarry children.

Open villages like Headington Quarry often originated in a squatter's settlement on the wastes, and the physical layout of the village continued to reflect the original conditions of settlement long after the title to land or dwelling had been secured. Cottages were much more scattered than in the nucleated manorial village, and sometimes they belonged to the natives themselves. Flora Thompson's *Lark Rise to Candleford* in North Oxfordshire describes a squatters' village enclosed in the 1850s – in the 1880s the hamlet consisted of about thirty cottages, not in rows but dotted anywhere in a more or less circular group. A deeply rutted cart track surrounded the whole and separate houses or groups of houses were connected by a network of pathways. Similarly in Headington Quarry, the village presented an appearance that was highly irregular with pits and hollows and strange peculiarities of level. Centuries of quarrying had turned an originally flat terrain into a warren of sudden declivities which even today fills the visitor with surprise, all holes and valleys and hills. Quarry seems to have been settled in the interstices of these manmade irregularities. Some cottages were built along the bottom of the pit, like those that can be seen today, presenting their roofs almost on a level with the pavement. Others were built into the sides, and yet others were perched alone on solitary mounds and levels.

There is another stereotype of the English village almost as widely held amongst the historically minded, and, as Ronald Blythe says, 'among manufacturers of picture postcards'. It is that of the forelock-pulling Hodge and his masters in the nineteenth-century village, the parson and the squire. You find it in the story of enclosure and the accounts of the last labourer's rising by the Hammonds; and so to the repression meted out to the agricultural labourer's union in the lockout of 1874. This account makes much of the tied cottage, the target of strenuous trade union and labour party campaigns in the present century, but arguably a much less characteristic feature of the nineteenth-century labourer's life. In this version, the story of the nineteenth-century village is one of almost unrelieved deference and servitude, punctuated only by an occasional and doomed revolt. Once again Headington Quarry offers a significant exception, for here one sees a village, a rare case, where enclosure may be said never to have taken place. Common land and wastes remained an integral part of the village's economy down to the memory of living man. And opposition to enclosures and property encroachments, where they were attempted, was by and large successful on account of the strength of the village's collective resistance as well as the peculiarities and difficulties of the terrain. Quarry had no parish church until 1861, no mansion house. At the time of the 1841 Census the village contained not a single person who might have been recognised in polite society as a gentleman. There was no servant-keeping household in the village. In 1851 only one appeared; in 1861 there were two. The number seems to have slightly increased in the following years, but the village is described by the Reverend C. F. H. Johnson in appealing for diocesan funds in 1897 as of almost wholly proletarian population. He claimed that in a population of 1,300 there were only three tolerably large houses of which one was almost always unlet, and the inhabitants were almost all working men, half of them being employed in the brick yards, most of the rest being bricklayers, carpenters, and in the building trade. The appearance during the last quarter of the nineteenth century of a house which proclaimed itself 'the

Manor' by no means betokened the late arrival of a landowning presence. The title seems to have been a mere fancy on the part of its owner John Coppack, a brick-master. The Manor consisted of no more than two old cottages put together and surrounded by a wall, and the scene upon which it looked out was Tommy Trafford's coal heap. This would be the first object to strike the observer's eye; a little further down was Piggy Baker's yard, and below that the Mason's Arms – the most plebeian of the four village pubs, with a fish and chip shop housed in a shed at the back, a sweet shop in the middle and a one-room parlour in the front, that is in the Edwardian years. In the middle distance was the Cuddestone College washing which Charlotte Webb took in. And the most conspicuous feature in winter time from Quarry Manor would be the gypsy wagons, as they regularly camped in the Mason's pit. Nell Appletree – who had held the manor in the years immediately before 1914, succeeding John Coppack – 'Squire Appletree' as he was sportingly called in the local pub – was a far from aristocratic man. He is said to have been a love-child and spent his early years as a working bricklayer, before inheriting the Manor from John Coppack. He is remembered as being alternatively a bit of a scallywag, and a farming type, and found his drinking companions in the bar parlour of the Six Bells. Quarry's surrounding farms, if they qualify for that name, for smallholdings would be a better description, shared in the village's fundamentally plebeian character. Only one farm in the 1861 Census was recorded with farm labourers, and at the turn of the century there were none. Instead there was a succession of small working farmers working the land as a source of immediate livelihood, rather than for surplus or for profit. 'It was just a scratch', I was told by Bill Trafford, who spent his early boyhood on Quarry farm.

In Quarry, losses as well as gains seem to have been curiously short-lived. No dynasty of brick-masters appears even in the heyday of the industry when bricks were needed for North Oxford's great expansion. Some of the brickyards were no more than one-generation ventures combined with farming, like that of Simeon Phipps, a man who was in trouble with the School Board in the 1870s for failing to send his children to school, and who in later years was said to have taken to drink. Another factor, which sometimes reinforces class status but in Quarry seems rather to have broken it down, was that in every family, even Coppack's, there was a variety of near relatives, from a man who was fairly poor to another who had an orchard and some money. As for quality labourers, there was little deference demanded by the local circumstances. Some of them were self-employed for part of the year, and in Edwardian times none except for boys in the three or four years after school worked as regular farm servants.

In the nineteenth century there were other villages like this, with no great resident proprietor, no squire or rich town farmer, but only little properties. They are often referred to, especially in Poor or Sanitary Inquiries, as open villages – a term which seems to have come into general use in the 1830s and 1840s. It does not seem to appear in Cobbett's *Rural Rides*. In a few counties they were overwhelmingly preponderant. Somerset, for instance, was a county very free from great estates, with many small manufacturers and many small freeholders, as well as much open moorland and heath where cottages could be freely or cheaply put up. In no part of the country were such places absent – even in Trollope's *Barchester*, readers will recall there was the ragged brickmakers' village of Hogglestock, which it would have required two Anglican clergymen to keep in order. Bleak and ugly, it had low artificial hedges and no woodland. The large parish included two populous villages abounding in brickmakers, 'a race of men very troublesome to a zealous parson'. And in Dickens's *Bleak House* also we read: 'I was glad when we came to the brickmaker's house, though it was one of a cluster of wretched hovels in the brick field with pig styes close to the broken windows and miserable little gardens before the doors.' There are industrial villages, brickmaker villages, plaiting villages in Bedfordshire and Hertfordshire, as well as quarry villages. They may not have the same social character, but certainly they were villages with a quite different character from that of the estate village. The open village was usually to be found at the edge of a more regular settlement and on the margin of the cultivable land, in places like Flora Thompson's *Lark Rise*. Quoting from Flora's father in *Lark Rise*, it was 'the spot God made when he finished creating the rest of the earth'. Many of them are not in fact villages at all but hamlets and ends, little clumps of dwellings, cottages or quite often cabins built to a very modest scale and settled on roadside strips. The wayside hamlet was very common because of the ease of squatting on roadside waste. There were two of them on Headington Quarry, one at Titup on the old London road and another by the Workhouse on the main London road, which has just been pulled down.

At Swanbourne in Buckinghamshire, the Children's Employment Commissioners noted in 1867, 'there are five low thatched and very poor cottages on the roadside. The rent for three of them one shilling per week, and two of them a penny the rent of their ground.' At Beachampton nearby there were more wretched hovels built by a squatter on the roadside adjoining Lord Carrington's property. The hamlet of Fivehouses in Cassell (Leicestershire) which Dr Hunter visited in 1864 was a little more substantial, but built up entirely of encroachments of the green roadside of old Watling Street, 'the little owners have to carry water about 200 yards up the hill and though they only average three in a cottage, the accommodation is insufficient and miserable'.[2]

A very interesting little roadside hamlet appears in some detail in the reporting of the Matfen Murder in Northumberland in October 1855. It was a place known as Waterloo in the parish of Stamfordham and was in the ownership and part occupation of Dorothy Bewick, a farmer's daughter.[3] The place had the reputation of being in the semi-permanent occupation of vagabond tribes, among them the Conroys, the family of besom makers who were charged with and then acquitted of Dorothy Bewick's murder. This little hamlet Waterloo consisted of about five small cottages adjoining the road. The property was in such bad repair that the owner, who was a farmer working with her own hands, keeping two cows, some pigs, and some poultry, was never able to improve it, having laid out all her money in the purchase. Even before she went there it had obtained an unenviable notoriety, owing to the frequent disorders which occurred among the roving characters from Scotland and Ireland who occasionally sojourned in the cottages – hence its name Waterloo. In these five cottages there was one farm servant, a man who worked as a drainer for a squire in a closed village, and there were the Conroys who were besom makers and 'broom-squires' as they are called sometimes in Southern England, and who led a nomadic life hawking their manufactures about the country.

Squatters' settlements are also frequently found at the edge of heaths and commons, some of them enclosed during the course of the nineteenth century, some still open, as for example the poor little village of Potten End, skirting the southern extremity of Berkhamsted Frith near Ashridge – the bitter and indeed rather riotous opposition of whose poor population Lord Brownlow had to face when he attempted enclosure in 1866. The Dorset Heaths, that vast expanse of moorland which stretches from Dorchester to Bournemouth, were fringed with little squatters' settlements, and so were the heaths of West Surrey. One particularly interesting example is the village of Tabley, which entered into a Gypsy occupation sometime in the 1870s and is said to have continued to this day to be peopled by migratory labourers who are at the same time also smallholders, and some of them seasonal craftsmen. They travelled the countryside to obtain piece-working jobs in the summer, going to the hop districts, the market gardens near London, and to a lesser extent to the fruit districts of Kent. In winter they returned to their holdings. The Gypsy family at Hicks held a number of the properties and there is a very good description here of their different jobs.

There were also squatters to be found at the fringe of forests, including disafforested woodland. There is a fine autobiography in the Hampshire Record Office of the village called, expressively, 'No Man's Land' settled again originally by Gypsies – a Gypsy named Willett who settled there. It is on the Wiltshire edge of the New Forest, and is a classic open village of people who worked as charcoal burners and fagoters, who went out hopping into Sussex, and of others who had a cycle of different harvests in the forest: form-cutting, hollying, and a succession of other activities. The villagers were thus left entirely in command of their own cottages and their own smallholdings, which had attached to them common rights in the forest.

While some of these open villages were survivals from a pre-enclosure past, many of them were part and parcel of nineteenth-century agricultural development. In the arable counties of the Midlands and the South, closed and open villages existed in close relationship to each other, complementing one another's deficiencies. Closed villages were the squire's village, the estate villages; the open village made up of labourers supplying the deficiency of labour in the estate village, which had been cleared by an improving landlord of all its hovels and its extra population. The open villages of the arable counties were usually much larger and more heavily populated than their dependent neighbours. The process of agricultural improvement in the nineteenth century augmented that population as landlords improved their cottages off the face of the earth. At the same time the extension of cultivation and the failure of mechanisation to make much impression on the harvest work before the 1870s produced an ever-growing demand for more freelance labourers, who went out to individual harvests from their village – 'job-men' or 'strappers' they are called in different parts of the country. Men who alternated between field labour and country navvying jobs, and in winter were quite often out of work.

To conclude my last ecology of open villages, one last place where one finds them in the nineteenth century, and where, too, economic development seems to have increased both their number and their population, is on the outskirts of rural towns and at the ragged edges of the large towns and cities. Such a place as Fordington, an outparish of Dorchester, which Thomas Hardy describes as 'the Durham of all the surrounding countryside, the hiding place of those who were in distress and in debt and in trouble of every kind'. Or the little village of Kinson, a place with many squatters, four miles out of Bournemouth, where many building workers and others employed in the town in the 1860s were able to get a cottage within walking distance. Notting Dale in London, settled by some refugee pig-keepers from Marble Arch to be joined later by Gypsies and brickmakers; or Gants Fields, Newton Heath, Manchester, the haunt of the town's slate butchers when they were being harassed by the sanitary authorities. Thame in Oxfordshire seems to have been surrounded by satellites of this kind, like Headington, a very poor village, most cottages of mud and built on the waste, at all times with a bad reputation. The women walked daily to Thame for their work.

Oxford, to the east of Magdalen Bridge, was ruined by such open villages. St Clement's, an outparish of the town, and Marston, and Hillingdon were all forest towns, and although disafforestation had been carried out, they still had something of their original character. Marston in the later seventeenth century had for a time boasted a manor house, but by the beginning of the nineteenth century it had lost its Lord and been converted into tenement dwellings and an alehouse. The village at that time was then recorded as having three classes: farmers, most of them living in a frugal manner; women labourers; and paupers. Later in the century it appears as a remarkably drunken village and one which gave the local police much trouble. The labourers besieged the police in their station on one occasion, and also the university authorities on Guy Fawkes night. Cowley, or Cowley Marsh, was largely occupied by cow keepers in the later nineteenth century with the addition of an iron and steel ploughworks. Some out-of-town building workers and dairymen also lived there. A little further to the east was Wreford, quite a famous black-sheep village. It was the resort of the more dissolute undergraduates from the university who went sporting on Sunday, and the vicar, the Reverend Edward Elton, was forced in 1849 to take refuge in the neighbouring parish of Grassington, because of rough music. All these villages stand in a definite relationship to the city. In Cowley's case it was the supply of milk to Oxford; in Headington Quarry's the fact that it was the Oxford laundry, just as Kensal New Town provided for the West End of London. The peculiar moral character of each of these places was also undoubtedly affected by the fact that they were resorts for sporting under-graduates. Open villages seem to have gained a bad reputation with nineteenth-century moral reformers, as much because of the truculent character of their population as because of the sanitary defects widely alleged against them.

Headington Quarry was a place like this, down to the Edward-ian years. It had a very bad name. It was a noted haunt of Gypsies, who were well known over a wide extent of the surrounding countryside, especially early in the present century when the Webbs and the Kerries, the two leading gangs, went on their foraging expeditions with the aid of a fast-trotting pony and cart. 'Quarry was a terrible place to us kids', recalls an eighty-year-old woman who grew up a few miles away in the by-then tamed village of Beckley, which is one of the Otmoor towns. An Oakley man, who as a boy once ventured to Quarry to watch a cricket match, remembers a tough sort of cricket, not much style, but plenty of barrels of beer. If you did not know someone there, you were wise not to go. And then there are complaints from the neighbouring village of Headington about the ferocity of Quarry's dogs! Politically too, the village's character was distinct. Its liberalism was strong, plebeian; it was said to be positively dangerous for a known Tory to cross the village borders. The story in Old Headington was that 'if anybody got across those fields that wasn't a Liberal, they never ever were seen again. If you were a Liberal you were all right mate, but outside that, life wasn't worth twopence.' And as you can see in a photograph, the Conservative van tipped into a pit during the People's Budget election of 1910.

The Quarry settlement originated on the wastes, and these first social conditions were successively reproduced first by the stone quarrying and then by the brickmaking. Because the quarrying was constantly changing the surface of the village, and as each quarry was exhausted, so cottages were put up in the pits and another quarry opened, the village was constantly unsettled, and the abandoned quarry land within the village itself became anybody's land.

There was an immediate perimeter of waste lands stretching from Shotover right down to Carremoss. Some of these were the subject of a long dispute running through the 1850s, 1860s, and 1870s, when a farmer called Richard Pether tried to enclose them. Such disputes are characteristic of Quarry, and continued in the later nineteenth century. The first appearance that Quarry made in history as a settled village was with the funeral path riots of 1805, when a wealthy banker of Headington tried to enclose what had been the villager's funeral path. It carried on like that until the First World War.

I think it is impossible to even undertake a historical inquiry of this kind into the social and moral economy of a village without extensive use of the spoken word of tradition. This is quite simply because there are not enough documents to go round. Histories of individual villages by local history groups tend to stretch back to the earliest records and to start where possible with the Romans, simply because with manuscript and political sources there is nothing else you can do. You cannot actually study a social structure or a social system within a limited small community, so deficient in records is an open village, except by using extensively the memories of old villagers. The parish chest, if it exists, will be of a comparatively recent date, there are unlikely to be farm records, there will only be occasional deeds not in sufficient number to indicate the interplay of property and economy, kinship and descent. The best manuscripts that I came across in this work were found in the course of collecting memories. And I want to give now three examples of ways in which I found that talking to people about certain events or about situations or social facts in Quarry helped me to make use of and understand the documents in the Oxfordshire Record Office, and elsewhere.

First of all, in the fight for the open Magdalens and open Brasenose – those two stretches of woodland and waste over which there were mass trespassings and a great struggle in the 1860s and 1870s. Now the written records provide a fine consecutive account of the struggle over common rights, but they tell us nothing of the later period, or about usage and what the commons actually meant to Quarry villagers. They do not record the grazing of cattle by the village cowkeepers, the horsebreakers who used the open Magdalens and the open Brasenose as their paddock, nor anything about the men who made a winter trade from the wasteland wood.

More important, the documents do not tell us anything about all the other wastes and commons whose common character was not in dispute in the nineteenth century. By far the most important common land for Quarry villagers was not these two well-documented commons, but Shotover, another limb of the ancient royal forest, very much larger in extent and more prolific in totting and foraging and grazing opportunities.

A second example is work. There is one rare document on the Merton College Stone Pit in Quarry, which records the names and period of employment of each labourer, and a stonemason's

diary for 1882 and 1883 which was found locally in the course
of the research. But the manuscript census returns available are
misleading. The great majority of Quarry's men were classed in
the 1861 census as 'labourers'. The description is stark and unin-
formative, though it may serve to suggest the villagers' general
social bias. But Quarry labourers were men of many occupations,
sometimes none, moving within a range of jobs rather than following a single employment. Where work was so seasonal and
jobs, even for a skilled man, often comparatively short-lived,
occupational statuses were necessarily fluid. The classification
of a man at any one time as a labourer thus ought to be seen as
highly provisional, and in fact it was rather a succession of jobs
or a network of jobs, which one can only establish by talking
to people about them. Moreover, inquiry about all the villages
discloses kinds of occupations which do not appear in the census
categories at all, and yet which figure largely in accounts of the
individual's working life. Well digging, for example – presumably
because well-digging jobs were comparatively short-lived; the
longest I have come upon was six weeks – shared many of the
technical and physical peculiarities of quarrying and provided a
frequent occupation for the village labourer down to the 1920s.
Small groups of men related to each other by ties of companionship or blood undertook to do the work in gangs. In the early
1900s it was possible to identify three more or less distinct
schools of well diggers, or sects as they were once described to
me. Two of them were largely based upon kin – the Washing-
tons and the Gurls who took on well digging when sacked from
work in the cinder quarries. One was recruited largely from the
village poachers. The country drainers also worked in this way,
hiring themselves out as independent companies of men, but for
comparatively short periods of time, and then taking on building work and other kinds of work. There were again men who
made their living, or at least part of their living, with a horse
and cart. There were a lot of these haggle-cart men, road hauling
for the stone quarries or the brick works or for local builders.
And at least five laundry carriers are remembered. For this part
of the inquiry almost all the worthwhile evidence was that of
people's memories.

The clearest example of the primacy of oral evidence is that of poaching. This is one of the first questions that I looked into: somebody said in the Black Boy pub that Quarry was a noted village for poachers. We went through all the Petty Sessions and other Court proceedings, tracking down Quarry poachers from about 1860 to about 1890, and sometimes beyond. This was a very long labour, and it was amazing how little it produced. It produced a list of convictions, but none of them had any kind of interest at all either on the formation of a gang, or as to who was the fence, or about the relationship of poachers to village life. Only one really regular poacher with many convictions appeared at all, a man called Green. I do not know whether he was convicted so frequently because he was the most active of Quarry's poachers or because he was not good at making getaways, but more recent evidence suggests the latter, because Quarry's most famous poachers – famous that is to say to the present day – have had very few convictions. Oral evidence made it possible to reconstruct in some detail the life of Quarry's latter-day poaching gangs, which were flourishing in the years immediately before the First World War. We were able to distinguish between the regular poachers, who went out with long nets and set about their work in gangs, and the more occasional poacher who, though he spoke enthusiastically about his youthful exploits, was not regarded as a real poacher at all by those who classed themselves as being skilled men. We recorded accounts of the door-to-door sales of rabbits and of orders being placed with the poachers before they went out, and of Milky Allum the weekly fence, who acted as the go-between for Quarry's poachers and the butchers in Oxford's Covered Market. The deliberate training-up of lurchers by Tod Kerry, a retired poacher who as a smallholder was at war with Colonel Miller and his keepers at Shotover, and the apprenticing of quite young boys to the craft, came out clearly and with a wealth of supporting detail. What is more, oral evidence made it possible to provide a context for this poaching, and to show how it fitted into the seasonal cycles of work and how it was dovetailed with a number of kindred totting and foraging activities such as mushrooming, briaring and rabbiting. One of the men I heard a lot about was Dusty Wright. Born of a Gypsy or part-Gypsy

family who went off to live in St Thomas in Oxford, he started
work draining for the Oxford City Corporation, but kept up his
allotment on Quarry, and his nephew Waggle Ward, a man in his
seventies, remembers him as a hero:

> Uncle Dusty'd walk from St Thomas's to Quarry, he'd go a-rabbiting
> all night, he'd walk back to St Thomas in the mornin', and he'd go
> to work all day ... that's what Uncle Dusty'd do ... He had allot-
> ment on Quarry Field, when he lived in St Thomas's, and he used
> to come up a-digging, and if the wind was a-blowin' at night, he'd
> leave that digging, and he'd go a-rabbiting all night, ... he'd have
> a cup of tea in Granny Webb's, he'd walk back down St Thomas's,
> he 'ood, and he'd go to work all day, and he'd be up a-digging on
> the allotment at night in Quarry. Tell me where another man 'd do
> that to-day? They ain't born to it. They was bred different, horses
> they was, I reckon that's the truth ... Uncle Dusty ... would walk
> from St Thomas's, to Quarry, on his 'lotment, if the wind was
> a-blowin' he'd go rabbiting all night, and he'd come back – carry
> about twenty rabbits on his shoulder – all round Waterperry and
> Shotover – he'd come back, he'd leave these rabbits there, and he'd
> walk to St Thomas's again in the mornin', and he'd go to work
> all day, and he'd be up there diggin' at night ... that's what Uncle
> Dusty used to do.

I want to raise a question about the use of the term 'oral
history'. Its chief help, it seems to me, is to direct attention to the
enormous resources of memory of the spoken word as opposed
to the written word. The bias it introduces into history is wholly
welcome since it will necessarily direct the historian's attention
to the fundamental common things of life: the elements of individual and social experience rather than upon administrative and
political chronologies. It makes it possible for the historian to
define his subject in the same way as the sociologist or the social
anthropologist, and to pick his themes before he starts in the light
of their substantive importance, rather than to leave himself at
the mercy of his documents, following them more or less compul-
sively because there is no other evidence on which he can draw.
The reason why history has so often a bureaucratic bias is not I

think because of the particular bias of individual historians, but very largely because bureaucratic documents are the ones most often preserved. The reason why so much of the history of the English land is the history of property is because in county record offices so many documents are deeds. Historians have very often simply followed the lines suggested by the documents. Here is a different kind of evidence which makes possible manuscript and printed sources, no less extensively, and yet does not leave the historian at their mercy.

There is another reason for favouring the use of the term 'oral history', whatever misgivings one might have, and that is that it will encourage discussion about method and particularly about the difficulties involved in collecting this particular evidence. It may help to establish common standards among those who feel themselves to be working together. I am sure, however, that it would be unwise to think of it as a peculiar or exclusive type of inquiry. In my own experience, part of the value of such work is that it makes it possible to bring to life documents which left to themselves would necessarily lie inert. The great strength of oral history from the point of view of the sociologically minded historian is that it allows him to recapture, in some detail, the humdrum circumstances in which economic action, political belief, and cultural expression were shaped.

On the other hand, I think it is much weaker, when it comes to social drama and social crisis: to those critical events when, as in a flash, the hidden resources and tensions of a community were revealed. Now nineteenth-century Quarry is quite rich in such events, starting from the Funeral Path Riots in 1805 and continuing down to the riot in the People's Budget Election of 1910. Each of the East Oxfordshire villages I have referred to has its own history and from these public events, from election riots, court cases, common rights disputes, from the little one can glean about their economies, although they are all open villages quite distinct from each other. But I suspect that if one had relied upon oral tradition alone, they might actually have appeared more similar to each other than the written evidence suggests. I found, for example, that talking to people in Beckley about secondary incomes, about the cottage, about keeping a pig, about going on to the common for fuel, one got very similar sorts of replies to that in Quarry, and yet other evidence shows that Beckley was by the late nineteenth century a village with a resident gentleman's family, a very different village indeed from Quarry.

Again, there are many memories of Quarry school at the turn of the century and particularly of Mr Bickley, whom a number of people remember as being very brutal, but a few remember as a fair man. There were also stories of resistance by Quarry children in the school. But it is only the log-book entries that make you see how serious that conflict was. In other words, in this case I feel that without that kind of outside evidence I would not have known how to evaluate the distinctiveness of this experience. Most people have wretched experiences at school, many people try to organise some kind of resistance in school, but in Quarry it does seem from this school log to have been different.

Another case in which I had to rely chiefly on manuscript and printed sources was the history of Gypsies in Quarry. Quarry villagers have affectionate memories of Gypsies, who were settled right in the heart of the village until very recent years, and when we were talking to Johnny Bucknell we asked about the relations between the Gypsies and the villagers. All we heard was, 'they were good to us', and that 'some of the villagers helped painting the wagons before the Gypsies set out', but nothing more. But when you look in the *Journal of the Gypsy Lore Society* which has a most detailed history of individual Romany families, and when you look at the 1861 Census which by a very happy error has actually got the enumerators' scribble 'gypsies' still visible there against two of the families, and when you see from the *Journal of the Gypsy Lore Society* and from gypsyologists who visited these Gypsies in Headington Quarry, that these families are in fact very well-known Romany families, and then through parish registers you trace their intermarriage with the village and can trace those who married out from the village to the Gypsies and went to live in caravans. You can see what assimilation meant and how nevertheless the Gypsies were able to maintain a distinct identity. It is also possible to show when a Gypsy fiddler played with the Quarry Morris-side. And with a murder that took place on open Brasenose in 1887, it is possible to see another kind of

Gypsy life, that is neither in the *Gypsy Lore Society* nor in people's memory, concerning relatives of the settled Gypsies, tent-dwelling Gypsies who periodically passed through Quarry because Quarry was a place known to have settled Gypsies.

In conclusion, I think it would be a great pity if oral history were regarded as something which superseded other forms of historical inquiry, taken on its own, without the restraint, encouragement, and provocation of manuscript and printed sources. In my opinion we should aim as far as possible to allow the interplay between the two. The actual balance of the one and the other will vary very greatly depending on the quality or otherwise of the documents. The use of oral history should not absolve the historian from his other more traditional tasks. On the contrary, it should make him attend to them with renewed zest, knowing that even from comparatively few pieces of written evidence, he may be able, with the aid of oral testimony, to make some quite substantial sense.

Comers and Goers

The 'migrating classes', as they were called by the promoters of the Leicester Square Soup Kitchen in 1850, have left remarkably few traces of their existence, even in the places which once served them as town lairs.[1] No railway hotels mark the terminal point of their journeyings. No imposing clubs stand as memorials to the seasons they spent in town. The back-street lodging houses where many of them put up have long since been swept away, though not their forbidding institutional successors – the 'Free Dormitories' and 'Night Shelters' promoted and endowed by late-Victorian philanthropy. The no-man's-land where the travelling showmen drew up their caravans and the Gypsies encamped – the wasteland edge of the nineteenth-century town – has been built over by houses and streets. It is not easy to imagine a time when men slept rough in the shadows of the gas-works, the warmth of the brick-kilns, and the dark recesses of places like London Bridge; or lined up their hundreds with tin cans or basins at Ham Yard, Soho, or the midnight soup-kitchens of Whitechapel and Drury Lane.[2] Perhaps the most complete change has been on the waterfront, which has been robbed of all its life. There is no Scandinavian settlement in Rotherhithe, no Tiger Bay in Cardiff. Rambling down Ratcliffe Highway, the curious observer is likely to find himself alone, flanked by derelict land and a low brick wall instead of the crowded dancing-saloons and rifle galleries, photographers' booths and boarding-houses of a hundred years ago. Then it was a great night-time pleasure strip, drawing sailors of all nations – red-shirted Americans, 'chewing indefatigably', Chinamen and Lascars, 'smoking Trichinopoly cheroots', 'shivering' Italians, 'piratical-looking' Greeks.[3]

Travellers in nineteenth-century England played a much greater part in industrial and social life than they do today. Among them were to be found some of the country's major occupational groups, as well as many hundreds of miscellaneous callings and trades. On the canals there were the boatmen and their families, who remained an important element in the carrying trade long after the coming of the railways – a half-Gypsy population who owed their very existence to the Industrial Revolution. Tens of thousands of navvies followed in the track of Victorian 'improvement' and the great public works, a class of men 'very fond of change', and forever on the move, especially the more skilled among them.[4] The building trades were chronically migratory, with men moving constantly from job to job, sometimes covering very great distances in the tramp for work. (Some hundreds of stonemasons emigrated seasonally to the United States, leaving in the early spring and returning in the fall).[5] The summer harvests depended to a considerable degree upon travelling labourers, most of them recruited from the countryside, but some coming out from the towns. James Greenwood met one of these on the road to Hitchin:

> He seemed to be a decent sort of man, and, for a wonder, was not an Irishman. He lived and worked, all the winter, at the Potteries at Shepherd's Bush, he told me, and every June set out on tramp, working his way at any kind of field labour, and winding up with the Northern late corn harvests, when he returned home with a pound or so in his pocket, besides what he was able to send, from time to time to keep his old woman.[6]

At the heart of the wayfaring constituency were those whom Mayhew called 'wandering tribes': people who had been either born and bred to a roving life (like the Gypsies and travelling showmen), or forced into it when settled occupations failed them, like the travelling Irish, who came over each year for the harvest, or the old soldiers and army reserve men who lived as trampers on the road, and were said to constitute not less than one-fourth or one-fifth of the whole class of destitute homeless persons.[7] It is possible to distinguish four different classes among them. First there were the habitual wanderers, who flitted about from place to place, with no regular settlement at all. Second there were those who spent the greater part of the year in the country, but kept regular winter quarters in town. Third there were the 'fair weather' travellers who went out on 'summer tours', but for the rest of the year stayed in one place. Finally, there were those who made frequent short turns into the country, but never moved far from their home base. Examples of these types could be found in each of the wandering tribes. Amongst the packmen and dealers, for instance, there were some who followed a weekly itinerary, 'pitching it' in town on Saturday-night markets, and going on country rounds during the week;[8] there were others who turned out only for special occasions, like the army of freelance hucksters who made an annual appearance on Derby Day at Epsom Downs; and yet others who left home for months at a time, like the 'muggers' and 'potters' who dealt in cheap crockery and earthenware, and the cheap-jacks, whose yearly round began in February and often did not end until November.[9] 'I used to go round the country – to Margate, Brighton, Portsmouth – I mostly travelled by the coast, calling at the sea-port towns', a cutlery seller told Mayhew; 'I went away every spring time, and came to London again at the fall of the year.'[10] Similarly among the gypsies there were comers and goers within every migration range, including the most limited (the Battersea Gypsies kept very close to London, and a few of them remained encamped all the year round).[11] Race-meetings and fairs attracted both short- and long-distance migrants, some following them round as part of a regular circuit, others going out on individual expeditions, with a basket, or a show, or with a tray suspended from the neck.

Wayfaring life had a definite place in the moral topography of the nineteenth-century town. Railway stations always attracted a floating population to the vicinity; so did the wholesale markets, especially those frequented by the drovers. Brickfields, on the outskirts of town, were regular dossing-places, along with gasworks, railway bridges, and viaducts. There were Irish quarters in every centre of industry and trade, 'Little Irelands', whose inhabitants remained notoriously migratory in their habits, 'exceedingly fluctuating and unsettled'.[12] The Irish were among the first to settle in the boom towns of mid-Victorian England (Middlesbrough, Barrow-in-Furness, West Ham). They were among the first to leave when there was a depression.[13] 'Our population is rather a floating one ... following the up and down ... of industry', wrote a Catholic priest of his Irish flock at Sunderland. 'St. Patrick's mission is not like many other ones.'[14] In the summer many of the Irish went off to 'counthry' work. A few of the York Irish were still doing this in Rowntree's time, while in London the Cockney Irish constituted a lasting element in the annual exodus of hop-pickers.[15] Waterfront districts, too, always bore a peculiarly migratory character, not only in the big sea-ports, where there were fully fledged sailortowns, but also inland, wherever there were wharves or docks. 'The quarters of every town that lie near the wharves and banks always seem to deteriorate', wrote Lady Bell, in her book about Middlesbrough. 'There is something in the intercourse of sailors from other ports who come and go, nomadic, unvouched for who appear and disappear, with no responsibility for their words or their deeds, that seems to bring to the whole world a kinship of lawlessness and disorder.'[16] Quite apart from the native sailors – perennial comers and goers – there were the sailors from other ports, an even more nomadic element. At Shields, for instance, it was computed that besides the fifteen thousand sailors belonging to the port there were no less than seamen from other places who annually visited the port.[17] On the Middlesbrough waterfront there were 'many ... foreigners'. 'Almost daily we come in contact with Germans, Greeks, Swedes, Danes, Norwegians, Arabians, Chinese, Lascars and Spaniards', remarked a chaplain to the seamen in 1892.[18] Sailors were not only more numerous and varied than their counterparts today; they were also more visible, spending far more time ashore, especially in winter.

Regular 'trampers' – 'comers and goers who ... prefer darkness to light' – had their own peculiar lairs. An example in Nottingham is Narrow Marsh ('this provincial Whitechapel') where J. Flanagan, the Bermondsey evangelist, once spent eighteen months in rescue work 'chiefly among the crimps, outcasts and tramps who were ever turning up'.[19] Another provincial example is Angel Meadow ('the lowest, most filthy, most unhealthy and most wicked locality in Manchester') whose inhabitants were accounted for by the *Morning Chronicle* special correspondent as 'prostitutes … bullies, thieves, cadgers, vagrants, tramps and … those unhappy wretches, the "low Irish"'.[20] In Merthyr Tydfil there was 'China', a maze of courts and tortuous lanes which the Education Commissioners of 1847 described as 'a sort of Welsh Alsatia'. It was, they said, 'a mere sink of thieves and prostitutes such as unhappily constitutes an appendage to every large town'.[21] There was a little enclave of this kind even in a sleepy place like Hitchin. James Greenwood came upon it in 1872, a long, narrow street which he describes as 'evidently the headquarters of the tramping fraternity':

> It is like a slice from the backslums of Whitechapel, or Kent Street in the Borough. As, in the delectable localities named, at least one house in a half-dozen throughout its length is a lodging house for travellers – travellers, however, who are not so worn-out and leg-weary but they prefer, on a sultry night in June, to sprawl in the house passages and on the steps …[22]

London had a number of little enclaves of this kind. Some of them were ancient haunts of the travelling fraternities (St Giles; Tothill Fields, Westminster; the Mint, Southwark); others were the accompaniment of the city's nineteenth-century growth. One of the newer tramp quarters was in Mill Lane, Deptford and its environs, 'known to tramps and low-class prostitutes throughout London', according to Booth.[23] Another was in the Arpley Road area of Anerley and Penge, 'a resting place for tramps entering London from the South'.[24] In the north there was Campbell Road, Islington, the occasion of much police and clerical disquiet.[25] To the south-east there was the 'Dust Hole', Woolwich, the subject of Canon Horsley's anti-vice campaign in the 1890s.[26] Booth wrote that it was a 'house of call' for tramps passing in and out of London on the high road to Kent, and a regular junction for the outer London tramp circuit. 'Policemen from Notting Dale', it was said, 'find old friends in Ropeyard Rails. The casual loafer floats between the two.'[27] Notting Dale, 'the resting place for tramps entering London from the North or West', was the largest

of these new tramp districts.[28] It was first settled by some refugee
pig-keepers from Marble Arch, in flight from the sanitary authorities, and they were soon followed by Gypsies, brickmakers, and
(in later years) lodging-house keepers. Bangor Street, the most
frequently noticed of its streets, was occupied by lodging-houses
from end to end, and we are fortunate to have a good account
of how a tramping family made its way there in the 1890s. It
comes from the autobiography of Sam Shaw, a little boy of ten at
the time. The family had set out from Birmingham 'without any
fixed stopping places or definite ... sleeping places'.

> Father told us that we were going on the road to a big place where
> matches and newspapers sold better than in Birmingham. So 'on
> the road' we went ... For weeks we tramped ... each stage was
> workhouse to workhouse where we were provided with bed and
> breakfast. If we arrived too late for admittance then we begged
> a shelter in a barn ... or slept under the stars ... Day after day,
> begging our way ... We reached Edgware ... and ... spent the
> night in a workhouse ... reaching London the next day ... While
> we children played in one of London's parks our parents searched
> for a room ... Bangor Street, Notting Hill Gate, eventually pro-
> vided us with a home ... It consisted of only one room and was
> furnished with two beds and two rickety chairs which were all
> the family exchequer could afford. Those who hadn't chairs to
> sit on sat on the bed.[29]

Within such quarters, and scattered on all the tramp routes of the
country, were the common lodging-houses, the night-time haven
of the wandering tribes or at least of the better-off portion among
them, hawkers and travelling labourers especially. Travelling
people used them as regular staging posts, and laid up in them
for the winter when the season's journeyings came to an end.
There were few towns without a street or two largely given over
to them. Around mid-century (a time when they were the subject
of much anxious investigation) Gloucester's lodging-houses were
concentrated in Leather-Bottle Lane;[30] Banbury's in Rag Row (a
back street of the proletarian suburb of Neithrop);[31] Huddersfield's in the narrow courts off Kirkgate and Castlegate (the Irish

ones in Windsor Court);[32] Doncaster's in Skinner's Yard, Far St Sepulchre Gate;[33] Brighton's in 'those bad streets', Egremont Street and Nottingham Street.[34] In Derby they were in Walker Lane, 'the St Giles of Derby'.[35] At Ashton-under-Lyne the twopenny lodging-houses were in Crab Street and the twopenny-halfpenny ones in Duncan Street.[36] London, of course, was full of them – no fewer than 988 were registered in 1889, with accommodation for over 33,964 people, quite apart from the coffee-shops which offered twopenny and threepenny beds, and the rooming-houses.[37] There were great numbers of them, too, in Liverpool, not only the sailors' boarding-houses of the waterfront, but also the 'emigrant houses' where travellers put up while waiting to make the transatlantic passage.

Common lodging-houses were condemned by sanitary reformers on account of the 'promiscuous' mixing of the sexes, and the crowded, impromptu conditions in which the inmates ate and slept. But to the footsore wanderer they offered warmth and a cheerful shelter. The kitchen was the hub of lodging-house life; it was usually to be found in the basement and served as a drying-room, a workplace (for those with a basket of merchandise to prepare), an eating room, and sometimes (though illegally) as a place to sleep. In the evening, when travellers returned from their rounds, it was turned into a common-room, thick with the fumes of coke cooking and tobacco, and warmed by huge, blazing fires. Even hostile observers had sometimes to admit that the atmosphere was companionable. 'The night being wet, enormous fires blazed in both rooms', wrote Dr Coulthart, investigating one of the low lodging-houses of Ashton-under-Lyne:

Groups of evidently abandoned creatures of both sexes, many of them dripping with rain, were drying themselves before the fires; while others, more jovial than the rest, were doing ample justice to the merits of ale, porter, porridge, beefsteaks, cow-paunch &c., nearer the door. Among the numbers was a woolly-haired negro who, the police officer with me said, had been driven from the streets a few hours before for balladsinging. In vacant comers were hawkers' baskets, pedlars' boxes, musical instruments, and beggars' crutches.[38]

Lodging-houses offered cheap overnight accommodation for prices ranging at mid-century from a penny to threepence, and in later years from fourpence to sixpence. Even so, they were expensive for travellers of the poorer class, who were able to use them only when they were 'flush'. There was a good deal of interchange between the lodging-houses, on the one hand, where accommodation had to be paid for, and the Casual Wards and Refuges, on the other, where it was free.

Men who slept rough (by no means only tramps) had an easy time of it in the country, when they made their summer rounds, and could pick and choose their places to sleep al fresco. Things were more difficult when winter drove them to the towns, and they were subject to a good deal of police harassment. But they were never without refuge. Police supervision was slight on the ragged peripheries of town, where many of them made a halt. The kilns on the Brent Brickfields at Willesden were an overnight stopping-place for men who tramped up to London. 'The cavities … afford warmth and shelter', says a police report, 'hence the … numbers.'[39] Outside Manchester, too, 'the numerous brick-fields on the outskirts of the city, were frequently resorted to by tramps.[40] In town itself there were certain places where men could escape the glare of the bull's-eye lantern: ruinous or abandoned buildings, shop doorways, omnibus depots, railway stables, coal-holes and boiler-rooms, cul-de-sacs and covered passageways, impromptu shelters arising, as it were, within the crevices of city life. In London, the wholesale markets were always a draw to tramps partly because of the all-night coffee-shops and stalls, and partly because they provided odd jobs, but also because of the shelter: any corner might be used for a kip – even the water-closets at Covent Garden.[41] There were certain other places, too, where tramps could assemble together more or less undisturbed. The Thames bridges served them for many years as 'Dry Arch' hotels, 'open houses for the houseless wayfarer'.[42] As late as 1869 Daniel Joseph Kirwan came upon a dozen people who had made their home in the underground recesses of London Bridge, and were burning driftwood for their fire: he called it a 'perfect Gypsy encampment'.[43] The most sensational of these shelters in inner London were the Adelphi Arches off the Strand, a series of underground chambers and vaults 'running here and there like the intricacies of catacombs'. Thomas Miller described them as a 'little subterranean city' and in the 1860s (according to one excited account) 'no sane person would have ventured to explore them without an armed escort'.[44]

Victorian 'improvement' swept away many of these nooks and crannies, but it created others in their stead. Street lamps yielded the homeless wanderer a certain starveling warmth; so did the boiler-rooms of the factories, the newspaper offices, and (in later years) the big hotels. Model dwellings, with their open landings, stairways, and passages gave a rudimentary shelter to sleepers-out.[45] The colonnade of St George's Hall ('our great municipal building') sheltered so many of Liverpool's homeless that it was described in 1890 as the 'lodging-house' of the destitute.[46] The Thames Embankment, the most spectacular of mid-Victorian 'improvements' in inner London, very soon became a by-word for the number of its tramps, some of whom filled the seats beneath the plane trees ('No. 2 bench' was recommended to Duckworth by a former *habitué*), and others of whom used it as an all-night promenade.[47] Its character was reinforced by the Shelters built at either end (the Salvation Army's 'Penny Sit-Up' at Blackfriars, and the *Morning Post*'s 'Embankment Home' on Millbank); by charitable distributions of food (such as the Eustace Miles Food Barrow at Cleopatra's Needle); and by the nightly distribution of relief tickets underneath the Craven Street arches (two thousand men were assembling there nightly in October 1908).[48] The 'lynx eyed metropolitan police' (as they were described by General Booth), after attempting to drive the tramps away, were by 1910 treating the Embankment as a 'kind of corral' where large numbers of tramps were conveniently assembled under the direct observation of law and order.[49]

Railway arches – both brick viaducts and iron bridges – were by far the most frequented of these new al fresco shelters, and they were resorted to by the homeless from their earliest days.[50] The Craven Street Arches at Charing Cross were a nightly assembly point for trampdom; so was Byker Bridge at Newcastle and (in later years, at least) the 'Highlanders' Meet' along Argyle Street in Glasgow. In Croydon the Windmill Bridge of the London &

Brighton railway was a night-time resort for sleepers-out; in Spitalfields the Wheler Street arches of the Great Eastern railway (a long, low, tunnel-like bridge) were used by some forty to sixty people a night, according to a police report; at Rotherhithe there were the 500 arches of the South Eastern and the London & Brighton railways, whose night-time *habitués* were not deterred by occasional prosecutions before the local magistrates.[51] The building of the Overhead Railway along the docks was a late addition to tramp facilities in Liverpool skirting the seven-mile length of the waterfront and open to all comers – it became locally known as 'the Docker's Umbrella'.[52]

Gypsies made their encampments on the outer edge of town, where streets and houses gave way to waste. The Everton Gypsies pitched their tents on a piece of waste ground near Walton Breck; in 1879 they were summoned before the magistrates for having failed to supply themselves with water 'as required by the Public Health Act' but the camp was still flourishing seven years later.[53] The Smethwick Gypsies occupied a piece of waste ground near to the Navigation Inn.[54] At Charlton the local Gypsies occupied an open space near Riverside – with six travelling-vans and a number of tents.[55] At Plumstead they camped out in the marshes – a stretch of land drained by deep ditches 'like the fen country' and used as a shooting range; their tents were made of old skirts 'stretched over like hurdles'.[56] In West London one of their camps was by Latimer Road, 'the ugliest place … in the neighbourhood of London … half torn up for brickfield clay, half consisting of fields laid waste in expectation of the house-builder'; another was in West Kensington (in the days before it was overrun by the bourgeoisie) close to the market-gardens and the brickfields, between Gloucester Road and Earls Court.[57] In north-east London the chief Gypsy settlement was at Hackney Wick, 'where the marsh-meadows of the River Lea, unsuitable for building land, seems to forbid the extension of town streets and blocks of brick and stuccoed terraces'; there was a smaller settlement near Finsbury Park, in the dust-heaps at the bottom of Hermitage Road.[58] The Battersea Gypsies camped in Donovan's Yard, a plot of ground near the South-Western railway, 'commanding an unpicturesque prospect of palings, walls, and arches'. The encampment, in 1900, was occupied for about six months every year, 'from October till the flat-racing season'. It was made up of two long lines of wagons 'broken here and there by a firewooddealer's hut'. The horses had been sold off 'to save the cost of keeping them in idleness during the cold months.' T. W. Wilkinson, writing about the camp, remarked on the

> curious air of domesticity: ... women, most of them stamped with their tribal characteristics, sit on the steps of the waggons, some at needlework, some merely gossiping. Other housewives are engaged on the family wash. Bent over tubs and buckets in close proximity to the fire, on which clothes are boiling briskly, they are rubbing and rinsing with a will, now and again going off for more water to a tap at one end of the ground.[59]

This 'domesticity' was less extraordinary than Wilkinson implies. However far they travelled, the Gypsies, like others of the wandering tribes, usually retained a base to which they regularly returned. The larger Gypsy-colonies were well established. At Notting Dale a nucleus of families (most of them Hearnes) remained in occupation all the year round. Thomas Hearne, the father of the community, and a chair-bottomer, had converted his van into a makeshift cottage, with an old tin pail serving for a chimney, and a signboard announcing his trade.[60] The Wandsworth Gypsies were also well entrenched. 'The houses are many of them owned by the richer members of the clan; and room is found for vans, with wheels or without, in which the poorer members crowd. The gypsies regard their quarter as their castle.'[61] They had been subject to some harassment in the 1870s when they were driven from the Common by the Metropolitan Board of Works and later on were hauled up before the local magistrates on account of the 'intolerable nuisance' of their tents, hovels, and vans. But a gypsy capitalist called Penfold had bought up cottages and lands in the vicinity, and twenty years later the colony was flourishing undisturbed, '3 families to a house'.[62] The Battersea colony too had acquired the status of semi-permanent residents when Booth enquired about them: 'These People, living in their vans, come and go, travelling in the country part of every year ...

They move about a good deal within the London area as well as outside, but are usually anchored fast all winter, and throughout the summer one or another always occupies the pitch.'[63]

The ebb and flow of wayfaring life in nineteenth-century England was strongly influenced by the weather. The months from March to October were the time when travelling people were to be found on the roads, and when they were joined by every class of occasional itinerant. With the approach of cold weather, in October and November, the season of journeyings came to an end and the wandering tribes returned to town. Spring was the time when long-distance travellers left town. Country labourers, who wintered in the metropolitan Night Refuges, were said to 'fly off' about March.[64] So did the men who sailed in the Greenland whalers, as one of their songs reminds us:[65]

> Twas eighteen hundred and twenty four,
> On March the eighteenth day,
> We hoist our colours to the top of the mast,
> And to Greenland bore away, brave boys,
> And to Greenland bore away.

The trampers' London season ended when the Night Refuges closed down:

> The winter is the homeless man's London season; and most of the refuges, especially the larger ones, are open only four or five months in the year, from November or December till about April. In mid-winter they are most crowded, by April they are usually comparatively empty. Still, even to the last there is a substantial number at the large refuges. What becomes of them when turned out is not very clear. Probably the majority go ... into the country.[66]

Travelling showmen began to leave town quite early in the spring. The peepshow caravans (Mayhew tells us) generally left London between March and April 'because some fairs begin at that time', and were seldom seen again until October, 'after the fairs is over'.[67] Some showmen had already travelled considerable distances by the time of the Easter Fairs. Manchester showmen turned up regularly at Blackburn for the annual fair which opened on Easter Monday: on one occasion there was even a troupe of strolling players from London.[68] Travelling circuses began their tenting tours in March.[69] Old Joe Baker's Circus, which wintered in the Bristol alums, had 'taken to the road for the Easter Fairs', and had already reached Worcester when the young Ben Tillett caught up with them.[70] David Prince Miller, 'weatherbound' one winter in Carlisle, began the next year's season with a February fair at Dumfries, then doubled back to Carlisle and worked his way over to Newcastle upon Tyne for the Easter Monday 'hopping'. Another year he had an indoor engagement in Birmingham, which kept him for the winter, and then proceeded to Manchester in the spring, to take part in Knott Mill Fair, 'the great Manchester carnival'.[71] Broadly speaking one may say that the showman's season began with the Easter fairs, but the starting-point was different on certain circuits. In East Anglia the season opened with the great Charter Fair at King's Lynn, which began on 14 February and lasted six days. It was here that Batty, the circus proprietor, began the 'outdoor business' of the season, after putting on a Christmas show indoors; here too, according to one of Mayhew's informants, cheap-jacks started their rounds.[72] In the Thames valley, when 'Lord' George Sanger was a boy, the season opened with the May-Day Fair at Reading. 'Showmen of all descriptions moved out of their winter quarters to attend it', Sanger recalls. Among them was his own father, who travelled the fairs with a peep-show during the summer months, and in the winter returned to his carrying-business in Newbury.[73]

All through the spring, men were beginning to move from indoor to outdoor jobs, sometimes taking the step of exchanging a fixed occupation for a roving one. Gasstokers ('regular winter men') were giving in their notices – or getting the sack – as early as February and March, when the retort-houses began to close down.[74] Only about a third of them were employed all the year round. 'What becomes of the extra men who are employed in the winter?' an official of the Gas, Light & Coke Company was asked by the Labour Commissioners in 1893, and he replied, 'They are only too ready to leave us in the spring.'[75] At the South

Metropolitan Gas Works the bulk of them went bricking. 'Our best stokers, at any rate, do', a Charity Organisation Society enquirer was told. 'They give us notice early in the year ... and then they go to the brickfields in the summer.'[76] The chimney-sweeper's town season ended in May, and both masters and journeymen were thrown out of employment. 'Some turn coster-mongers, others tinkers, knife-grinders &c., and others migrate to the country and get a job at hay making or any other kind of unskilled labour', wrote Mayhew.[77] Those who still worked in the trade went on country rounds, travelling from job to job, and making up their money by the country sale of soot.[78] The maltings season in the breweries ended about the same time, and some thousands of country labourers, who had come up to town for the winter, and spent seven or eight months at the work, returned to their native villages. 'We used to finish at the maltings towards the end of May', a Suffolk labourer told George Ewart Evans, 'but before you went home you had to have a new suit. You dussn't come home from Burton wearing the suit you went up in ...'[79]

The spring migration out of London occurred in stages it began with an outward drift from the city to the suburbs rather than with a single clean break. Regular trampers hung about town as long as they could after the Night Refuges closed down, 'tiring out' the London and suburban workhouses (as one of Mayhew's tramp informants put it) before finally cutting adrift.[80]

The outward movement of the London Gypsies only became general in May, and those who gained their living as itinerant agriculturalists moved out even more slowly: 'Christians who wish for opportunities of doing good to the Gipsies in and about London will find many of them in the suburbs in ... April, May, and June, when they find work in the market gardens. In ... July and August they move into Sussex and Kent, and are engaged in the harvest.'[81] Showmen also frequently spent a month or two in the suburbs before 'pitching it' out in the shires. Stepney Fair ('then the biggest gathering of the kind in England') was the first place where the Sangers pitched, when they wintered in Mile End, and they followed it up with King's Cross Fair, one of the new impromptu fairs which had grown up on the wasteland edge of the city.[82] In later years (when the city extended outwards), the

Easter Fair on Wanstead Flats took its place: it was known as the 'Gypsy Fair' from the number of them who made it the first 'gathering' of their season.[83]

By the beginning of June, a fresh series of migrations was under way. Gangs of mowers moved about the country, and haymakers followed in their wake. Later on in the summer the corn harvest set up demand for extra helpers on all sides. At Kenilworth the extra men who came to do the work were from 'Coventry, Ireland, Buckingham and Berkshire.'[84] At Holbeach, Lincolnshire, they included numbers of Irishmen from the big towns of the Midlands – the 'English Irish' as they were called locally; at Goldstone in Surrey there was an immigration from London, Croydon and elsewhere – 'frequently travellers on their way to the hop-picking in Kent'.[85] Some of this movement took place within a short migration-range, the surplus labour of the towns being absorbed in the fields of the immediately surrounding countryside. But some of it occurred over longer distances. A town missionary who boarded a steamer at London Bridge in August 1860 found that a 'considerable number' of the three hundred passengers were labourers from the southern counties 'going to Yorkshire for the harvest' (the steamer was bound for Hull).[86]

During the summer months there was big money to be earned in the fields, for the man who was prepared to rough it, and to try his luck on tramp. Early in July 1872, for instance, wages were said to have risen as high as eight to ten shillings a day in some of the suburban hayfields of Middlesex.[87] Harvest rates could be nearly as high, even in a low-wage county like Oxfordshire: in August 1872 two builders' labourers at Woodstock were demanding seven-and-six a day to dig the site of a new gasholder 'because the harvest was about to begin'. When the rate was refused as 'exorbitant' they went off to find work as harvesters instead.[88] For a few brief months industrial and agricultural employments faced one another as direct competitors, and the worker who was disgruntled, or ill-paid, or out on strike, was not slow to take advantage of the situation. Those who worked in the 'dangerous' trades, for example the lowest class of Victorian town labour – had a chance to escape from the wretched conditions in which they worked. 'It is surprising to me how persons can breathe here', a factory inspector wrote of a London enamel-ler. 'One man is sensibly affected; he goes away each year hop picking, for the purpose (as he says) of cleaning himself from chalk.'[89] Amongst London fur-pullers the escape into hopping was general. 'The work, disagreeable at best, is unendurable in hot weather, and when hop or fruit picking in the country offers as an alternative, it is gladly accepted.'[90] There was a similar efflux of labour from some of the white-lead factories, with their dust-laden, poisonous atmosphere. At H. & G. Grace's, Bethnal Green, for example, as many as a third of the employees were said to go off hopping, even though there was no summer short-age of work.[91] Similarly, at the Millwall Lead Company, 'All of them go hopping in the autumn for a month or two, that is one of their chief occupations, but of course that lasts only a short time; and they hawk fruit about if they can; but when they have nothing of that kind to do, then they come back to the white lead works.'[92] In the Brough Lead Works, Sheffield, haymaking rather than hopping provided a seasonal escape. 'Have you any difficulty in getting men to come here?' the manager was asked by the Labour Commission in 1893; 'only just in the summer time', he replied, 'in the middle of the summer, when there is hay harvest and other jobs'.[93]

The summer harvests prompted a whole series of different itin-eraries. Some labourers followed the harvests round – haymaking in June, turnip-hoeing or pea-picking in July, corn-harvesting in August, hop-picking or fruit-picking in September. Others went out only for a single crop or relied upon the odd jobs in the countryside to support them on the road. Those who went for one harvest sometimes stayed for two, either because the work was available or because they had given up their lodgings in town. Others alternated between town and country. Even those who followed the 'long' harvest were by no means all of one type, and there seems to have been a broad division between those who visited a variety of places, travelling from county to county, and those who did a variety of jobs, all of them within a single district. In Lincolnshire and the East Riding, for instance, migrant labourers were divided between those who worked the country in regular rounds, 'beginning further south and working northwards as the harvests successively ripen', and others, 'less migratory than this' who came into a district at hay harvest 'and manage to find sufficient work at odd jobs in the same district to keep them till corn harvest commences'. Both, it may be added, hailed from the Midland manufacturing towns.[94]

Haymaking was the starting point for many of these summer rounds. Cobbett called it the 'first haul' of the 'perambulating' labourer, and the London tramp regarded it as 'just the proper season' for leaving town.[95] 'Down I strolled into Sussex, towards the border of Hampshire, and soon got a job', one of Thor Fredur's informants told him, 'half-a-crown a day, my food, a corner of a barn with clean straw to lie at night, as much beer as I would drink while at work ... I ... always begin with a spell at haymaking'.[96] The Irish came over for it *en masse*, leaving the mowing for native-born labourers, but following closely behind them. Haymaking in the nearby countryside was one of the resources which enabled the Padiham weavers to support themselves during the long strike of 1859.[97] It was still a standby for out-of-work labourers in York when Rowntree and Lasker made their study for *Unemployment*, along with 'carting', 'droving', 'farm work', 'snow sweeping'; the weekly itinerary of an unemployed grocer's assistant shows the way in which it was dovetailed into the local network of odd jobs:

Monday – Called on ... [grocer] in answer to an advertisement. Was told I had been too long out of the trade. Then searched advertisement in the Library.
Tuesday – Got job of digging up sand at boat landing-place (having drawn owner's attention to need for the job).
Wednesday – Same.
Thursday – Worked for boat owner. Earned 3s. 6d.
Friday – Library for advertisement.
Saturday – Applied for work at stores and for horse clipping at ... without success. Spent afternoon outside the town looking for a job haymaking.
Monday – Started at 4 a.m. seeking haymaking job at three villages [named]: got work at 9 a.m. Came home early owing to rain. Earned 3s.[98]

Market-gardens, too, drew upon migrant labour from the towns. The London Irish were prominent amongst them, and according to 'A Wandering Celt', writing in the *Labour News* for 1874, did most of the pea- and fruit-picking for the London market. 'Young Irish women, who in London during the winter are fruit-sellers or working in dust-yards, pickle-factories, sack-making, etc., go into the market-gardens for the summer.'[99] In Essex there was a regular influx of Londoners in June and July – most of them rough women from the East End, who took on summer employment as market-garden hands, and then crossed over to Kent in time for the start of the hopping. James Greenwood came upon a little colony of them at Rainham in 1881, 'browner by many shades than gipsies'. 'There ain't no men among 'em', a local told him, 'only women, and girls, and a few lads.' The work (chiefly pea-picking) lasted from eight to ten weeks, and was paid at a flat rate of eighteenpence a day. But much of the work could be done piece-work, which suited a woman with children to work alongside her: 'in fine weather and at certain work – onion-pulling for instance – some families earned as much as four shillings a day.'[100]

Summer was the height of the travelling season. There were more navvies on the road, moving from job to job, more tramps, more travelling hawkers and dealers.[101] Street-arabs left London in shoals, traversing the country in every direction, and trading (or thieving) as they tramped: 'they sometimes sleep in low lodging-houses … frequently "skipper it" in the open air … and occasionally in barns or outhouses'.[102] Vagrants, too, preferred to spend the summer out of town, and 'seasoned it' al fresco, or staged their way across the country with the aid of the Casual Wards. In the workshop trades the tramping artisan, who trudged along under his oil-skin knapsack, was a familiar figure at this time, as Thomas Wright, the journeyman engineer, reminds us. According to him, it was a 'frequent practice' for men to tramp to do their travelling by night (when the weather was hot) and to have their sleep by day, in an orchard or a field 'conveniently near the roadside'.[103]

The wayfaring constituency was further enlarged by summer newcomers. There was a seasonal influx of Italians for example.

Some seven or eight hundred of them crossed over to England every year for the ice-cream trade. 'Each spring brings a contingent', wrote Ernest Aves in his notes on the Italian colony in Clerkenwell. 'They come in small parties from all parts of Italy, travel slowly, take their food with them and when autumn comes go back to their wives and their vineyards.'[104] The organ-grinders arrived a little later. 'June July Aug. Sept, are the busiest months, when a great number migrate and travel the country through visiting Birmingham Bradford, even Scotland, Wales & most seaside resorts ... It is then that a great number of fresh arrivals are seen, but as winter arrives they gradually depart.'[105] On a larger scale there was the annual influx of harvesters from Ireland who began to arrive in large numbers at the end of May and followed the harvests round. The coming of really warm weather, in May and June, also tempted a weaker and more occasional class of traveller to venture out of town. Some hundreds of sandwich-board men, for instance, took to the roads at this time, most of them army pensioners and 'beyond middle life'; 'in the summer ... numbers of them go into the country and by pea, hop or fruit-picking, or in some other way, obtain a livelihood until September or October, when they return to their old haunts.'[106] Even in the workhouse there was a class of inmate who had their summer 'tour' – old men and women, who laid up in the 'house' for most of the year, but enjoyed a brief spell of freedom when conditions outside allowed it. Booth came upon some of them in Stepney Union workhouse.[107]

Male	Married	69	Carpenter	Wife left him and went to her son's. Man goes on tramp during summer months.
Male	Married	56	General Labourer	Man was doing casual work when relief was first given ... admitted in 1886 ... Only out for short periods in the summer since.
Female	Married	63		Woman had medicines in 1882. She goes out nursing or fruit picking in summer, winters in workhouse.
Female	Widow	60	Washing	Husband died (1849). Woman had out-relief, but it was stopped. Goes hopping with daughter.

The largest movement out of town took place in August and September. It was the season both for feasts and fairs ('Wakes' weeks in the Potteries and Lancashire), and for holidays on the sands. All kind of opportunities opened up for those who followed the track of holiday-spending and the regular showmen were joined by a whole army of itinerant hucksters ministering to the pleasure-goers' needs. It was also, in a different branch of summer activity, the height of the harvest season. The corn harvests which began in August and which lasted (until the coming of the mechanical reaper and binder) for up to six weeks, set up an enormous demand for extra hands and, as in the case of haymaking, some of this was supplied from the towns. Fruit-picking and hopping, the September harvests, offered a choice of less strenuous opportunities.

The late summer exodus corresponded to a general slackness in town employment. August and September were the 'dead months' of the year in many of the indoor trades (especially those which depended upon the world of rank and fashion), in heavy industry (on account of the heat), and in certain branches of factory work. During the 'Long Vacation' even the occasional law-writer was said to go off hopping.[108] In the London docks 'very many men' found work elsewhere in the months from July to September, 'the time of the harvest, and … the militia … in training'.[109] The same was true in the coalfields, an important source of harvest labour in the Midlands and South Wales. In the Black Country many smithies were closed up when the inhabitants took themselves off *en masse* to the fruit-picking in the Vale of Evesham, and the hopping in Herefordshire. Women and girls found work particularly hard to come by at this time. A 'little army' of ironers and laundresses was thrown out of work when the middle class went off on holiday (some followed them to the seaside); the tailoring trade was invariably dull at the end of the London season, and the number of women and girls thrown out of employment was said to be 'incredible'.[110] Factory work was also scarce. At Allen & Hanbury's, Bethnal Green, one of the biggest factories in the East End, something like a quarter of the girls were sacked every summer; the same was true of the match-factory girls (some found alternative employment in the jam factories, others went hop-picking or fruit-picking in Kent), and in the bundlewood yards on the Surrey side of the Thames: 'Nothing is made up for stock ... the women go fruit and hop picking, and the men find casual employment as best they can.'[111]

This is no doubt one of the reasons why women and girls figure so largely in the late-summer movements out of town. Another was that the work was of a kind which gave them a positive advantage over men – work for the nimble-fingered. Hopping was often undertaken by family groups with a woman in command and the husband (if he existed) elsewhere. It was piece-work, and children could make as great a contribution to earnings as grown-ups. Fruit-picking seems to have been largely in the hands of itinerant girl labourers. London work girls who went 'fruiting' in the orchards of West Middlesex were joined by others who had come south from Staffordshire and Lancashire: there is a good description of them in Pask's *Eyes of the Thames* (1889):

the North Country girls ... look forward to this fruit harvest ten miles from London to find them the means to form a little nest-egg to help them through the coming winter. Their work, when they choose to take over time, which they generally do, is, in the early summer, from half-past three in the morning until eight at night. By this custom, they can always, if they choose, earn over eighteen shillings a week, doing piece-work, or, as it is termed in market-garden parlance, 'great' work ... In their short print dresses and with their red cotton handkerchiefs tied over their heads, the girls look well enough to form a pretty study for any follower of the Fred Walker school. Still, despite rosy cheeks, blue eyes, and agile forms, the romance is soon broken when they open their mouths. If ever a rival could be found for Billingsgate, it would be some London market-orchard. Even the Irish girls, who can boast a far higher standard of morality, are as foul-tongued as a lighterman on the Pool.[112]

The September hop-picking was the Jamboree of the wandering tribes. Mayhew called it the 'grand rendezvous for the vagrancy of England and Ireland'.[113] Gypsies came to it from every part of southern England – 'nearly all the gypsies in England', according to one inflationary account.[114] In London the common lodging-houses were said to be 'almost deserted' on account of it, 'the Bohemian inmates having betaken themselves *en masse* to the pleasant fields of Kent'.[115] Even the workhouse population was notably affected.[116] The Irish poor had a 'positive mania' for hopping, and the 'wild unrestrained kind of life' which it allowed; for those who travelled the harvests it was the climax of the summer's round; for many more it was the one departure of the year from town: 'it is no uncommon thing for the houses of rooms to be shut up and for whole families to go off together', wrote Denvir.[117] 'In the season of 1891 as many as eight hundred, chiefly Irish, went from Poplar alone, and it is the same among our poorer fellow-countrymen in other parts of London.'[118] Trampers were moving off to the hop-fields fully a month before the picking season began. 'They are gone for about two months and then we have to another rush', Mr Ruffus, the Superintendent of St Giles workhouse, told an enquirer in 1891.[119] In September they 'infested' the hopping counties of Hereford and Kent, a ragged army of followers, some of them quite indigent: when an inspection was made of the casual ward at Hollingbourne in 1868, only two of the 289 inmates ('all hoppers') had a sum of money amounting to twopence on them.[120] 'The great majority had nothing, and were partly without clothing.'[121]

The social composition of the migrant picking-force gradually changed in the course of the nineteenth century, partly because of the greatly increased demand for hopping labour, partly because of improved methods of cultivation (which shortened the season to as little as three weeks), and partly because of the cheap trains promoted by the railway companies which put the hop-fields within reach of the proletarian family group, instead of only its more able-bodied members. In earlier times the French, the Welsh, and later on the Irish migrant labourers had been prominent: in the second half of the nineteenth century the hopping became increasingly an affair of women and children from the towns. Long-distance migration did not cease (a man from Warrington who went hopping in Kent in 1893 found himself working alongside two Yorkshire colliers who were out on strike) but most recruitment was from nearer localities.[122] At Martley in

Worcestershire the extra hands were reported as coming from 'Stourbridge, Dudley and the mining district', those at Bromyard in Herefordshire were from Cradley Heath.[123] In East Kent many of the hoppers came from Sussex villages and the seaport towns.[124] In mid-Kent and west Kent the immigration was more Cockney, being drawn from the Medway Towns (two thousand hoppers came from Gravesend in 1876), from Croydon, and, above all from Inner London (according to one account, Poplar sent to East Farleigh; Bermondsey to Wateringbury; Shadwell to Paddock Wood).[125] The Farnham hoppers in Surrey (said to number about five thousand in 1887) were attributed by Sturt to 'the slums of Reading and West London', in earlier years they had come from Portsmouth and the south-coast towns.[126] There were slum districts in which something like a general turnout took place as hop-picking approached. Ellen Chase, one of Octavia Hill's property managers, says that, 'exciting rumours' of the size of the hop harvest filled her Deptford street for weeks beforehand; and George Meek, who went hopping in Mayfield, Sussex, in 1883, remarks on the 'rough lot from the purlieus of Edward Street Brighton' whom he found there.[127] Many of the hoppers travelled down together in family and neighbourhood groups, and worked together for the same farmer in their own companies. The frequency of hop-pickers' strikes, one of the more affecting if least noticed features of this seasonal migration, may be partly accounted for by the fact that many of them were already closely knit together.

After the harvests the movement from town to country was reversed. Country occupations began to grow scarce, while in the towns, on the other hand, there was a general revival of trade. The season of journeyings came to an end, and with the approach of cold weather the wandering tribes returned to town 'with the instinct which sends some birds of passage southwards at the same season'.[128] 'I like the tramping life well enough in summer', a girl tramp told Mayhew, 'cause there's plenty of victuals to be had then ... it's the winter ... we can't stand. Then we generally come to London.' Her sentiments were echoed by another of Mayhew's informants – a girl who passed the winter in the Metropolitan Asylum for the Houseless Poor. 'I do like to be in the country in the summer-time', she told him. 'I like hay making and hopping, because that's a good bit of fun … It's the winter that sickens me.'[129] Travelling in winter was 'an unusual thing for the gipsies': it was very little practised by vagrants, or by tramping artisans.[130] Even the regular tramper, who moved about for the sake of keeping on the move, rather than with any particular destination in mind, deserted the roads.

Travelling people began to drift back to town in October, and by November the movement was general. 'All over England', wrote an observer in 1861, 'a characteristic migration sets in … tens and hundreds of thousands … driven by necessity … swarm into the towns.'[131] The largest movement, and certainly the most frequently commented on, was in the direction of London, the winter Mecca of the wandering tribes. But it had its counterpart in a whole series of local migrations from country to town, and in a general change-about, which continued right through the autumn, from outdoor to indoor jobs, and from summer to winter trades. General labourers took their navvying skills into the gas-works. Travelling sawyers exchanged the saw-pit and the woodland clearing for a workshop bench ('towards winter time … a roof over their heads became desirable').[132] Migratory thieves, who conducted summer business al fresco, at the race grounds and the fairs, turned to a spell of safe-cracking or burglary in town aided by the long dark nights. (November, according to Manby Smith, was the month when many of them came back to London.)[133] Cheap-jacks rented shops and conducted mock auctions from their own premises instead of from temporary pitches in the open air.[134] Not all the exchanges were as regular or predictable as this: Booth gives us a glimpse of one or two in the street notes he collected from London School Board visitors: 'Punch and Judy show in summer and makes iron clamps in winter'; 'Works at watercress beds in season, and sweep chimneys in winter.'[135]

A first wave of travellers returned to London immediately after the hop-picking. 'Within a few days' (according to one account) some of the Gypsies were back in town: 'hopping over, they go, almost *en masse* … to buy French and German baskets in

Houndsditch.'[136] In the Kentish suburbs (Gravesend, Woolwich, Greenwich) there was 'always' an influx of labourers at this time, 'men who ... resort to the casual labour afforded by the revolution of the seasons'.[137] Some of them found local employment as rubbish-carters and scavengers, others drifted on into town. In Notting Dale, the common lodging-houses, 'comparatively empty' during hay-making, hop-picking, and fruit-picking, filled up with returning travellers: Bangor Street ('one of the most dangerous streets in London') was said to be inhabited 'almost entirely by' them.[138] St Giles, *'le quartier general des vagabonds'*, was very soon packed: tenements, closed up for the summer, were once again reoccupied, as the inhabitants returned with their summer earnings from Kent; the lodging-houses took on their winter complement of sandwich-men, loafers, and touts; and the casual ward of the workhouse was crammed with travellers (many of them country labourers) making their way back home.[139] The Holborn Irish returned home in mid-October, much to the dismay of the local Medical Officer of Health, who complained of 'crowds of squalid Irish people ... returning from the country to their winter haunts in the Courts and Alleys'.[140] Even on the London waterfront the end of hopping made itself felt: 'I never saw so many callers', wrote a correspondent of the *Labour News* in October 1874, 'the dock labourers having returned from the hop gardens ... seem to have grown in number.'[141]

Not all the travelling harvesters returned at this time. Some of them jobbed about the country until the frosts came, or worked their way home in stages. Potato-lifting kept some of them out of town until November – the West Ham Irish in the early nineteenth century, for example, and the travelling Irish of York in later years.[142] Trade tramps, too, sometimes delayed their arrival in town. Travelling coopers had a mid-autumn season at Lowestoft and Yarmouth where they were employed in the herring trade.[143] In the Northampton shoemaking trade there was a 'very large influx' of travellers a little before Christmas 'when the better sort of work is more brisk, and when there are generally more orders in the "bespoke" department'.[144] Cheap-jacks and showmen were among the latecomers. Many of them followed the great autumn cattle fairs and the Michaelmas and Martinmas 'Hirings', or wound up their season by 'pitching' at the late town fairs. Some showmen delayed their wintering almost till Christmas, when the 'World's Fair' ('the great event in the showman's year') opened at Islington and van-dwellers from all parts of the country made a winter camp in the yard of the Agricultural Hall.[145]

'Wintering in town' was a regular part of the showmen's round, and the difficulty of making it pay was one which cost them much ingenuity. Some, it seems, let out their shows, and lived upon the proceeds, like the little 'half gypsy' colony whom Hollingshead came upon in Owen's Yard, Lambeth, settled in the midst of dust-heaps and factories.[146] The more enterprising adapted themselves to the conditions of town life by hiring temporary premises and putting on their shows indoors (the penny sideshows and 'gaffs' which figure so largely in description of nineteenth-century street-life were often promoted in this way). 'Lord' George Sanger, who seems to have been very successful in making wintering pay, has left an excellent account of his repertory. One winter he went in for *poses plastiques* and conjuring, and hired a warehouse in Bethnal Green Road where the crowd sometimes was so great 'that we had to square the policeman not to interfere'. Another year he took on an empty chapel in Clare Market, and fitted it up as an impromptu theatre, playing a round of pieces, 'gaff fashion', and for Christmas put on a pantomime. Wintering in Liverpool, during the Crimean winter of 1854–5, he took on a large piece of ground near 'Paddy's Market' ('the lowest part of Liverpool'), and built a board and canvas theatre, with admission charges of a penny:

> Here we had a semi-dramatic-cum-circus sort of entertainment that exactly suited the neighbourhood ... what we mostly did was acting on the gaff principle, and there was nothing we were afraid to tackle in the dramatic line, from Shakespeare downwards ... One of our best and most popular actors ... was Bill Matthews. He ... made a big hit ... by his impersonation of Paddy Kelly, an Irishman who had distinguished himself as a soldier at the Alma, news of which battle, fought on September 20th, had thrilled the nation. Well, Matthews did a riding act, 'Paddy Kelly, the hero of the Russian war' and in his uniform, slashing at the enemy with a

sword and plentiful dabs from a sponge of rose-pink, excited the audience to frenzy.[147]

Trampers 'led by an instinct somewhat analogous to that of ... animals who lurk in holes from the inclemency of the season', came up to town for the shelter and the warmth. In London, according to Mayhew, they turned up each year 'as regularly as noblemen' to season it in town.[148] 'In the winter season', the Chief Constable of Manchester complained,

> Tramps flocked to large towns such as Manchester, whether they can obtain warm sleeping-quarters in the various brick-yards, boiler-houses, and different buildings connected with factories and workshops; also they can generally obtain free meals, which are provided by the various philanthropic societies in Manchester during the cold season. In the summer month they migrate to the country ... sleeping out in the open when the weather is good.[149]

Night Refuges ('strawyards' as they were known to *habitués*), brought many of them to town.[150] In London, critics alleged, there was an immediate increase in vagrancy when they opened up for the winter (usually in November, but the precise date depended on the state of the weather).[151] 'A great number of persons come to London in November, when the refuges are generally opened', an officer of the Mendicity Society complained. 'It is not an unfrequent answer, when they are asked, "How is it you have come to London again? You were here last year." "Oh, I thought the Houseless was open".'[152] Night refuges (which were financed by private subscription) were much more popular with travellers than the workhouse, and, while they were open, slept many more people than the metropolitan Casual Wards.[153] The regime, though spartan, was comparatively kind. The stranger was offered warmth and shelter without any of the humiliations and restraints associated with the Poor Law. Inmates could stay for as long as a month at a time (in the Casual Wards the rule was two nights only), and they were allowed to go out when they liked (in the Casual Wards shelter had to be paid for by hard labour and forcible detention for a day). At the Playhouse Yard

Asylum, Cripplegate, the oldest and largest of the metropolitan asylums (it later removed to Banner Street) the dormitories were kept 'always ... heated', and there was a gigantic communal fire. 'As these are lighted some time before the hour of opening, the place has a warmth and cosiness which must be very grateful to those who have encountered the cold air all the day, and perhaps the night before.'[154] Night Refuges existed in a number of the larger towns: Manchester, Birmingham, and Edinburgh each had one; in London there were seven (more, when the Salvation Army embarked on its social work), quite apart from such specialised institutions as the Destitute Sailors' Asylum, in Well Street, Ratcliffe Highway, and critics may well have been right to hold them responsible for so many homeless men making London their winter retreat.[155]

The autumn migrations, like those of the spring, took place in stages, and once again it was the outskirts and environs of the town which felt them first. Vagrants, it seems, made their way into London sideways, circling the outer ring of the metropolis, and testing the hospitality of the brickfields – or the suburban Casual Wards – before making their way into town. Travelling prostitutes seem also to have arrived back in this way, with preliminary comings and goings. 'They travel round the country in summer and come into London in November' an officer of the Mendicity Society told an enquiry in 1846. 'If they come before the refuge is open they go to Peckham, then they go to St. Olave's, and then to Greenwich and other unions.'[156] Gypsies ended their autumn journeys on the outer peripheries of town ('as close as you please to the skirts of civilization'), but as the weather grew more severe some of them moved further in, and went to live in rooms.[157] 'They leave the country, and suburban districts of London', wrote a City Missionary in 1860, '... and make their dwelling in some low court ... 2 and 3 families ... in one small room.'[158] George Smith came upon a little colony of this kind when he visited Canning Town the winter of 1879–80, seventeen families crowding together in two small cottages, where they had crept 'for ... the winter'.[159] Families like this occasionally visited Deptford. Ellen Chase recalls that they would 'tide over the rough weather by renting temporary accommodation. The walls would remain as bare as they found them ... young and old sat upon upturned boxes about the small grate, as contented as if it were a camp fire.'[160]

As well as the travellers, returning to base, the towns received a large winter influx of refugees. Some came for the charities and shelter. Many were winter out-of-works, who came up to town (sometimes unwillingly) when every other resource had failed them. 'It was when the snow set in ... I thought I would come to London', an inmate at the Houseless Poor Asylum told Mayhew:

The last job I had was six weeks before Christmas, at Boston, in Lincolnshire. I couldn't make 1s. 6d. a day on account of the weather. I had 13s., however, to start with, and I went on the road ... going where I heard there was a chance of a job, up or down anywhere, here or there, but there was always the same answer, 'Nobody wanted – no work for their own constant men'. I was so beat out as soon as my money was done – it lasted ten days – that I parted with my things one by one. First my waistcoat, then my stockings (three pair of them), then three shirts ... After I left Boston, I got into Leicestershire, and was at Cambridge and Wisbeach, and Lynn, and Norwich; and I heard of a job among brickmakers at Low Easthrop, in Suffolk, but it was no go. The weather was against it, too. It was when the snow set in. And then I thought I would come to London, as God in his goodness might send me something to do.[161]

London was full of such winter refugees, caricatured, and yet in some sense truly represented, by the 'froze out gardeners', who regularly appeared in winter as beggars, or buskers, about the city streets. Night Refuges ('the outcast's haven') catered largely for men of this class. 'Travelling tradesmen' were said to compose the bulk of the inmates of the Ham Yard Hospice – trade tramps who had been reduced to a state of complete destitution and could not afford even the price of a lodging-house bed; country labourers figured largely at Banner Street, 'a very rough class of men, who will work if they can get it ... digging among fruit trees and market-garden work – in the fields'.[162]

A certain number of farm labourers, turned off after harvest, drifted into the towns, and they were joined by others as country employment grew scarcer and the weather more severe. In Norfolk and Suffolk there was a class of freelance labourers, known as 'joskins', who went off after harvest to Lowestoft and Yarmouth and got work in the autumn fishings (October and November were the height of the East Anglian herring season); another class migrated to the breweries of Burton-on-Trent.[163] Farm labourers in Monmouthshire and Nottinghamshire took up winter employment in the pits; in Carmarthenshire, at mid-century, some of them went off to the ironworks ('in the summer they return home or go to England for the harvest').[164] In Sussex, according to a report of 1895, 'the more helpless' made for Brighton and Hove, 'large towns ... where there are many charities'.[165] Most of these migrants disappeared, for the season, into obscurity – mere 'birds of passage' in the town – and the historian is fortunate when he comes upon an individual case, like the one recorded by Steel-Maitland and Miss Squire in Jenner's Row, Birmingham:

> Mr. J. and his wife, in third floor front, were occupied in making strawbaskets, which they sell to some of the family shops. Mr. J. about fifty, seemed a superior type of man. He said he should not take to regular home-life now. For the last twenty years he had tramped from town to town. During the winter he and his wife took a furnished room, and in the summer they walked into Herefordshire, where he did apple-pulling, and other odd jobs at the cider harvest, for a farmer. They were allowed to lock up a few pots and pans and a bed in a shed on the farm, and to this they returned every summer. Mr. J. said he had wintered in Plymouth, Manchester, Bristol and in London. They generally reckoned to be in the country for about five months of the year. If times were good, 'The missus' might perhaps go by train, but he always walked ... He thought he should go to Cardiff next winter, if all was well ... He had found Birmingham an expensive place, and did not think he would return. (This was his first visit.)[166]

One of the most enduring of these autumn migrations was that which brought many hundreds of country labourers to work in the breweries. It has been vividly documented from oral tradition by George Ewart Evans, and his account can be supplemented by documentary references from earlier years. Maltsters were usually taken on at the beginning of October and continued till about the latter end of May, 'being about seven months of the year'.[167] The great majority of them were drawn from the country – 'big-framed men, strong enough to handle the comb-sacks (sixteen stones each) of barley'. At Hertford and Ware, according to a *Morning Chronicle* account in 1850, 'nearly the whole of them are employed as agricultural labourers when not engaged in malting'.[168] At Newark, where 460 maltsters were employed in the 1890s, only about a third of the men were engaged all the year round, 'the rest go into the kilns in September, and remain till May or June'.[169] Farm labourers in Derbyshire went up to Burton-on-Trent. 'The winter employment in Burton helps to keep wages up', the Agricultural Employment Commissioners were told in 1868, 'especially for the hired single men.' 'A good many men go to Burton in the winter, where they get 13s. a week and beer ... many of them would be out of work in winter if they didn't.'[170] The catchment area for Burton was very wide indeed. In the later nineteenth century it extended as far as East Anglia, and George Ewart Evans has collected some remarkably detailed testimonies from labourers who made the last of these autumn journeys in the years 1900–30. He has also recovered a Burton labour list for 1890–1 which shows the extent of the East Anglian

Name of worker	Home village	Nearest railway station
ADDISON, George	Melton	Woodbridge
ASHEN, Henry	Flempton	Bury St. Edmunds
ASHEN, William	Flempton	Bury St. Edmunds
BALDWIN, William	Aldburgh	Harleston
BARBER, Walter	Martlesham	Woodbridge
BEAUMONT, Peter	Baylham	Ipswich
BETTS, Arthur	St. Cross	Harleston
BACKHOUSE, Jesse	Sutton	Woodbridge
BLOOMFIELD, Richard	St. Lawrence	Harleston
BRAGG, John	Bardwell	Bury St. Edmunds
BRETT, Charles	Martlesham	Woodbridge
BROOKS, Alfred	Pakenham	Bury St. Edmunds

hirings. It is taken from the records of Messrs Bass, Ratcliff & Gretton. Here are the first twelve entries.[171]

Building-workers flocked up to town when the frosts put a stop to the country trade. In London they figured very largely among the winter refugees – pick and shovel men, who tramped the metropolitan building-sites looking for work ('*bona fide* navvies, up to "Lunnun" in search of a job'); country craftsmen like the 'strong and handy carpenter' whom the roving correspondent of the *Labour News* met in Greek Street, a 'most desponding' man who had left Watford just after Christmas, and tramped it inside and outside the town, without finding himself a place; painters and decorators 'calling at every job, and offering, in many instances, to work at half-starvation wages'. 'Outside the heavy jobs on hand', he writes in January 1873 '… maybe seen building hands and labourers … asking the foreman to put them on, and the reply is that they have already too many men.'[172] Painters were particularly badly placed, and are often singled out for attention in distress reports. At the Newport Market Refuge for instance, they were by far the most numerous group of inmates – 57 of the 644 men admitted in 1889.[173]

The months from November to February were always a bad time in the building trade, but it was only in the country and suburban branches of the trade that the standstill was complete.[174] In the towns there were big contract jobs where work continued in all but the worst of weather. Stonemasons, 'though apt to be severely hit by a really hard winter', stood a fair chance of getting work; so did navvies. The ordinary builders' labourers were less well placed, but some got employment with the vestries, some went into the gas-works, and there was always a chance of employment wherever there was a heavy job in hand. In the mid-Victorian years 'no end of work' was provided (even in winter) by town improvement schemes, by the building of Board Schools and Model Dwellings, churches and chapels, town halls and commercial offices, by extension work on the railway terminals and the docks; by road-widening, tramways and the laying out of drainage works and sewers.[175] In London such great undertakings as the building of the Metropolitan Railway (where the writer of the *Reminiscences of a Stonemason* was taken on for tunnelling work in January 1866), the Thames Embankment, and the Law Courts, were a continuing source of winter employment.[176] Cubitt's, one of the largest London builders, seem actually to have put on extra men in winter: 'when the summer comes they go brickmaking', a branch manager told an enquiry in the 1890s, 'the Brick men are very good workers, and we always give them a job. They come and go.'[177] It was the same in some of the big provincial towns, to judge from a trade report which appeared in January 1882.[178]

> LIVERPOOL ... the works in hand are of almost unexampled importance and magnitude. The City Corporation is proceeding actively with its immense operations for supplementing the present water supply with water from the Vyrnwy reservoir. Each of the railway companies having a terminus at Liverpool is making extensions. The Mersey Docks and Harbour Board is engaged in improving at various points its vast system of docks. The scheme for tunnelling the Mersey is being pushed forward actively. A new university is being erected. New commercial and trading edifices are springing up in all directions.

> MANCHESTER. In this district the building trade is fairly active so far as heavy work for public and business purposes is concerned but in housebuilding, either of the cottage, or in the better class of dwellings, there is comparatively little doing ... The Manchester Corporation have several important works in hand. A new free library and reading-room with the basement occupied by shops ... recently erected on the old Knott Mill Fair ground, are on the point of completion ... New baths are ... being erected by the Corporation for the Rochdale Road district ... the contractor ... Mr. James Hind ... has also in hand for the Corporation the erection of women's swimming baths, as an addition to the present Leaf Street baths ... Amongst other important work at present in hand ... is a new General Post Office, a new railway station for the London and North Western Railway Company, and new business premises for the proprietors of the *Manchester Guardian*.

Perhaps sailors might be classed among the winter refugees. There were many more of them on shore in winter than
in summer, weather-bound or without a berth. Some found
shore-going occupations for the season – for instance as dock
labourers or as shipwrights – but most of them swelled the ranks
of the unemployed: at the Destitute Sailors' Asylum, Well Street,
London, established in 1827 to supply shelter, food and clothing
to distressed seamen, 'and to keep them until they can obtain
employment', winter admissions were more than double those
of the summer months.[179] The months of December, January, and
February 'usually' found the shipping trade at its lowest point in
the West Coast ports – at Fleetwood in Lancashire, for example,
at Liverpool (where the emigrant traffic seasonally collapsed),
and at Milford Haven, where a great number of vessels, 'large
and small', and manned by men of many nations, sheltered for
the winter.[180] Many thousands of sailors were shored up in the
East Coast ports, when the Sound froze over and the Baltic trade
came to a stop. The period of this winter standstill varied from
year to year, depending on the state of the weather: in 1895 it
was causing unemployment among the seamen of North Shields
and Grimsby as late as May; in mild winters it could be quite
brief.[181] Bagshawe has left a vivid description of the winter scene
at Whitby when the Baltic traders laid up:

> The old quays were thronged with ... lads ... home from long
> cruises ... Grave old skippers stood in knots at the Bridge-end and
> fought their battles with gales and bad holding-ground over again,
> and discussed the chances of good freights in the coming spring,
> when the ice should loosen its hold on the northern waters, and
> each of them would strive to be the first of the year to break into
> the silent fiords and gulfs.[182]

For the man who was looking for work, October was a good
time for coming up to town. Vestries were beginning to recruit
sweepers and street orderlies, in anticipation of the late autumnal
muds; extra men were taken on at the public parks for end-of-
season gravelling and repairs.[183] The gas-works were making
up their winter labour force; the breweries were beginning their

'regular busy season' (in London the biggest brewings took place in October, immediately following the arrival of the hops).[184] In the building industry there was a late burst of employment – 'an early covering-in process seems to be the one thing aimed at', wrote the *Labour News* in October 1876.[185] Some of the work-shop trades enjoyed a 'second season' in mid-autumn (hatters and brushmakers, for example);[186] in others it was the peak period of the year, notably amongst the journeymen coopers,[187] the bookbinders, and in the printing trades, where the produc-tion of Christmas numbers, almanacks, and the 'great variety of … literary productions that usually crop up about this season of the year', kept 'grass hands' in full work.[188]

A certain amount of extra employment became seasonally available on the waterfront. In the Liverpool docks some 2,500 extra porters were taken on when the cotton season began: 'A certain number of these are men who systematically follow another trade in one season or go to sea and come back for the busy period between October and March.'[189] In the London docks there were more men employed in December than at any other time of the year. Waterfront industries too were seasonally brisk, notably the oil mills at Hull, 'the largest seed-crushing centre in the United Kingdom', and cotton-picking at Liverpool.[190] There was a steadily increasing volume of work at the riggers, the sail-makers, and the shipwrights as the weather more severe. Winter was the height of the repairing season, with many ships laid up for the purpose of dry docking or put on the slip to have their bottoms caulked, coal-tarred, and blackleaded. At Whitby, when the Baltic traders laid up, the town presented a 'stirring scene', with the ships moored in tiers across the upper harbour, and many men at work. 'The caulking mallets rang merrily in half-a-dozen shipyards; rope-walks and sail-lofts worked overtime, and the air was redolent of pitch-kettles and new timber.'[191] Deep-sea ships continued to be treated in this way in the days of steam: the *Great Eastern* was put on the gridiron after its first transatlantic cross-ing, and laid up at Milford for the winter.[192] The winter harvest of wrecks brought more work to the repairing yards as well as providing salvage men (Such as the Yarmouth beachmen) with a full-time occupation. 'Seamen seem more abundant than berths, but not more so than is usual at this season', wrote the west of England correspondent of the *Labour News* in January 1873, 'the many shipping casualties having found temporary employment for many of them, and abundant work for the shipwrights and sail makers.'[193]

Industrial employment was less open to the wayfarer, but a limited amount of it became seasonally available. For example, oil mills ('very warm work') recruited their winter labour force from those who followed the summer trades.[194] So did some of the coal-mines. Both steel-smelting, which was slackest in June and July, and iron-puddling, which was at full stretch in November, were to a certain extent winter trades, with extra jobs at times for the rough class of general labourer.[195] Gas-works were by far the most frequent employers of this class of labour. They began putting on extra men 'about the latter end of August', and took in many more in midwinter, when the 'dark ... days of fog and cold' drew in.[196] The work (stoking and firing) was intensely laborious (there was said to be no other trade in England where a man lost weight and size more quickly), and the hours were incredibly long (a seventy-eight-hour week was quite normal in 1882).[197] But it was very well paid. Winter 'so much dreaded by others', was hailed by gas-stokers as an old friend (wrote an observer) 'the harbinger of ... plenty'.[198] Winter hands at the gas-works were largely recruited from migrant labourers who spent the summer out of town, brickmakers especially, but also a 'good proportion' of builders' labourers, navvies, and 'many ... who ... go into the country for farming work in the summer'.[199] Will Thorne, who went navvying and brick-loading in the spring and summer has left a very good account of the way men tramped up to town for the work:

> I had always wanted to go to London and ... my desire ... was stimulated by letters from an old workmate who was now working at the Old Kent Road Gas Works ... I finally decided to go ... in November, 1881. With two friends I started out to walk the journey, filled with the hope that we would be able to obtain employment, when we got there, with the kind assistance of my friend ... We had little money when we started, not enough to pay

for our food and lodging each night until we arrived in London. Some days we walked as much as twenty miles, and other days less. Our money was gone at the end of the third day … For two nights we slept out – once under a haystack, and once in an old farm shed … On arrival in London we tried to find … my friend … but … were unsuccessful. Our money was all gone, so there was nothing for us to do but to walk around until late at night, and then try to find some place to sleep. We found an old building and slept in it that night. The next day, Sunday late in the afternoon, we got to the Old Kent Road Gas Works, and applied for work. To my great surprise, the man we had been looking for was working at the time. He spoke to the foreman and I was given a job.[200]

Quite apart from the regular winter trades, such as gas-stoking and cotton-portering, there was a multitude of chance occupations and residuary employments which the migrant classes were well-placed to take up. Street-trading was a major resource to which many of them turned during their winter stay in town. Gypsies hawked their clothes-pegs and basketry about the suburbs, canvassing from door to door; and they turned up in force on Fridays for market day at the Caledonian Road. Travelling Italians took up position, with tin cans and braziers, outside the pubs, selling roast potatoes or hot chestnuts; organ-grinders perambulated the streets. The migrant Irish often turned trader for the season when winter drove them back to town. The street trade in cutlery, which was particularly brisk in winter, seems to have been largely in the hands of those who went on summer rounds, like 'Showman George', the man who makes a brief appearance in *The Life and Adventures of a Cheap Jack*: 'a big, stout, free-spoken, and rather jolly fellow, who kept a large drinking-booth at the fairs and races during the summer months, and in the winter hawked butchers' cutlery'.[201] So was the winter sale of nuts and oranges, which in London was the special province of the Irish. 'When we got to London', one of Mayhew's informants told him, '… we got to work at peas-picking, my wife and me, in the gardens about. That is for the summer. In the winter we sold oranges in the street, while she lived, and we had nothing from the parishes.'[202] The development of Christmas as a great spending holiday increased the possibility of impromptu sales, and produced its own fugitive callings, such as the kerbstone trade in novelties and toys (especially penny toys), the crying of almanacks and Christmas numbers, and the street-sale of holly and mistletoe. Christmas also helped to loosen the purse strings of the rich, and made life temporarily easier for the 'griddlers' and 'chaunters'. As children were taught in the nursery:

> Christmas is coming
> The goose is getting fat
> Please put a penny in the old man's hat.

London in the weeks before Christmas was a paradise of odd jobs. Extra hands were taken on at the Post Office, to cope with Christmas deliveries; at Covent Garden, where there was a 'second season' in fresh fruit and flowers; at the railway stations; and at the docks. The Christmas pantomime season gave temporary employment to a whole army of 'extras' – scene-shifters, stage-hands, ballet-girls and 'supers'.[203] Christmas was the height of the advertising season, and men of the lodging-house class were widely employed in delivery work on tradesmen's hand-bills (a winter refugee from Stockton, lodging in St Giles, was earning 2s. 6d. a day for this in November and December 1877); also hand-bill distribution at the street corners, and board-carrying.[204]

In London something like six or seven thousand men were employed as board-carriers at this time, more than twice as many as at other times of the year, 'the extra contingent being provided by those who have spent their summer months in agricultural pursuits'.[205] The work was paid for at rates varying from one shilling to one-and-eightpence, the 'highflyers' (who carried over-head boards) being paid at a somewhat higher rate than the others ('except for theatrical & publisher's work which is always the worse paid').[206] Some of this work was done on a casual basis, but Nagle's, one of the leading London contractors, employed men for as long as a month at a time, and according to Booth's investigators, a man, if known to the contractors, might reckon on employment 'throughout the season'.[207] The chief employment office for the West End boardmen was at Ham Yard, Leicester

Square, where an enterprising contractor had established himself next door to the soup-kitchen. In the early morning it served as the sandwich-board equivalent of the dock-gate call. A forest of grimy hands shot up for each of the jobs, and little knots of the chosen came forward from the throng. At night a 'Doré-like' group of figures were to be seen, 'camping ... as near as they can to the office which doles them out their jobs'.[208] On 29 January 1904, when the L.C.C. enumerators of the homeless counted forty-nine of them, they were sleeping out (or making themselves comfortable for the night) by the air vents of the Palace Theatre 'on account of the heat coming from the boilers through the grating'.[209]

Christmas was the winter harvest of the wandering tribes. When it was over, things changed for the worse. January and February were bad months for the working man, and especially for the poor and insecure. Almost every trade experienced a lull after the Christmas rush of work, and unemployment became widespread as the weather grew more severe. Even so, the balance of advantage, from the point of view of the homeless, remained overwhelmingly on the side of the town – in fact it was after Christmas that the last of the migrations to town took place. There was warmth and shelter in the town, even if work was impossible to come by, soup to be obtained at public kitchens, open to all comers, Night Refuges and Asylums in place of the workhouse, public works (always started up by the vestries when the season was particularly severe) in place of the humiliations of the parish stoneyard.[210]

Bad weather itself, in the conditions of town life, was a prolific source of occasional opportunities. Wintry weather added urgency to the street beggar's cry. Rainy days were a godsend to the cab touts who loitered about the railway stations and the theatres, and to the crossing-sweeper, who levied a small tribute on the wealthier passer-by. After a big snow thousands of hard-up opportunists took to the streets. Augustus Mayhew noticed how 'the whole town seems to swarm with ... sweepers, who go about from house to house, knocking at the doors, and offering to clear the pavement before the dwelling, according to the Act of Parliament, for twopence.'[211] Frosts, too, had their collateral advantages for the wide awake. In London the 'ice harvest' on the northern heights brought some hundreds of men foraging, with ice-carts and shallows, to Finchley Common and Hampstead Heath, while at the frost fairs which sprang up in the public parks, the hard-up could earn odd pennies by sweeping the ice for the skaters, putting on and hiring out skates, or by trading in comforters and sweets.[212] 'Lord' George Sanger, wintering in London one year during the 1840s, found this a profitable line:

A terrible winter it was, with an unusually hard, long spell of hard frost. Our funds in hand were not very heavy, and seeing all our cash going out and none coming in made me very unhappy. At last, however, I struck a new line with considerable success. Wandering on to Bow Common and Hackney Marshes I found numbers of people sliding and skating on the large ponds there. They were trying to keep warm in the bitter weather, and I noticed that, despite the crowds gathered there, nothing was being sold or hawked. That gave me an idea.

I knew how to make rock and toffee, such as was sold at the fairs, for I had assisted in the process many times. Here was my chance. I went and bought about ten pounds of coarse moist sugar, at that time sevenpence a pound, and some oil of peppermint, borrowed some pans to boil it in, and very soon had a nice little stock of strong, good-looking peppermint rock. Then I took it to Hackney Marshes near the biggest piece of ice, and at a penny a lump it sold like wildfire. I was cleaned out in an hour, and had made several shillings profit.

I could see I had hit on a good thing, and at once went to work on a bigger scale. I borrowed what little money my brothers William and John had saved, added my stock to it, and then went and purchased a big parcel of sugar from a grocer in the Whitechapel Road and more oil of peppermint. This I boiled into rock, which was cut into penny lumps, and having pressed my brothers William and John into the service we started out. The rock sale proved as brisk as ever, and we came home with our pockets loaded with coppers and silver, having made over two pounds profit.

The problem of how to live through the winter in London without trenching on the savings from the summer show business, savings that were always needed to give a good start to the caravans when the time came for the road again, was solved.[213]

With the return of spring the wandering tribes began to stir. Sailors, no longer weather-bound, signed on at the Registry Offices. Showmen put their caravans in harness, and set off for the early fairs. Cheap-jacks and packmen resumed their country rounds. By March the emigrant traffic, almost at a standstill in the three winter months, was moving to the first of its seasonal peaks. In the work-shop trades the 'regular roadster' – the congenital nomad – showed signs of restlessness as soon as the sun began to rise higher in the sky. Such a man was Dominic McCarthy, the travelling composi-tor affectionately recalled in W. E. Adams's *Memoirs of a Social Atom*.[214] Every winter he came to London and supported himself as best he could by getting an occasional job as a 'grass hand'. In the spring his wandering life was resumed. He was a good workman, Adams tells us, but incurably nomadic, 'whenever the proper season came round'. George Acorn, recalling his childhood in Bethnal Green, describes a similar type, a tramp shoemaker called 'Old Bill', who turned up in the neighbourhood every winter, 'bronzed and tattered', and left again in the spring. He was employed at 'Little Wonder', a back-street cobbler's shop, and while winter lasted, and the nights were long, he would sit contentedly at his bench, heel-balling or sewing 'as patiently as anybody':

But as soon as the sap began to rise, and the buds to burst in the trees, he would get fidgety, would rise from his stool, and, going to the door, would look at the sky, with his hand shading his eyes.

'Weather breaking, eh?' Jordan commented.

'Yes', the old cobbler would reply, as if a new spirit had entered into him.

'Want to be off?' His employer took a delight in putting these leading questions to him.

'Not just yet', 'Old Bill' replied, 'but very soon, very soon.'

As the days lengthened his eyes fairly glowed with anticipation, his restiveness increased.

One evening I called in at Jordan's to find a vacant chair.

'Where's Old Bill?' I inquired.

'God knows', was the reply. 'Somewhere in the country by now, getting fresh air, and seeing things.'

'Does he go away every year?' I asked.

'He has, ever since I've known him, George. He's got the wandering spirit, and when he sees the green leaves a-coming on the trees he has to go out and taste the country air; it would kill him to stop here all the year round.'[215]

The wandering tribes found their place in the underlife of the nineteenth-century town, and it is not easy to log their comings and goings with precision. Their circuits were innumerable, their settlements obscure, and their interconnections with more settled lives can often only be conjectured. Numbers are difficult, perhaps impossible, to arrive at, since they varied with the changing of the seasons and the ups and downs of trade. Nor is it easy to define the boundaries of each individual group. The wayfaring constituency was in a constant state of flux. The tramp, the navvy, and the pedlar might be one and the same person at different stages of life, or even at different seasons of the year; the 'gaff' proprietor might spend his summer on the roads; the freelance labourer turn to busking, or board-carrying, or gas-stoking, when winter drove him into town. The distinction between the nomadic life and the settled one was by no means hard and fast. Tramping was not the prerogative of the social outcast it is today; it was a normal phase in the life of entirely respectable classes of working men; it was a frequent resort of the out-of-works and it was a very principle of existence for those who followed the itinerant callings and trades. Within the wandering tribes themselves the nomadic phase and the settled were often intertwined, with men and women exchanging a fixed occupation for a roving one whenever conditions were favourable.

One thing at least is clear. The wandering tribes (like other nomadic peoples) followed well-established circuits, and journeyed according to a definite plan. There were relatively few who moved about the country simply for the sake of keeping on the move, or who travelled hither and thither, as the spirit moved them without a springboard, a haven or regular ports-of-call. Some kept a foothold in town all the year round; many of them wintered there, and turned up again 'as regularly as noblemen' when the long nights drew in. Their comings and goings were closely bound up with the social economy of the town, and the openness (or otherwise) of its employment and its trades. The wandering tribes were often the object of hostile legislation, whether to bring their lodging-houses under inspection and control, to bar them from using city wastes, or to harass them from pursuing their callings about the city streets. Their children, after 1870, were subject to the eager ministrations of the School Board Visitors; the camping sites of those who lived in movable dwellings fell one by one to the enterprise of the speculative builder, or the railinged enclosure of the public parks. But it was economic change, in the later Victorian years, which really undermined them: the growth of more regular employment, especially for the unskilled, and the decline of the 'reserve army of labour' in both the country and the towns; the mechanisation of harvest work, and the displacement of travelling labourers by regular farm servants; the rise of the fixed holiday resort in place of the perambulating round of wakes and feasts and fairs; the extension of shops to branches of trade which previously had been in the hands of itinerant packmen and dealers.[216] Towards the end of the century the towns began more thoroughly to absorb their extra population, and to wall them in all the year round.

Workshop of the World

Steam Power and Hand Technology in mid-Victorian Britain

There is no doubt whatever that the people of England work harder, mentally and physically, than the people of any other country on the face of the earth. Whether we take the town or the country population, the same plodding industry is apparent, and the respites enjoyed by either in the shape of holidays are few and far between ... We have no desire in stating the fact that Englishmen work harder than their neighbours to make them discontented with their lot; far from it. It is due to their untiring industry and to the natural advantages of the country of which we are so justly proud, that England holds the foremost rank among the nations of the earth.

– Mechanics Magazine, vol. III, no. 280, 27 April 1860

The genius of Great Britain is mechanism; the master-spirit the civil engineer; her tendencies, to relieve labour from its drudgery, and delegate to iron, and steam, and water, the real weight and burden of toil.

– Illustrated Exhibition, 7 June 1851

Nowhere do we find a more shameful squandering of human labour-power for the most despicable purposes than in England, the land of machinery.

– Marx, Capital, Dona Torr ed., I. 391.

The Messrs. Whitehead send their Buenos Aires wool to be picked in the prisons of Manchester, that species of raw material being so coarse and dirty that it is difficult to find free labourers to meddle with it. A great deal of the ordinary picking is, however, done by the women in their cottages in the neighbourhood.
    – *Morning Chronicle*, 'Labour and the Poor, Manufacturing Districts XIII: Saddleworth', 29 November 1849

Introduction. The Machinery Question

Whatever their disagreements about the origins of the industrial revolution, economic historians are in little doubt about its effects.[1] Steam power and machinery transformed the labour process, and acted on society as an independent or quasi-independent force, demonic or beneficent according to the point of view, but in any event inescapable. Commodities were cheapened and new markets opened up for them; labour was made enormously more productive at the same time as the physical burden of toil was eased; mechanical ingenuity took the place of handicraft skill. David Landes's summary in *The Unbound Prometheus* is both influential and representative:

> In the eighteenth century, a series of inventions transformed the manufacture of cotton in England and gave rise to a new mode of production – the factory system. During these years, other branches of industry effected comparable advances, and all these together, mutually reinforcing one another, made possible further gains on an ever-widening front. The abundance and variety of these innovations almost defy compilation, but they may be subsumed under three principles: the substitution of machines – rapid, regular, precise, tireless – for human skill and effort; the substitution of inanimate for animate sources of power ... thereby opening to man a new and almost unlimited supply of energy; the use of new and far more abundant raw materials, in particular, the substitution of mineral for vegetable or animal substances.[2]

This account has the merit of symmetry, but the notion of substitution is problematic, since in many cases there are no real equivalents to compare. The fireman raising steam in an engine cab, or the boilermaker flanging plates in a furnace, were engaged in wholly new occupations which had no real analogy in previous times. So too, if one thinks of the operations they were called upon to perform, rather than the nature of the finished product, were the mill-hands of Lancashire and the West Riding. And if one looks at technology from the point of view of labour rather than that of capital, it is a cruel caricature to represent machinery as dispensing with toil. High-pressure engines had their counterpart in high-pressure work, endless chain mechanisms in non-stop jobs. And quite apart from the demands which machinery itself imposed there was a huge army of labour engaged in supplying it with raw materials, from the slave labourers on the cotton plantations of the United States to the tinners and copper miners of Cornwall. The industrial revolution, so far from abridging human labour, created a whole new world of labour-intensive jobs: railway navvying is a prime example, but one could consider too the puddlers and shinglers in the rolling mills, turning pig-iron into bars, the alkali workers stirring vats of caustic soda, and a whole spectrum of occupations in what the Factory legislation of the 1890s was belatedly to recognise as 'dangerous' trades. Working pace was transformed in old industries as well as new, with slow and cumbersome methods of production giving way, under the pressure of competition, to overwork and sweating.

Nor is it possible to equate the new mode of production with the factory system. Capitalist enterprise took quite different forms in, for instance, cabinet-making and the clothing trades, where rising demand was met by a proliferation of small producers. In agriculture and the fisheries it depended upon an increase in numbers rather than the concentration of production under one roof. In metalwork and engineering – at least until the 1880s – it was the workshop rather than the factory which prevailed, in boot and shoemaking, cottage industry. The distributive trades rested on the broad shoulders of carmen and dockers, the electric telegraph on the juvenile runner's nimble feet. Capitalist growth was rooted in a sub-soil of small-scale enterprise. It depended not on one technology but on many, and made use, too, of a promiscuous variety of profit-making devices, from the adulteration of soot (in which there was an international trade with the West Indies, as well as a local one with farmers for manure) to the artificial colouring of smoked haddocks.[3] Bread was dosed with liberal sprinklings of alum to disguise inferior wheats; low-grade cloths were camouflaged with 'size'.[4] In domestic housebuilding, scamped workmanship kept the speculative builder afloat, while in the East End furniture trade orange boxes provided the raw materials for piano stools and Louis Quatorze cabinets. The 'Golden Dustman', immortalised by Charles Dickens in *Our Mutal Friend*, is as representative a figure of mid-Victorian capitalism as the Bradford millionaires pilloried by John Ruskin for their taste. So too – from the same novel – are the Veneerings, whose provincial counterparts rose to affluence by cotton 'corners' on Liverpool or Manchester Exchange. One thousand needlewomen made the fortunes of Nicoll, the Regent Street sweater, while the railway speculations of the 1840s rested on the muscle power of three hundred thousand navvies.[5]

Economic historians have had remarkably little to say about either labour process or the relationship of technology to work. They are much more concerned with business cycles and measuring rates of growth. Commercial achievement excites them, and whole histories will be written to celebrate the achievements of individual firms. Railways are discussed as a source of investment, and their comparative contribution to economic growth is a subject of hot debate; nothing at all is said about how the rolling stock was made or the engine cabins staffed or merchandise unloaded. Bricks, too, are treated as an index of investment, without so much as a word being said of the primitive conditions in which they were made, or the ferocious toil imposed on the men, women, and children who made them.[6] Production is seen at second or third remove, in terms of inventory cycles and aggregate profitability: we do not learn how the furnaces were de-clinkered, or the iron steam ships coaled.

Except in the 'heroic' age of invention, economic historians have very little to say about machinery. They may tell us what it did for production, but not what it meant for the producers, and their preoccupation in recent years with 'takeoff' – 'that decisive interval in the history of a society when growth becomes its normal condition' – means that they give far more attention to the progress of mechanisation, and the constellation of circumstances favouring it, than to measuring its human costs. The plight of the hand-loom weavers in the 1830s is admitted, even insisted upon, but since they are regarded as a solitary and to some extent exceptional case, they do not seriously obstruct the linear march of improvement, and once they have been disposed of the historian passes quickly to the problems of a 'mature' economy, and the triumphs of Free Trade.

For labour historians, the machinery question attracts attention chiefly in the 1820s and 1830s, when Cartwright's loom was throwing thousands out of work, and when the rival merits of an agrarian and an industrial society ('past and present') were being vigorously canvassed on all sides. The scenario is arresting, with midnight raiding parties, rickyard incendiaries and factories besieged. But the drama is short-lived, and once the protagonists have performed their parts they are quickly shuffled off-stage. Opposition to machinery is assigned to the pre-history of socialism, when it was 'utopian' rather than 'scientific'; and the machine-breakers, despite Eric Hobsbawm's pioneering attempt to interpret their action in the light of modern collective bargaining (machine-breaking as a form of strike) take their place in the gallery of 'primitive', pre-industrial rebels, along with such other early-nineteenth-century martyrs to oppression as Jeremiah Brandreth and Dic Penderyn.[7] Luddism appears as a doomed, if heroic, resistance to the ineluctable forces of change – a fight against the inevitable – the Swing Riots of 1830 as 'the last labourers' revolt'. Yet in industry after industry the machinery question was still being fought out in mid-Victorian times, and there was a whole spectrum of occupations where mechanisation was still being resisted, or its scope drastically curtailed, in the 1890s: the last great machinery strike in the boot and shoe trade did not take place until 1895; while as late as 1898 a steam saw mill was blown up in the Forest of Dean.[8] There were also striking regional variations in the application of invention and progress of the machine, and in some cases at least the strength or otherwise of the workers' opposition seems to have been the deciding factor. In carpet weaving, for instance, the 'extra speeded' Moxon (an improved power loom of the 1870s) was kept out of Kidderminster entirely, where the weavers' organisation was strong, but installed with apparent ease in Rochdale, Halifax, and Durham, the northern centres of the trade.[9] In printing, the Hattersley, an early mechanical typesetter, was widely employed by provincial newspapers (the first was installed in the offices of the *Bradford Times* in 1868) but the London Society of Compositors was successful in keeping it at bay.[10] Similarly in boot- and shoemaking, the 'stabbing machine' – an application of the sewing machine to waxed threads – was excluded from Northampton, the metropolis of the wholesale trade, after three general strikes against it, fought between 1857 and 1859; but it was widely employed at Leicester, Norwich, and Bristol.[11] In metalworking, the treadle-worked 'Oliver', a semi-mechanical stamp which had been common in Staffordshire for 'generations', was still apparently unknown in Manchester in 1865, and when in that year a local manufacturer attempted to introduce it, the nut-and-bolt makers (or, at any rate, the anonymous correspondent who wrote on their behalf) threatened to kill him.[12]

Even when machinery was eventually installed, the struggle to control it remained unresolved, and one of the most common complaints of employers in the later nineteenth century was that tools were not run at their proper speeds, but were being sabotaged by worker lethargy or resistance. In a cotton mill every spindle was potentially a battleground as mules increased in size: in an ironworks, every attempted economy in fuel or alteration to the 'heat'. Often the machine proved disappointing to its patentees and promoters, either for want of precision, or because of the recalcitrance of the raw material, or because of the irreplaceability of handicraft skill. Patent could follow patent without anything like profitability being achieved, and the employer's dream of a 'self-acting' mechanism – equal to the best hand labour, but driven by itself – remained elusive. Mechanisation, in short, was a process rather than an event. It did not begin with the great inventions of the eighteenth and early nineteenth centuries; nor did it end with their application. The process itself was neither linear nor smooth but, on the contrary, discontinuous and subject to a whole complex of competing claims, pulling in opposite directions. For the most part it advanced by small increments rather than by leaps, and forward movements were often followed by retreat, as workers reasserted their claims. In the study of which this article forms a part, I want to argue that the machinery question, so far from being settled by the defeat of the Luddites, is in some sense coterminous with capitalism itself; that resistance to machinery, though often opaque and only intermittently recorded in the documents, was an endemic feature of nineteenth-century industrial life. I also want to look at the repercussions of machinery on skill, and at the ways in which the labour process was reconstructed both from above and below, under the impact of technical change. Finally I want to look at machinery in relationship to the 'reserve army of labour' and the demographic changes of the early and middle years of the nineteenth century, and to consider the relationship of factory industry to capitalism in the countryside, domestic outwork and the workshop trades.

Readers of *Capital* will know that such a discussion inevitably bears on Marx's 'stages' of capitalist development. In Chapters XIII to XVI of *Capital* Vol. I, he proposes three great epochs of capitalist development, which are both chronologically and analytically distinct.

1. The handicraft stage, or that of petty commodity production – the chrysalis from which later capitalism grew.
2. Capitalist 'manufacture' – the concentration of artisan and handicraft production under the control of a single capitalist, and the systematic extension of the division of labour.
3. 'Modern' industry – the epoch inaugurated by the coming of machine tools and the factory system.

In Marx's discussion each of these epochs appears to supersede its predecessor and in the case of 'manufacture' and 'modern industry' at least a clear chronology is suggested, the first being assigned to the period from the middle of the sixteenth to about the middle of the eighteenth century, the second to the age of invention. But as Marx's lengthy chapter on 'modern industry' unfolds – it takes up fully 150 pages of the book – it becomes clear that modern industry incorporates older systems of production rather than superseding them, and that it is in fact a mixed development, in which 'modern' domestic industry and 'modern' manufacture play no less distinctive a part than the machine-based factories.[13] Here, as elsewhere in *Capital*, there are plainly shifts of emphasis in Marx's discussion, and one way of elucidating them – as well as of determining their theoretical status – would be to consider the historical phenomena to which they were addressed. The discussion of such questions has in recent years been left to the philosophers and the economists, each of them concerned, in their own way, with the theoretical consistency of Marx's texts rather than the industrial reality which he was attempting to dissect. The historian may be ill-equipped to undertake a work of epistemological clarification, or to explore the more problematical reaches of the law of value. But that does not or should not mean that he or she has no contribution to make to theoretical discussion. The territory of *Capital* Vol. I is, after all, a historian's territory, one whose landmarks are in many cases familiar, and whose signposts the historian will sometimes be better placed than an economist or a philosopher to read.

Another theoretical question which this discussion poses is the relationship of ideology and class struggle. There is no doubt that so far as public agitation is concerned historians have been right to focus upon the 1820s and 1830s as the crucial period for the debate on machinery. All the major questions still seemed open, and the debate was uninhibitedly pursued, with Macaulay and the political economists upholding the 'march of improvement', Cobbett as its most eloquent critic, and Carlyle as the prophet of doom. Even after the defeat of the Luddites, the inevitability of mechanisation was by no means accepted. In the 1830s there were widespread working-class demands for a tax on machinery, and a vigorous agitation for short-time which was quite openly directed against factory 'slavery'. The economy plunged wildly from hectic bouts of activity to devastating slumps, and in the depths of the 1842 depression even the prime minister seemed uncertain as to what the outcome would be.[14] The labour movements of this time openly regarded machinery as an enemy force, one which they held responsible for the huge increases in the reserve army of labour and which, if left to continue unchecked, would make every class of worker redundant. Alternatives to the factory were eagerly canvassed and whenever the opportunity arose they were put into practical effect – spade husbandry and smallholdings on the land, producer co-operatives in the towns. As a public issue the machinery question was settled by the defeat of the Owenite trade unions in the 1830s, and the failure of the producer co-operatives to establish themselves; by the growing confidence of the industrial bourgeoisie; and by the retreat from socialist theory which marked the Chartist years (a subject to be discussed by Gareth Stedman Jones in a future issue). Once the opposition to machinery had been abandoned there was no turning back, and in mid-Victorian times resistance was characteristically fragmented. Trade unions re-wrote their rule books to expunge the anti-machinery clauses; trade union leaders adopted the language of 'improvement' as though it were their own. But at the level of the shop floor the machinery question was not settled at all, either in theory or in practice, and the battle of ideas continued to be waged around the workshop stove long after it had disappeared from the public stage.

Finally, there is the whole question of whether technology should be seen as a cause or an effect, an outside neutral force, or what the sociologists call a 'dependent variable'. It is one of the great unresolved questions about the industrial revolution itself, and it is certainly one which should be posed of the mid-Victorian economy, when Britain was the workshop of the world. Marx's texts are ambiguous on this point. In Chapter XV of *Capital* Vol. I, he begins with a purely technical explanation for the rise of modern industry, identifying it with the replacement of hand tools by machine-based technologies. The machine is more than just a giant tool. It is a process, a demonic power, a whole productive system – 'Modern Industry'. Machinery takes over from man the role of tool-bearer, manipulating numbers of tools simultaneously, synchronising separate detail processes as one. Instead of labour power, it is the instruments of labour which dominate production. 'It is now no longer the labourer that employs the means of production, but the means of production that employ the labourer'. But as Marx's lengthy discussion of 'modern industry' unfolds, machinery seems less and less essential to its hegemony, which is no less clearly established, and no less exploitative, in manufacture and domestic outwork than it is in factory industry. Mechanisation comes to appear more a result of modern industry than a cause – the capitalist's way of escaping from worker resistance.[15] Earlier, in a letter to Annenkov (28 December 1846), Marx distinguished between two great epochs in the progress of machinery:

> One can say that up to the year 1825 – the period of the first general crisis – the general demands of consumption increased more rapidly than production, and the development of machinery was a necessary consequence of the needs of the market. Since 1825, the invention and application of machinery, has been simply the result of the war between workers and employers ... This is only true of England. As for the European nations, they were driven to adopt machinery owing to English competition both in their home markets and on the world market. Finally, in North America the introduction of machinery was due both to competition with other countries and to lack of hands, that is, to the disproportion between the population of North Americas and its industrial needs.[16]

Marx did not go any further in exploring the first of his two epochs of machinery and they remain unexplored by historians to this day. It is possible that research will show that the rise of machinery in eighteenth-century England was much more closely related to class struggle than Marx believed: that, for instance, the migration of the silk trade from Spitalfields to Essex was intimately bound up with the strength of the weavers' combinations, and that similar factors were involved in the migration of the woollen trade from the West Country and Norwich to Yorkshire. Conversely, it is by no means clear that mechanisation in mid-Victorian times can be explained by class relationships alone. All these questions remain properly open. The general bias of these chapters is to reduce the part assigned to machinery in the making of modern industry, and to look for wider changes both in technology and in the capitalist organisation of work; it is also to reject the idea of mechanisation as a self-generating process, and to look instead at the complexity of competing claims which nineteenth-century capitalism faced, and with which the workers' movements of the time had to contend.

So far as economic history is concerned, one of the main general questions raised by these articles concerns the relationship of mechanisation to overall capitalist growth. It should become clear as the argument proceeds that the two are in no sense one and the same. Not only is the tempo of change different in different trades, but its character is polyglot. Increased investment was by no means synonymous with the growth of large capitalist firms or the installation of elaborate plant. In some trades – classically in the building industry – it was accompanied by a proliferation of small producers. The response to market competition was also exceedingly various, and impossible to account for simply in terms of economic rationality. The conservatism of the Sheffield employers, which in the 1870s and 1880s exposed them to heavy competition from Germany and America, cannot be separated from the extraordinary power of the workers' trade societies in mid-Victorian times, and the very special claim of their skills.

Another question in economic history which these articles address – more particularly the third, which will be about 'sweating' – is that of the standard of life. This is usually discussed statistically in terms of household budgets, or else of take-home pay. 'Optimists' – i.e. nineteenth-century capitalism's academic partisans – point to the progress of the nation, measured by the statistical indices of consumption; 'pessimists' point to the vast numbers living at or below subsistence, or to the sanitary condition of the towns. Neither, however, address themselves centrally to the question of work, or to the momentous transformation which nineteenth-century production imposed on working pace. Yet it is surely impossible to consider the standard of life apart from the conditions under which it was earned. The modest prosperities of mid-Victorian Lancashire were purchased at the cost of putting whole families to work in the mill; those of Victorian railwaymen – as Frank McKenna pointed out in *History Workshop*

Journal I – at the price of working hours which turned day into night, and working shifts which could extend to twenty-four hours at a stretch. High wages in mid-Victorian England were quite often a species of death money, for those who could not hope to live long at their trades; or else a compensation for the fact that they had to work like horses: the Sheffield grinders and the Staffordshire iron puddlers might come into the first class, railway navvies into the second, while the coal miner, with more and more dust in his lungs as deeper shafts were sunk, and more explosives used, could qualify for either. Low wages, as Henry Mayhew pointed out, were in the London trades inseparably associated with over-work and sweating. It is hardly in question that the nineteenth century saw an enormous deterioration in working conditions, yet the matter has inspired little research. Historians are willing to delve into the remotest crevices of the stock market, in searching for the origins of railway investment or the effects of overseas trade, but so far as I know there is not a single modern article attempting to compute the comparative mortality of the trades, or to reconstitute the aetiology of industrial disease, despite the mass of evidence bequeathed to us by the more radically-minded nineteenth-century doctors.

The materials for an inquiry into nineteenth-century work are inexhaustible. Quite apart from the ordinary printed and manuscript sources available to historians, there is a huge technical literature, very little of which is used, and it is hoped that this article may indicate something of its potentiality. There are literally hundreds of treatises devoted to the 'rudiments' of individual trades – over a hundred titles in Weale's series alone.[17] Then there are the compendious dictionaries of manufactures, such as those of Tomlinson and Ure, which are often very well illustrated with prints; the industrial surveys undertaken, from time to time, by provincial newspapers (examples can be seen in the Goldsmith's collection of economic literature in the University of London library, Senate House); and the guides to industrial 'curiosities', a genre of investigative writing, developed around the time of the Great Exhibition, which in subsequent years kept many a Grub Street hack employed, as well as providing Sunday School superintendents with useful prize books: *The Busy Hives Around Us*

(1860?) is a representative title. Trade newspapers, ranging from the *Horticultural Times* to the *Iron and Coal Trades Review* have been a rewarding primary source. They are often more informative about industrial conditions, though written from the point of view of capitalists, than labour movement journals. Periodical publications such as the *Journal of the Society of Arts* act as a sensitive register to some of the 'intermediate' technical changes; so too, for heavy industry, do the 'transactions' and 'proceedings' of the various societies of civil and mechanical engineers. As well as reprinting papers, these latter journals also contain the discussions which followed them, so that you can sometimes hear the Victorian engineer thinking aloud about his work. Finally, there are the Patent journals which, together with the Board of Trade papers at the Public Record Office, make it possible to track the course of speculative invention, and the euphoric hopes invested in self-acting mechanisms of all kinds.

The historian can only be grateful for such a wealth of documentation. Yet at the same time he or she should be on guard against its bias. The technical treatises, for instance, rarely deal with the industrial and commercial setting, so that it comes as something of a shock to turn from, say, James Facey's *Elementary Decoration* (1882) with its detailed specifications about the nature of the painter's craft, to the realities of 'scamping' in Robert Tressell's *Ragged Trousered Philanthropists*. And beyond an occasional reference to 'the operator' they may tell one nothing about labour at all. Tilt-hammers rise and fall, with never a gang of men to position the metal; convex parts are jointed as by an invisible hand. The trade journals, too, are unsatisfactory as a guide to work. They persistently exaggerate the importance of invention, so that even in the most resolutely handicraft sectors of production it often seems – on the evidence of single instances – that mechanisation is about to take off. The trade reports from Sheffield in *The Ironmonger*, for instance, are filled with trials of machinery in the 1860s and 1870s yet the Sheffield trades remained overwhelmingly handicraft right down to 1914. *The Boot and Shoe Trade Journal* is even more misleading: to read it in the 1870s is to have the impression of an industry on the very edge of automation rather than one in which domestic outwork was still, in the leading centre of manufacture, a major part of the production process.

The Factory Inspectors' reports, another major source for any inquiry into nineteenth-century work, also need to be treated with care. Their evidence is strongest on the textile mills, the first great object of factory legislation and, until the Extension Act of 1867, its only subject. But even here it is limited and partial. The Inspectorate's investigations were largely confined to the objects specified by the Factory Acts: working hours and industrial safety. The historian concerned with job control and machinery, or with the class struggle at the point of production, will have to look elsewhere. Another limiting bias is the restriction of the inspectors' activities to the sphere of women's and children's employment. As a result they have little to say about industries, such as shipbuilding and engineering, where adult male labour predominated; while artisan trades are in many cases neglected, and the building industry ignored. Backyard industries and domestic outwork are also excluded from notice, because the small scale of the production unit disqualified them from protective legislation. It is not until the sweating inquiries of the 1880s that they were exposed to investigation, and then as a special problem rather than as an integral part of nineteenth-century production. The map suggested by the factory inspectors' reports is thus cumulatively misleading; the lateral spread of 'modern' (factory) industry is exaggerated, while its artisan components arc ignored, and comparatively little notice is taken of production in the workshop and the home.

To correct these biases the historian can make use of other more fugitive sources. Strikes throw up a great deal of incidental information about working arrangements, and show how custom and practice was shaped in the crucible of struggle; so do the arbitration proceedings which in the 1860s and 1870s were sometimes reprinted verbatim. County Court cases tell one a great deal which could never be learned elsewhere, prosecutions can often illumine the flashpoints of resentment which at other times are hidden. Medical evidence can take one closer to the realities of industrial life than the Factory Inspectors' reports, as in Dr Greenhow's 1861 survey of industrial lung diseases, or Dr Edward Smith's report on the sanitary circumstances of tailors, printers, and dressmakers. A rare though valuable source of evidence is that of workers writing about their own industries at the time, as in the reports by English artisans on the Paris Exhibitions of 1878 and 1889, or the accounts (mainly from the industrial crafts) collected by F. W. Galton in *Workers on their Industries* (1896). Branch reports in trade union journals can tell one a good deal about bargaining conditions, while the proceedings of annual or quarterly trade union meetings often contain extensive reference to the ways the machinery question was discussed. Above all there is the priceless evidence of autobiography, which makes it possible to translate technical process in terms of the individual's experience of work. Enough of them survive for the nineteenth century – or can be reconstituted through oral history – to provide the historian with a benchmark against which every other class of evidence can be measured.

These articles are based on an unwritten chapter of a half-finished book. The material had been lying fallow for some years and was brought to life as a result of discussions in the History Workshop collective. We were looking for a piece which would address itself to some area that was central in history teaching. 'The Machinery Question in 19th Century England' – the subject of my unwritten chapter – seemed to fit the bill, and was adopted in place of other alternatives on which I had been working. The piece was started in April 1976, but as a result of critical discussion in the collective, each of the sub-sections began to grow into chapters, and the piece is now far too long to be published in the journal, even in serial form. We have finally taken out three closely-related studies. The first, published in this issue of *History Workshop Journal*, is about the balance of steam power and hand technology in the 1850s and 1860s. It offers an epitome, brief, but in intention comprehensive, of the situation in the main areas of industrial activity, and discusses some of the obstacles to mechanisation. Its basic argument is that labour power was much more important than capital equipment in making Britain, at mid-century, 'The Workshop of the World'. A second article, to be published in a future issue of *History Workshop*, is called 'Industrial Design and the Rise of Alternative Technologies'. It is about the consumer goods industries of mid-Victorian Britain and the ways in which mass production methods were pioneered. It also attempts to relate work to Victorian industrial design, and to show how the simplification of labour process was accompanied by an increasing elaboration of the product, as manufacturers competed with one another for the market. A third article, called 'Sweating', is primarily about factory industry, though it also discusses the domestic outworkers to whom the writings on 'sweating' usually refer. This argues that the capitalist achievement of the nineteenth century was accompanied by a radical deterioration in working conditions, which can be measured by the incidence of industrial disease, the rise in workplace temperatures, and the intensification of work-loads. It looks at some of the hidden components of industrial activity, such as industrial haulage and cleaning, the stoking and charging of furnaces, the sorting and packing of goods, and argues that mechanisation in one department of production was usually accompanied by an increase of drudgery in others.

Labour Power

Capitalism in the nineteenth century grew in various ways. Mechanisation in one department of production was often complemented by an increase of sweating in others; the growth of large firms by a proliferation of small producing units; the concentration of production in factories by the spread of outwork in the home. Sugar was refined in factories like Messrs Tate and Lyle's at Silvertown; but sweets were manufactured for the million in back-street kitchens and courts, as also were such popular children's purchases as ginger beer, sarsaparilla, and ice-cream (among the manufacturers, in 1890s East London, were out-of-work dockers, victimised by the employers as a result of their activities in the Dock Strike).[18] Timber was sawn at the saw mills, where steam-driven machinery was, by the 1850s, very general; but it was shaped at the carpenter's bench, on the cabinet-maker's trestles, and at the cooper's coke-fired cresset. In ironmaking, the giant furnaces of the Black Country existed cheek-by-jowl with thousands of back-yard smithies, complementary in their action, yet radically distinct. The same was true of steelmaking and the cutlery trades in Sheffield, where thirty or forty rolling mills supplied the working material of some sixty handicraft trades in which production was organised by outworking journeymen-masters.[19] Textiles were mechanised and accounted for far more steam power than any other trade – as can be seen from the figures in Table 1 – but the clothing trades, which increased by leaps and bounds in the 1840s and 1850s, depended on the poor needlewoman's fingers.

The most complete triumph of the machine was in the cotton trade of industrial Lancashire. Elsewhere its progress was more halting, and there were major sectors of the economy – as Table 1 suggests – where down to the 1870s steam-power had made very little impression at all. Often its effects were secondary, applying only to the preparatory process of manufacture – or to the finishing – while leaving the main body of the work untouched: the case, for example, with firebricks.[20] In other instances it served to make handicraft labour more productive without impairing its skill – as in the example of glass cutting, where steam power turned the grinding wheels, previously worked by a man or boy assistant, but the delicate work of grinding, smoothing, and polishing remained in the hands of the craftsman who had traditionally performed it.[21] In yet other instances steam power and machinery were chemical rather than mechanical in their action, and fuel-saving rather than labour-saving in effect. This was the case, in ironmaking, with Neilson's Hot Blast, which cut down coal consumption by about a half, and in glassmaking Siemens's tank furnace.[22] Even when machinery was extensively applied, it by no means necessarily reduced workers to the status of mere hands; often its role was ancillary rather than commanding, and it may be useful to suggest a broad line of distinction between the textile industries on the one hand where, by mid-Victorian times, repetition work largely prevailed, and metalwork and engineering on the other, where the production process was discontinuous, and depended on craftsmanly skill. Mechanisation and steam power, in short, were by no means inseparably linked, and a vast amount of nineteenth-century work was affected by them only at second or third remove.

Table 1 Steam Power in 1870

	Number of Works	Steam H.P.
Textile Trades		
Cotton factories	2,371	280,602
Woollen factories	1,550	45,148
Worsted factories	599	47,140
Silk factories	692	7,465
Lace factories	223	998
Flax factories	155	8,670
Hosiery factories	126	777
Bleaching, dying, calico printing	341	14,789
Other textile factories	369	9,159
Clothing Trades		
Millinery; mantle, stay, corset, and dress making	9,625	110
Tailoring	5,918	79
Ironmaking		
Blast furnaces	511	164,551
Iron mills	201	36,970
Foundries	1,310	20,022
Metal Working Trades		
Nails and rivets	1,424	3,925
Cutlery	379	447
Files, saw, and tools	738	3,634
Locks	111	378
Brass finishing	256	1,786
Electro-plate	102	873
Buttons	254	353
Iron ship-building	48	3,536
Manufacture of machinery	1,762	36,473
Leather Trades		
Tanners and curriers	569	2,054
Saddlery	1,144	82
Boots and shoes	8,865	420
Gloving	68	8
Mineral Working Trades		
Potteries	517	4,679
Bricks and tiles	1,630	7,614
Other earthenware	446	2,797
Glassmaking	213	3,944
Glass cutting	81	110
Building Trades		
Builders	2,890	3,391
Marble and stone masons	1,213	1,372
Carpenters, joiners, etc.	5,518	3,016
Woodworking Trades		
Cabinet and furniture makers	1,821	718
Boatbuilding	167	114
Coopers	712	383
Food Manufactures		
Bakehouses, biscuits, confectioners	4,381	724
Breweries	860	4,466
Sugar Refineries	33	2,356

(Source: P.P. 1871 LXII (440), Return of Factories and Other Manufacturing Establishments)

Even in textiles the progress of mechanisation was uneven. It was faster in spinning than in weaving, in worsteds than in woollens, in cotton than in linen or silk. Silk was mainly a hand-loom trade at the time of the Cobden Treaty of 1860; so were many branches of West Riding woollens, while in the linen industry the power loom had only recently made its first appearance.[23] The Nottingham lace trade was a factory trade almost from the start (though much of the machinery was hand rather than steam-powered).[24] But in hosiery, the other great East Midlands staple, the manufacture, so late as 1861, was 'largely ... domestic', and though the steam-powered rotary made swift progress in the following two decades, the finishing branches of the trade – seaming and stitching – remained almost entirely in the hands of out-workers.[25] In cotton spinning itself, the original site of the 'industrial revolution', hand-mule spinners held their own in the cotton mills right down to the 1870s, where they were employed on the finer counts, and maintained their own trade union organisation. Before the Cotton Famine of the 1860s 'only the more venturesome' manufacturers would trust their fortunes to the self-actor mule entirely, and down to the 1880s the self-actor and the hand-mule, instead of competing with one another, were allotted separate departments of the work.[26]

Many trades in mid-Victorian times remained divided between machinery and handicraft sections. In armaments, for instance, the Enfield Rifle was manufactured by machinery on a system of interchangeable parts. But ammunition continued to be made by hand – at Woolwich Arsenal, when Andrew Wynter visited it in 1860, some eight hundred children 'aged from 8 to 12' were employed at packing cartridges – while in the 'Gun' quarter of Birmingham the small arms trade was diffused among a multitude of small producers, with lock, stock, and barrel as separate handicraft trades.[27] In newspaper printing, press work was transformed by the steam-powered cylinder machines, installed at *The Times* in 1814, but typesetting down to the 1860s, and in London until the introduction of Linotype in the 1890s, remained a work of the individual hand compositor, piecing together letters from a case.[28] In brewing, the twelve big London firms were among the largest manufacturing establishments in the kingdom.[29] They had been among the very first to order James Watt's steam-engine, when it was still in its patent stage, and they conducted operations on a factory scale.[30] But in the 1850s there were still thousands of handicraft brewers – no fewer than 1,800 in Birmingham alone.[31] Steam-powered flour mills were built on the waterfront to process imported wheat, but in the 1850s and 1860s by far the greater part of flour was ground by stone – in some places still in hilltop windmills.[32]

Dual technologies also existed together – in large establishments – under the same roof, as in the example already given of hand mules and self-actors in different departments of cotton spinning, or that of hand looms and power looms in silk mills and woollens.[33] At the Atlas Works, Sheffield, armour plates were tempered in the furnace, but dragged about the factory floor by teams of men in chains.[34] Another striking example from Sheffield is that of steelmaking, where the ingots were melted in the furnaces, but the crucibles which held them were hand-made on the same premises, and the ganister or clay from which they were made was prepared for manufacture by puddling it underfoot. Pot-making is a well-remembered Sheffield occupation, of which we are fortunate to have an excellent autobiographical account, and the process of treading it underfoot – very much akin to the wine-growers trampling of grapes – remained a skilled occupation down to at least 1914.[35] Here is an account of it incorporated in a technical treatise of the time:

> When the materials are to be mixed by treading, they are spread out on a concrete floor and are sprinkled with water. The mass is turned over repeatedly with spades and, when it becomes too pasty to be worked in this way, it is again spread out and is trodden by men with bare feet, who squeeze the clay between their toes, and so mix it thoroughly. Each portion of the clay has to be squeezed between the toes, compressed and then pressed on to the previously worked paste. The treader stands in the middle and, working his toes, goes over the whole surface of the clay in a spiral direction, always working towards the edge. Having reached the edge, he turns round and walks m the opposite direction until he arrives at the starting point. Some treaders prefer to

walk in straight lines instead of in a spiral direction. The trodden mass is then made up into balls of 40 to 45lbs. weight, and is afterwards beaten into a dense mass. In some works it is 'pugged' after being trodden.[36]

In transport, too, dual technologies existed side by side. Iron steam-ships shared the coasts with thousands of collier brigs and sailing drifters and their cargo was taken ashore by dumb barges and dockers walking planks.[37] Railway engines revolutionised passenger transport, but road haulage remained the province of the one or two-horse cart. Goods carried by rail increased from 60 million tons in 1851 to 410 million tons in 1900, while those carried by carts, wagons and vans increased in the same period from 106 million to 671 million tons.[38] Over the same period the number of railwaymen increased from 29,000 to 318,000, while those in road transport from 139,000 to 565,000.[39] The greater part of the mineral traffic was carried by canal, long after the coming of the railways.[40] At Messrs Chance Brothers, Smethwick, the largest glass factory in the world, 'not a few' of the barges bringing iron, coals, and glassmaking materials were drawn by human beings: a visitor in December 1850 noticed, in a very short journey, 'no less than five barges, to each of which a man and an ass were yoked together' (the factory was engaged at the time in making the Crystal Palace).[41]

'Improvement' in nineteenth-century industry – as the above paragraphs may suggest – by no means worked in a single direction, and in the following pages I want briefly to indicate, industry by industry, some of its characteristic paths.[42]

A. Mining and Quarrying

In coal-mining, steam power transformed the scale of operations, while leaving the technology of hewing unchanged. Steam-driven fans were applied to ventilation, and allowed working places to proliferate, instead of being tied to the foot of the shaft. Steam-driven pumps were applied to underground drainage, and allowed the mining engineers to explore new and deeper levels, more especially in the second half of the century, as the shallower seams showed signs of exhaustion. But there was a total absence of mechanisation at the point of production, where the coal was still excavated by shovel and pick – 'tools of the most primitive description, requiring the utmost amount of bodily exertion to render effective'.[43] Mechanical coal-cutters were frequently patented and in times of strike high hopes were entertained by employers of the 'revolution' they might affect; but in 1901, forty years after the first wave of patents, only 1.5 per cent of total output could be attributed to them – a percentage which had still only risen to 8.5 per cent in 1913.[44] Output was increased not by mechanisation but by recruiting extra men. More and more hewers were needed as workings were extended both laterally and in depth. The numbers of hauliers (mainly boys) also increased: there was more coal for them to handle, and longer galleries to travel. Longer galleries also meant more roofs to prop, more roads to keep up, more rails to be laid down, while the increased use of blasting meant more hand-bored holes. The nineteenth century saw the creation of whole new classes of underground worker – 'stonemen' or rippers who had the job of extending the levels, timbermen to do the propping, shot-firers to bore the holes.[45] The mining labour force, which had stood at little over 200,000 in 1841, rose to 1,202,000 by 1911.[46] Animal power, too, was brought to production's aid, with the introduction of pit ponies for underground haulage: there were an estimated 11,000 of them in 1851, 25,000 in 1881, 70,000 by 1911.[47]

Stone quarrying, like mining, was a sweat-and-muscle job, and little that took place in the nineteenth century impaired its labour-intensive character. Technological change characteristically took the form of 'improved' hand tools rather than of steam-powered machinery, as with the introduction of the 'patent axe' ('an instrument composed of thin slips of steel tightly bound together'), which first found its way into Scotland about 1818 and by the end of the century was in use at granite-working centres all over the country; or the spread of the 'feather and tare' method of stone-splitting, which replaced the old method of wedge and groove, but still required the quarryman's whole strength (the 'tares' had to be repeatedly hit with a sledge-hammer until the rock eventually broke).[48] Gunpowder was increasingly used in quarrying for the rougher class of stone, but boring boles for them was hardly less taxing than working with crowbar and pick: in Clydach Vale, a foot an hour was considered a workmanlike progress ('you kept on turning and twisting the bar ... like buttermaking in a churn').[49] The most widespread measures of 'improvement' were in haulage. Cranes were introduced into the Aberdeenshire quarries as early as 1835, and by the 1900s there were few large quarries without at least the hand-operated version, while in some the stone was carried away on the overhead rails known (after the acrobat of that name) as 'Blondins'.[50] But in the smaller quarries – still by far and away the most common – the stone was dragged about by main force with men or horses to provide the traction. Fred Bower, who worked there briefly in the 1880s, describes the laborious procedure used on the Isle of Purbeck: the quarrier, having cut his stone, loaded it on to a "bogie" or trolley, to which be harnessed himself "just like a horse" and dragged it to the foot of the incline, from where it was drawn up to the top by a donkey or mule-driven windlass.[51]

Clay-getting, though providing two major industrial raw materials, for pottery and bricks, was less affected by nineteenth-century 'improvement' than any other branch of extractive industry, with the possible exception of salt. In the china clay industry of Cornwall, which shipped vast quantities of working materials to the Potteries of North Staffs., there were no mechanical aids and only the most primitive plant. The clay was puddled (i.e. sifted, washed, and homogenised) in open-air pans, 'forty feet in diameter, and from six to ten feet deep'; it was dried by the wind and sun, with reed thatches to cover it when it rained.[52] Pumping engines (bought second hand from bankrupt tin and copper mines) were an innovation of the 1860s and 1870s; kilns came even later. The clay diggers worked with a heavy pick (the heaviest pick in Cornwall, according to an authoritative account published in 1875), and a long, square-mouthed shovel.[53] In the settling pans they stirred the mass of slime with a 'dubber' and brought it to consistency by trampling. The boy-runners, who had the job of haulage, carried the blocks of clay on boards, with a stiff leather shield 'to keep the wet clay from reaching one's chest'.[54] 'Balmaidens' (the women workers who cleaned the final impurities from the clay) used a small iron scraper 'resembling a

... Dutch hoe'. In the 1860s they were expected to clean two or three tons a day for the princely sum of 1s.

In the Devon ball-clay industry, another major source of raw materials for North Staffs., the clay was cut dry in open-cast or underground pits, and the intermediate processes of puddling dispensed with, but the technology was no more sophisticated than that in china clay. When it came to carrying the clay down the Stover Canal to Teignmouth, men were used instead of horses for haulage, dragging the barges by rope.[55] Loading the ships at Teignmouth was also primitive, the clay being hoisted aboard by a simple expedient known as 'jumping': 'A rope was suspended from a pulley-block attached to the ship's rigging. One end was attached to the basket while the lumper grasped the other ... end and jumped from the ship's deck into the barge below with the effect that the laden basket was raised by his own weight.'

B. Agriculture and Market Gardening

In agriculture, cheap labour rather than invention was the fulcrum of economic growth, and the changes inaugurated by the agricultural revolution were accompanied by a prodigious increase in the work force, as well as by an intensification of their toil. Heavier crop yields needed more hands to harvest them, new methods of cultivation demanded a more intensive preparation of the soil – more draining and ditching, deeper ploughing, heavier and more frequent dressings of manure. Turnips in particular, the pivot of the new rotation of crops, demanded an almost gardenly care. The soil had to be in such a state of pulverisation 'as to fall from the plough like meal', with ploughings, harrowings, rollings, pickings, and liberal dressings of manure before it was ready for the seed, and once the crop had begun to appear the earth had to be continually prodded and poked; sometimes there would be three different hoeings.[56] The extension of arable farming into upland, heath, and fen – another feature of the 'New Husbandry' – also made heavy demands on labour, with more claying or marling to bind the sandy soil, more manuring to bring it into a state of cultivation, more stone-picking and weeding to keep it clean.[57] This was the origin of the gang system in Norfolk and the Lincolnshire Wolds.

In harvesting, the most labour-intensive sector of farm work, the main innovation in the early and middle years of the nineteenth century, the replacement of the sickle by the scythe, took place within a hand technology.[58] Although reaping machines had been in use since the 1820s, it was not until the last quarter of the nineteenth century that they began to make serious inroads into the work, and not until the coming of the reaper-binder, at the very end of the century, that farmers could dispense with the seasonal need for extra hands.

Market-garden crops were even more labour-intensive than wheat. Wage rates, even by the miserly standards of the British farmer, were exceptionally low, and much of the labour was performed by the grower and his own family; even so labour costs per acre were calculated at anything up to £11 per acre in the 1870s, compared with between £1 and £2 per acre on an arable farm.[59] Much of the ground was dug by spade husbandry – i.e. trenched rather than ploughed; many of the seeds were dropped by hand rather than sown by horse-drawn drill; potatoes were individually planted.[60] Heavy and frequent dressings of manure were administered to offset the intense exploitation of the soil. In rhubarb farming, wrote Shaw in 1879, describing the practice in the Surrey market gardens, 'rank litter' was used, but because of the softness of the newly dug soil it had to be carried by basket, some people being employed to fill them, others to carry them on their heads, 'and a few more to empty their contents over the crowns of the plants'.[61] Earthing-up was by hand-held trowels: it had to be done two or three times in the case of celery 'to suit the growth of the plants'.[62] Other crops, too, needed an individual treatment: cauliflowers had to be transplanted, onions and cucumbers tied, rhubarb pruned of leaves 'sometimes thrice in the season'.[63] Weeding – generally a job for women and children – was done with a sharp-bladed knife rather than a hoe, in order to get close to the crops, and baskets rather than wheelbarrows were used to carry the weeds away.[64] Much of the harvesting was done on all fours.

A great deal of market-garden work was done by contract. The grower, who bore many resemblances to a peasant proprietor (and some to a kulak), worked by rule of thumb. For much

of the year he might employ no regular labour at all except for
that of his family. But he would engage poor people in the locality – women and children especially – to take on particular tasks,
and for the larger jobs he would engage with labour contractors
or itinerant labourers, drawn from further afield.[65] They would
be employed not only for picking and pulling but also for other
jobs, such as hoeing and weeding. Patrick MacGill was one of
those who engaged at it, working with a gang of men and women
for a potato farmer in Buteshire, Scotland. The men would dig
potatoes from the ground with a short three-pronged 'grapis',
a kind of fork. The women followed behind, crawling on their
hands and knees, and dragging two baskets apiece into which
they lifted the potatoes thrown out by the men:

> The job, bad enough for men, was killing for women. All day long,
> on their hands and knees, they dragged through the slush and
> rubble of the field. The baskets which they hauled after them were
> cased in clay to the depth of several inches, and sometimes when
> emptied of potatoes a basket weighed over two stone. The strain
> on the women's arms must have been terrible ... Pools of water
> gathered in the hollows of the dress that covered the calves of their
> legs. Sometimes they rose and shook the water from their clothes,
> then went down on their knees again. The Glasgow women sang
> an obscene song, 'Just by way o' passing the time', one of them
> explained ... Two little ruts lay behind the women in the black
> earth. These were made by their knees.[66]

C. Food Industries

Food processing in mid-Victorian England was perhaps less
subject to technological improvement than any other branch
of production. Vegetables were dressed for the market by hand.
Earth-stained crops, such as celery and radishes, were washed and
bunched by women and children, working for market gardeners in their sheds.[67] At Covent Garden, peas were podded in the
market itself and sold 'ready for the saucepan' according to their
respective size (the work was chiefly in the hands of old women,
working at the rate of 1s. or 18d. a day and recruited by salesmen
from the local workhouse).[68] Pickling too, though increasingly

a factory trade, was mostly done by hand. The vegetables had to be soaked in brine, diced or sliced to size, liberally sprinkled with vinegar and then 'artistically arranged' in jars.[69] It was cold winter work (the vegetables had to be kept in the cold for fear that they would rot) and chapped hands and cuts are remembered occupational hazards.[70] Onions were particularly labour-intensive as they had to be individually peeled. 'Consequently in a bottle of pickles every onion is always visible from the outside though perhaps a cabbage may fill up the middle – an onion is never allowed to enjoy oblivion.' There was more machinery in jam-making, where by the 1880s steam-jacketed boilers reduced the fruit to pulp, but the preparatory stages were performed by hand. The fruits were sorted out into their respective qualities and the damaged parts cut away, oranges peeled, lemons squeezed, soft fruit separated from brambles. Extra labour was taken on at the jam factories during the height of the fruit-picking season, and sacked when it was over.[71] In the meat trade, cattle continued to be brought live to market and to be sold by dealers 'on the hoof' – i.e. for the purchaser to kill. The great majority were taken by family butchers, who did the slaughtering on their own premises (it took four men to kill a bullock, fewer for pigs or sheep).[72] Not until the 1880s did anything like a wholesale trade develop on any scale, though in the 'bad meat' trade – whose physiognomy can be studied in the cases which came before the police courts – it seems that there was a class of travelling dealers who supplied the 'slink' butchers with their wares.[73] Cheese, one of the very few proteins to form a regular part of the labourer's diet (even workhouse inmates had a ration), was made by a long and protracted process in the farmhouse. Stilton required up to half a year for ripening; Cheshire and Cheddar cheeses had to be turned daily for three months. Cheese-malting involved a great deal of heavy lifting and carrying, and for the dairymaids who performed the work – or the farmer's wife and daughters – the process was intensely laborious, as well as long drawn-out: 'in many dairies ... not only the hand, but also the whole arm is immersed in nearly every operation.' Most farms seem not to have made use of either chemical or mechanical aids. The heat of the milk was tested by finger-tips rather than thermometers;

curds were broken by hand or knife. A semi-mechanical separa-
tor was patented in 1834, but farmers were very slow to take
it up, even when it proved successful, and down to the 1880s it
seems to have been very little used in Somerset and Cheshire,
two of the leading cheese-making counties. 'The women do all
the work', wrote Acland in his report on Somerset, the home of
Cheddar cheese:

> It is true the men see the cows milked at a very early hour in the
> summer, and have some trouble with them in the winter, but the
> real hard labour falls on the women; and very active and industri-
> ous they are, but it is a sad sight to see a man standing by doing
> nothing, while his wife or daughter is turning many times a day a
> weight above half a cwt ... Cheese-turners used in the Midlands
> are not in use in Somerset ... the farmers who have heard of them
> say they would occupy too much space.[74]

In the fish trade, too, a purely hand technology prevailed. In the
middle years of the nineteenth century more and more boats were
engaged at it, especially in the East Coast herring trade, and there
was an enormous increase in the volume of the catch. New docks
and harbours were laid down to cope with the increased traffic,
while the coming of the railways opened up the inland markets.
There was a vast increase, too, in fish manufacturing (over half a
million barrels of herring a year were being cured in the 1860s),
but working practices remained primitive. The Scotch herring
girls, who followed the herring down the coast, from North-East
Scotland to Lowestoft and Yarmouth, worked ankle-deep in the
fish, equipped with nothing more than a short-bladed knife. (The
barrels themselves were hand-made by journeymen coopers who
migrated to the herring ports for the season.) Smoked haddocks –
'the especial dainty of the breakfast table' – were cured over peat
and sawdust fires. (Coke was substituted in the back slums of
Limehouse and Camberwell, where fish curing remained a cottage
industry down to the 1900s.) Bloaters, the favourite fish of the
London working class, were prepared in even simpler conditions,
since they did not need so much fire. Whelks and winkles were
boiled and salted in the backyards of the dealers, and made more

attractive by polishing the shells (one of Mayhew's costermonger informants employed children at ½d. an hour to do the works). The potted shrimp trade, which provided the working class of Lancashire and Yorkshire with a tea-time relish, was hardly more advanced: for the most part it was conducted in the outhouses of Marsh Side, Southport.[75]

In baking, the only mechanical triumph which nineteenth-century capitalism could record was the mass production of biscuits. Milling remained dispersed among thousands of local millers, and depended for motive power on wind and water rather than on steam: not until the spread of roller milling in the 1880s, and the massive importation of foreign wheats, did modern capitalist industry take their place. Bread-making itself was notoriously backward. Marx in *Capital* scathingly described its technology as 'pre-Christian', and Seymour Tremenheere, in his report of 1862 on the journeymen bakers of the metropolis, was hardly more complimentary. 'There is probably no trade supplying a vast and constant demand which has so completely remained in its primitive condition ... as the baking trade.' Numerous projects for improvement were canvassed, but except in Birmingham, where steam bakeries seem to have been established in the 1860s, results were disappointing: Dr Daugleish's much trumpeted 'aerated' bread – which used carbonic acid instead of yeast – proved both expensive to manufacture and taste-less; Mr Stevens's 'Patent DoughMaking Machine', though it impressed Seymour Tremenheere, seems to have been ignored. Rising demand was met not by mechanisation, but by a pro-liferation of 'under-cutting' bakers, and a marked increase in over-work and sweating.

The London bakehouse of the 1850s and 1860s was as often as not the underground appurtenance of a shop, a single cellar which served simultaneously as storeroom, manufactory and oven, as well as providing the journeymen with planks to take their naps on, and sacks to serve as pillows, while they waited for the dough to rise. The only machinery in use was the rotary action of the workers' hands and fists. Blending was in many cases performed by manual labour entirely, the different flours being emptied into a bin or trough and 'thoroughly mixed' by hand or spade. 'Making the ferment' involved mashing boiled potatoes, and then mixing them with yeast, flour, and water, as a thin, runny mass in a trough. 'Putting in the sponge', the next stage of the process, involved 'very hard work' in a swill. 'Making the dough', which followed, was by far the most laborious part of the work.

> This process is usually carried on in some dark corner of a cellar, by a man, stripped naked down to the waist, and painfully engaged in extricating his fingers from a gluey mass into which he furiously plunges alternately his clenched fists.[76]

The bakehouse visited by Andrew Ure was little different, it seems, from those described by Eddie Dare.[77]

In the sweet trade, as in bread, increasing demand was met by a proliferation of small handicraft producers. In some cases they worked out of their own kitchens – like William Luby, the Ancoats sugar-boiler, whose early experiences are recorded in John Burnett's collection of autobiographies of working people, *Useful Toil*; others used the back of a shop. Apart from access to a fire, very little was needed in the way of plant. Syrups and creams were made with a spatula, boiled sweets with a ladle and pan, lozenges with a rolling pin and cutters. Technology was not necessarily more sophisticated in the little factories which enterprising capitalists began to put up in the 1850s and 1860s. Messrs Wotherspoon, for instance, the Glasgow confectioners, who produced 'really fabulous' quantities of sweets – their trade list included no fewer than fifty-two different classes of lozenges – patented several machines for superseding hand-cutting, but they were all found impracticable 'in consequence of the difficulty of keeping the cutters clean', and when J. D. Burn visited their works in 1858 they had reverted to cutting by hand. Messrs School-ings of Bethnal Green were equipped, according to an admiring observer in 1866, with 'the most perfect' steam appliances in the trade. But 'Surprise Nuts', one of their most popular selling lines, were all individually filled by hand, and the nuts themselves hollowed out by girls with pen-knives and rosecutters. Here is an 1858 account of comfit-making at an Edinburgh sweet factory:

A large copper pan, probably 3 feet in diameter, containing the seeds, is suspended by a double sling from the roof over a low fire or stove. A quantity of sugar is dissolved in water and kept standing in a vessel by the workman's side. He then pours over the seeds a spoonful of this dissolved sugar, and, by a process of shaking and mixing in the hot pan, every seed is made to take on an individual layer. The heat and ... friction soon cause the water to evaporate and the sugar to dry on the hot seed. Another dose of the liquid is then given, another process of shaking and mixing, and thus the manufacture proceeds, until at length the seeds have attained to an enormous bulk, and then the heat is slightly diminished, and the friction increased for the finishing coat. The whole process ... requires great skill in the manipulation, and it also requires the most severe and continuous muscular labour. We know, indeed, of no other kind of labour that requires more. Not a muscle joint of the whole body remains inactive. It has quite a marvellous affect in taking down superfluous fat. It is well known that a stout man, taken perhaps from lozenge-making, and put to work this hot pan, becomes in six weeks convened into a living skeleton.[78]

D. Building and Construction

The building industry, like mining and agriculture, was labour-intensive and increased output was achieved by putting on extra men: the work force recorded in the census was 376,000 in 1841; by 1901 it had risen to 1,216,000. Building and construction was one of the fastest-growing sectors of the economy in mid-Victorian times, and accounted for between 20 and 30 per cent of gross domestic fixed capital formation, rather more than twice the amount attributed to cotton.[79] But the scale of enterprise was characteristically small, and investment, whether by master-builders or sub-contractors, went on labour and materials, not on plant. The main thrust of technical innovation, such as it was, came in the direction of labour-saving materials rather than of mechanical devices. In the 1850s and 1860s their influence was comparatively slight. The painter still mixed his own colours; bricklayers still cut and shaped their own bricks (so late as 1874 it was considered a more important part of their work than setting); carpenters and joiners worked, very often, to their own designs.[80]

Road-making, one of the earliest 'improvements' associated with the industrial revolution, was transformed by the coming of the turnpikes, and the new surfaces of Telford and Macadam. Large numbers found employment at it, both paid and unpaid: among them, in 1832, were some 32,000 parish paupers.[81] But though road surfaces were revolutionised, the technology of labour was unchanged. Stones were broken up by sledge-hammer, a weary labour at the roadside or in the parish pits; and the new surfaces were trodden down by foot and pitched and packed by hand (the great turnpike roads had to be very closely wedged, 'so as to form a regular convexity' between the centre and the channels).[82] The coming of asphalt seems to have made the work, if anything, more severe. Smoking loads of it were shot from wheelbarrows, raked to and fro to eliminate the harder knobs, and then pressed with red-hot irons, hissing and scorching as the surface set.[83] Many English workmen refused to be employed at the work (despite comparatively favourable wage-rates) on grounds of the intolerable heat; and the London companies who pioneered the process used French and Italian workers to take on some of the more fiery work.[84] Steam-rollers, first manufactured and marketed in England by Aveling and Porter in 1867, were slow to be adopted, and it seems that stone-crushers, too, were little used.[85] In Chamberlain's Birmingham, a go-ahead city when it came to 'improvement', they were grudgingly accepted by municipal officials: the Corporation Surveyor, in a report of 1874, complained that with Blake's Patent Stone-Crusher, one of the most advanced models on the market, some 16 per cent of the stone was lost in dust.[86]

Paving stones were entirely hand-made, and notwithstanding the vast increase in their manufacture, little seems to have been done to alter the character of the work. At Mountsorrel, Leicestershire, one of the great centres of the industry, a variety of hammers were used: the 'burster', 'an immense tool weighing 30 lbs', which was used for breaking up the large blocks and irregular lumps; the 'knob hammer' for knocking off the larger knobs; and the 'squaring' hammer, 'universally employed' for squaring setts. In Aberdeenshire too, the other great centre of granite paving, sett-making remained a work of the hammer down to the end of the nineteenth century. 'The dressing of granite by mechanical means is a problem that has engaged the attention of engineers for many years', wrote Powis Bale in 1884, 'and is still, practically speaking, unfulfilled'.[87]

Mid-Victorian town 'improvement' owed more to artisans than to civil engineering, and the monumental art forms favoured at this time gave a wide field for the exercise of their skills. Banks competed for grandeur in columns of Bath and Portland stone, Doric, Ionic, or Corinthian, according to the architect's whim. Churches – a major growth industry down to the 1880s, and by far the wealthiest of the architect's clients – blossomed out in revived Gothic; warehouses and offices went baronial, with turrets, gables, and keeps. Stonemasons were very largely responsible for these ornate façades, though bricklayers played more part in the revived Queen Anne style of the 1870s. Stonemasons also serviced the mid-Victorian boom in town halls and exchanges, the rage for civic statuary and clock towers, and the proliferation of museums, galleries, and halls.[88] All of their work was hand-tooled, and it was not until the very end of the century that stone-working machinery began to make serious inroads on their craft. Most of the decorative work was done by banker masons in the yards, but the stone carvers worked on site, as did the 'roughers out' – the walling masons who shaped the stones for fitting.[89]

Railway building was very largely pick-and-shovel work, notwithstanding the achievements of the civil engineers. Contractors were niggardly in their fixed investment, lavish in their use of hands, and at the height of the 'mania' of 1845–7 were thought to have had some 300,000 men in their employment. Bricks were manufactured for the viaducts and embankments on site. Millions of tons of earth, sand, and gravel were shifted by the spade – twenty tons a day was the normal navvy stint in the 1850s.[90] In tunnelling, the rock was shifted with gunpowder, but bored by handworked drills; heavy clays, such as those encountered by the London and Birmingham railway at Primrose Hill, were broken up by hatchet and cross-cut saw.[91] Hoisting devices were primitive, with nothing more elaborate in the way of handling equipment than cumbersome horse-drawn gins. On deep cuttings, like the Tring works of the London and Birmingham line, where some 1,400,000 yards of chalk had to be removed before the track could be laid, tipping was conducted on the principle of the seesaw, with a man and horse as weights. There is a vivid description of the work in F. S. Williams's *Our Iron Roads* (1852):

> Runs, as they are called, are also made by laying planks up the sides of the cutting, on which barrows may be wheeled. The running is performed by stout young men, round the waist of each of whom is a strong belt, fastened to which is a rope running up the side of the cutting, and turning on a wheel at the top, whilst to the other extremity a horse is attached. The barrow being laden ... a signal is given to the driver, who leads the horse quickly out a given distance into the field, and thus the man is drawn up the acclivity; the contents of the barrow are emptied, and the horse being led back the rope is slackened, and the man runs down the plank again, drawing the empty barrow after him.[92]

In domestic housebuilding, activity expanded with little more in the way of mechanical aids than the wheelbarrow (even this could be controversial – Manchester building workers came out on strike against it in 1864).[93] There were no pile drivers to dig the footings, or, in many cases, hoists to raise the parts: 'it was quite customary to see labourers staggering up a ladder, carrying a window-head or a sill balanced on their shoulders, using both hands to grasp the sides ... of the ladders'.[94] All of the work was done by hand tools. House carpenters would have an elaborate set of them, which it could take them an hour or two to grind.[95] Others were simpler: the slater worked with an all-purpose hatchet, pointed at one end, called a 'zax', the gas-fitter with soldering-irons and a blow-pipe, the bell-hanger with a pair of combination pliers which in the 1880s could be bought for as little as 2s. 4d.[96]

Despite the existence of a few large contractors, such as Thomas Cubitt in London, and Johnson of Manchester (the man whose home was blown up by the local brickmakers in

1870), domestic housebuilding fell very largely within the province of the small master economy, with jobbing men acting as subcontractors for portions of the work, or venturing into business on their own. Often the master would be an enterprising carpenter with nothing to lose by failure except a return to the journeyman's ranks, or a man out of work for whom starting up as a 'capitalist' was an alternative to unemployment.[97] 'A £5 note and plenty of cheek' was said in the 1880s to be enough for a man to set up on his own. The plumbing and the slating could be fanned out, the scaffolding hired, the raw materials obtained on tick (the initial load of bricks had to be paid for on the nail, but the cash for that could be borrowed).[98] Rowland Kenney has left a good example of a job like this which he took on, together with a mate, in the 1890s.

Fred learned of a possible job at Standish, a few miles the other side of Wigan. A small local contractor had been offered the job of building a couple of cottages ... a considerable cut above the small places in which most of the local miners lived. The 'contractor' was a joiner who had the sense to see that there was going to be some building development in the neighbourhood, and that he would do better contracting than following his trade as a journeyman joiner; but he had no knowledge of bricklaying ... It suited him better to sub-let the bricklaying part of the job, and here was where I could perhaps be useful. I was 'quick' at figures and Fred was not; so the suggestion was that he should contract to do the brickwork at so much a square yard. I should be labourer, and also do the measuring up and generally act as clerk of the works. As occasion served I was gradually to take over trowel. We had visions of becoming masters instead of men, and tramping and roughing it seemed likely to be things of the past for me. The scheme did not work out well at all. Whether we had taken the job too cheaply I do not know – the amount Fred had asked per square yard struck me at the as remarkably small ... he had been very reassuring when I questioned about it ... but the job never paid even full wages.[99]

E. Building Materials

In the building materials industry, as in building work, increased activity was not matched by technical change. Of the major building materials, only wood was seriously affected by machinery, and its influence – for reasons which will be indicated later – was definitely limited. Window-glass was hand-blown at the furnaces, window fittings and door furniture (in ways which will be described in a subsequent article) were hand-hammered at the forge. Builder's lime, the chief ingredient of stuccos and mortar, was reduced to powder at hand-charged furnaces; builder's sand was dug by spade.[100] Cement technology was a bit more advanced, with clays being washed in a mill, but most of the work seems to have involved heavy digging, lifting, and carrying, in dismal conditions (at Harwich in 1849 some 500 people were apparently engaged at dredging the harbour to get stones for a local cement works).[101]

Except for marble (extensively used in the manufacture of chimney pieces), almost every class of builder's stone was hand-dressed.[102] Aberdeen granite, a popular architect's embellishment for the more imposing class of shop-front, was both shaped and polished by hand, with emery paper to produce the final gloss when the surface had been smoothed. The hearthstone raised at Godstone, Surrey, was hewn into shape by a peculiar double-headed axe.[103] The window sills and doorsteps manufactured on the Isle of Purbeck, and exported by stone boat to the southern English towns, were shaped by mallet and chisel.[104] Slates, which in the third quarter of the nineteenth century largely displaced tiles as roofing materials, were both hewn and shaped by hand, principally in the slate quarries of Bethesda and Dinorwic. Each slate had to be individually treated, according to the peculiarity of the rock. 'The splitter, the real aristocrat of the quarry craft, had to be able to tell at a glance what size and quality ... he could coax out of a particular block ... to glance at a slab and recognize ... posts, crychs, bends, sparry veins, faults, joints and hardened rock.'[105]

Bricks, like slates, were individually hand-made, though manufactured in prodigious quantities (150 million a year, for instance, on the great Cowley brickfield, which stretched from Southall to Slough).[106] The work, which was sometimes undertaken by family groups or gangs, sometimes sub-contracted, was dirty and laborious, and involved a whole series of exhausting tasks, from the clay digging of the autumn and winter months to the setting of the clamps or kilns (20,000 bricks was an average firing in the 1850s). Stones were picked from the clay by hand, and the puddling or tempering, which reduced the clay to plasticity, depended on bodily weight, the clay being turned over repeatedly by the spade, mixed with water, and then trodden underfoot: the labourers who did this (sometimes horses, sometimes men, sometimes children) were said to develop 'puggers' feet' from the sensitivity with which they could detect the slightest intrusive pebble.[107] Moulders, too, worked in close physical proximity to the clay, pressing their bricks into shape with rapidly working fingers, and taking off surplus pieces with a scraper, or dextrous flicks of the thumb ('wrist-up' or 'lack of joint oil', according to a Chesham brickmaker, was an occupational hazard, 'if you started off too rash').[108] Numbers of different machines were projected to streamline the work – in 1856 over 230 patents were in existence for machine-moulding alone – but down to the 1880s (and in the southern brickfields a good deal longer) most of them came to grief, either because of the obduracy of the raw materials (London clays were particularly unyielding) or because of the inferiority of the finished product.[109] Only the pug-mill, a horseginned mixer, was widely adopted, but it was too expensive for the smaller yards, and in the 1870s there were still many districts where it was comparatively rare. 'Pug mills are not general in Essex and Suffolk', Factory Inspector Lakeman reported in 1872, 'the earth is trodden by children who are kept at work tempering a heap of clay from morning to night'.[110]

The ingredients of the brick were also got by hand. In London they were drawn from a wide hinterland, though the clay itself was dug on site. Lime, which the moulder used to bind his clay together, came from places like the Merstham limeworks, Surrey.[111] Sand, sprinkled on the inside of the moulds to prevent the clay from sticking, was dredged from the River Thames at Woolwich, spread out thinly to dry, and repeatedly raked over 'so as to expose every particle in succession to the sun's rays'.[112]

Ashes, 'thoroughly incorporated' with the brick earth while the clay was being puddled, both to prevent the warping of the bricks while they were drying, and to assist in their colouring when burnt, came from the great metropolitan dust heaps at places like Paddington Basin.[113] So did the 'breeze' or cinders which the brickmakers used as fuel (the larger suburban makers would order as many as 155,000 chaldrons at a time). Sifting the dust for 'breeze' was a woman's occupation in mid-Victorian London, paid for at a rate of 1s. a day plus a perquisite of cinders. The 'hill women' who performed the work had the job of sorting out the cinders according to their respective size (the larger ones were reserved for the laundries), making separate piles for the different classes of debris (linen rags went to the papermakers, woollen ones to the shoddy mills of the West Riding), and heaping up the ashes and the 'breeze'. They were armed with large iron sieves which they held waist-high and riddled, while the men threw up the stuff.[114]

Painter's colours were produced in even more barbarous conditions – those of the Victorian lead works the most poisonous, perhaps, of all the 'dangerous' trades.[115] Paint was a standard product used in great quantities. It should have been a prime candidate for self-acting machinery, especially in view of the known dangers of lead-colic and 'drop-hand'. But in fact, machinery was only used for crushing and grinding – in most factories all the other processes were done by hand. The women who did the stacking (men, it seems, could not be found to do the work because it had such a bad name) had to carry heavy pots of lead on their heads, from 30 to 50 lbs in weight, and to climb ladders from 10 to 15 feet high. They did the work, as a Newcastle manufacturer gratefully acknowledged, with 'truly marvellous skill and rapidity'. Lifts were installed in place of ladders at a leading Glasgow works, partly to save the women fatigue, and also because it was 'upon all accounts … a very much more respectable way of doing it than going up ladders for women'. But the Newcastle manufacturers refused to follow suit, partly, it seems, on grounds of productivity, and partly on that of cost ('ladders would be, perhaps … less expensive … because they last a long time, and it is not like machinery that wants to be put in order ... I think we could fill a stack almost as rapidly by ladders as with the hoist'). The puddling and firing of the lead, to reduce it to powder, also involved a more or less continuous risk of poison. Mechanical stoves had been invented to take on portions of this work, but manufacturers in 1893 were still making little use of them, both on grounds of quality ('there was a prejudice in the trade as to the lumps') and also on grounds of cost. 'No perfectly satisfactory mechanical stove has yet been devised, and their very high price is also a bar to their general introduction.'[116]

F. Glass and Pottery

Manufacturing in other classes of mineral work was as labour-intensive as it was in lead or bricks, though demanding varying degrees of athletic strength and skill. In chemicals the crucial operations were performed by men with long iron rods stirring vats, and furnacemen sifting the powder in kilns. In saltmaking, the lumpers, who had the making of the finer class of salt, worked as high-speed rakers over boiling pans of brine. In glassmaking everything was made by hand, whether it was destined for the sideboards of the aristocracy, the shelves of the pharmacist, or the counter of a back-street bar. Even in glass bottlemaking, a manufacture for the millions, every item was individually made, the gatherer taking the 'metal' from the furnace at the end of an iron rod, the blower shaping the body of the bottle with his breath, while the maker who finished the bottle off ('the most difficult task') tooled the neck with a light, spring-handled pair of tongs. Glassmaking was a factory industry in which, however, as late as 1895, 'no machinery' had been applied at all, in spite of the vast proliferation of its products. The glassblower's tools were few and simple, indeed the fewer he used the better so far as the quality of the work was concerned: 'the more these shape the article, the more imperfections are likely to be produced by the scratching and rubbing of the irons'. The chief instrument of production was an iron blowpipe – 4 or 5 feet long, and with a slightly enlarged nose at the end. In bottlemaking the glass was gently rubbed against a small metal plate known as a 'marver' or blown into a mould; in window-glass rolling, the sheets were first blown up into cylinders and then flattened on a rolling table, 'a cast-iron slab of sufficient size to accommodate the largest sheet which has to be rolled'.[117]

Sheet or 'cylinder' glass, the great innovation of early Victorian times (it was first introduced to this country by Messrs Chance Brothers of Smethwick in 1838), cheapened production by making it possible to use inferior sands in the mix, and brought a whole new trade in window glass.[118] But it owed everything to skilled workmanship, nothing at all to plant. On the part of the blower, swinging and rotating a molten mass of glass, it required both delicacy and strength, delicacy to prevent the glass being misshapen or marked, as it swelled on the end of his blowpipe, strength to blow with sufficient force to make a six-foot cylinder.[119] The sixteen acres of glass which covered Mr Paxton's 'Palace of Industry' were blown into shape in this way, and there is a vivid description of it by George Dodd, written after visiting Messrs Chances's works at Smethwick:

The workman takes up, on the end of his iron tube, a large mass of glass, and whirls it about in an extraordinary way. He swings it round in a vertical circle, blows into it, swings it again, rolls it, until at length it protrudes beyond the end of the tube, as a cylinder, perhaps four feet long by ten metres in diameter. This cylinder is easily opened at the two ends and detached from the tube. A hot iron wire severs it in a line from end to end; and the cylinder by careful heating and running, opens out into a square sheet, flat, but slightly wrinkled on the surface.[120]

Glass finishing – i.e. ornamentation and polishing – was also a handicraft work, though steam power was applied to the turning wheels. It was a distinct class of labour, carried on for the most part in separate establishments, and had more of both drudgery and art than glassblowing. In the best class of ware, such as wine decanters or cut-glass chandeliers, the worker was his own designer, shaping the vessel on the wheel. Accuracy of eye and steadiness of hand were indispensable. 'Those arabesques, stars, running lines, vandykes, and often intricate traces which appear on the most costly glass fittings ... are produced ... without any previous drawing ... the workman, holding the glass in his hands, with no more indication of the pattern than two or three pencilmarks dividing the globe or plate, grinds out the pattern on a wheel of Craig Leith stone, guiding the brittle material by eye and hand with a precision and rapidity perfectly marvellous.' In the cheaper classes of ware, such as hall lamps for boarding houses, or frosted glass for pubs, much of the work was done by women, pressing palmfuls of wire and sand against the globes. Polishers, who made the dull surface bright, rubbed it up with pumice stone, and then gave it a finishing sheen with jeweller's rouge or putty. This was largely women's and children's work, and involved a series of processes that were wet, monotonous, and, in the case of the puttying, poisonous, since the putty was made of lead. (Puttying was especially a feature of high-class work, and was used to bring out the fine gloss and white colour 'so much admired in cut glass of the most expensive qualities ...')[121]

Despite the absence of mechanisation, glassmaking was subject to a whole series of developments which cheapened production and led to a proliferation of new lines. One important influence was the removal of the Excise Duty in 1845, which led to a great burst of activity – the bottle manufacture is said to have increased fourfold in the following twenty years, while the population of Castleford, a new Yorkshire centre of the industry, increased from 2,000 to 10,000 in the same period.[122] Another was the introduction of the Siemens tank furnace, which allowed for a much more continuous working than the clay pots it displaced, as well as bringing substantial economies in fuel.[123] Then there was the development of new types of commodity, such as the stained glass windows fostered by Ritualism and the Gothic Revival. In the flint glass trade the most striking improvements were in what an 1866 commentator described as its 'artistic' development – the adoption of engraving as a method of ornamentation, the introduction of coloured glass and the use of new decorative processes, such as embossing.[124] None of these changes affected the basic technology of work. The blowpipe, 'invented sometime during the three centuries preceding the Christian Era', remained the fundamental tool in every class of manufacture except for pressed glass.[125]

The manufacture of chinaware and crockery presents an even more striking instance than glassmaking of mass production on the basis of hand technology. In spite of the early appearance of a factory system (pioneered in the 1760s and 1770s by Josiah Wedgwood), and an intense development of the industry in North Staffordshire, a very simple technology prevailed – 'the same essential appliances as were used in Egypt four thousand years ago'. 'There are none of the noisome adjuncts and deafening sounds of the huge cotton or woollen factory, where hundreds of hands are working together, and have to feed the gigantic machinery which dwarfs them all', an American visitor to the Potteries wrote in 1871. 'There are a large number of rooms, and only a few operatives in each. Each potter works independently.' In the 1870s machinery, in the form of steam-powered 'jiggers' and 'jollies', was slowly making its way. But it advanced faster in the out-potteries, such as those of Glasgow and Newcastle-upon-Tyne, than in the hinterland of the industry, at least partly, it seems, because of the strength of the workers' opposition. In 1889 its impact was still sufficiently limited for a Factory Inspector to report that 'by far the larger number of china manufacturers do not employ steam power'.[126]

Pottery work was very physical, and involved, in every department of production, a more or less continuous personal handling of the clay. The thrower shaped his ware on the wheel 'by the exquisitely fine touches of ... thumb ... finger and palm'. He had to keep his hands constantly wet 'so as to mould the clay with the least possible friction'. So did the handlemakers. 'The operator ... gives it the required shape ... with no other tools than his wet fingers, a drop of adhesive liquid, and a moist sponge.'[127] Platemakers worked in a similar way, except that the final shape of their ware depended on flicks of the wrist. Dippers prepared the ware for firing by steeping it in a glaze tub. 'The right hand and arm ... are plunged nearly up to the elbow as he passes the piece of ware through the liquid ... Then with a rapid circular movement of the hand ... a movement that only years of practice can teach ... he makes the glaze flow thin and even over the surface, and shakes off what is superfluous.'[128] Motive power in the Potteries, such as it was, also depended on the human body.

The thrower's wheel was turned by a 'baller' ('generally a female') whom he employed full-time to keep the wheel on the go, and feed him with small lumps of clay.[129] The turner's wheel was kept moving by a lathe-treader, again a woman, who was paid (in the 1890s) 4d. for every 1s. that he earned.[130] She rested the weight of her body on the left foot while turning the wheel with her right – Dr Arlidge described her work in 1878 as a sort of 'perpetual jumping on one foot'.[131] Platemakers also had a wheel turner, though in their case boys were employed rather than women or girls.[132] Attempts to introduce steam to these departments of the work were bitterly resisted by the operatives, and also found little favour with the Staffordshire manufacturers: 'With steam it was difficult to regulate the different speeds required', Clara Collet was told in 1893, when enquiring into this particular branch of women's employment.[133]

G. Leather Trades

In the leather trades, every process of production, from the preparatory work to the finishing, depended on manual dexterity and strength. The industry employed some quarter of a million people in the 1830s, and McCulloch, in his *Statistical Account* of 1837, estimated it as third or fourth in the kingdom, 'inferior only ... to ... cotton, wool, and iron'. But then and down to a much later date the peculiar nature of its raw material seemed to make it impervious to the machine. 'I do not think you will ever get machinery into our trade', a clicker told the Royal Commission on Labour in 1892, 'until you can grow all the animals of one size with just the same blemishes.' Tanning (the preparation of leather from raw hides) was a dirty business, and for the yardsmen who had the job of lugging heavy animal carcasses in and out of pits, it was also a wet one, which needed a strong constitution (in Bermondsey, Mayhew tells us, the majority were Irish). The hide took a tremendous beating when it was not soaking in the pits. The flesher and the unhairer slashed away at it with their pokes and knives, the shedman pummelled it with a double-headed stave, while at the end of the process the creases were taken out of the leather by a triangular steel pin, with a labourer's weight behind it. Tanning was a protracted process, though the period varied according to the stoutness of the hide, and the manufacture for which it was destined: in the case of sole leather it could take a year or more to complete. Patent improvements abridged the period of the work ('almost every tanner has some process peculiar to his establishment') but they did not alter its essential character. Even in such a large tannery as the Avonside works of Messrs Evans, 'the most modern and complete' in the Bristol region, according to the *Boot and Shoe Trade Journal* in 1887, it took more than twelve months for a hide to progress through the successive stages of its treatment. The firm used a Tangye pump for pumping water; there was a machine for grinding bark; and there were three boilers, though more than one was rarely used at a time. But beyond these the sound of machinery was 'scarcely heard'.

Currying – i.e. the softening up of leather for saddlery, coach linings and shoes – was classed as a superior trade, but it required a labourer's strength to perform it, as well as an artisan skill. 'Shaving', for example, 'the most difficult part of the work, which none but the best workmen can perform', involved long heavy strokes with the knife – 'driven with great force' from the top to the bottom of the beam – while the rest of the worker's strength was devoted to keeping the hide in place by the weight and pressure of his knees. As in the case of tanning there was a great deal of pummelling and slashing away with knives, though the more delicate nature of the material required a greater care: 'The unskilful currier is constantly liable to injure the leather by cutting through it, as well as by failing to produce a regular substance.'[134]

In the manufacturing branches of leatherwork, machinery was hardly more in evidence than it was in tanning and currying. In gloving, 'getting ... the stretch of the leather' was the great point, and the finer and more flexible the leather, the more individual care and attention was needed. Yeovil, Torrington, Worcester, and Woodstock were the centres of the trade, which largely depended on outwork. The delicate work of cutting out – 'anything but ... mechanical' – was done on the master's premises, the rest of the work was farmed out. In Worcester, where the famous 'dogskin' glove was made, the fingers and thumbs went to women in the villages, while the back and 'topping' went to outworking sewers in town. Saddlery and harness were hand-stitched down to the

1870s, and workers in the trade enjoyed a large measure of self-government; many worked at home, and those who worked on the master's premises elected their own shop constable to govern workshop affairs, and owned their own tools. In Walsall, which established itself as the centre of the trade in the third quarter of the century, the sewing machine was introduced to the work in the 1870s, but as late as 1898 W. J. Gordon could describe saddle-making there as 'a genuine trade of the old sort ... all handwork'.[135] In London the introduction of the sewing machine was bitterly and successfully resisted. 'Through the saddlers' windows', wrote Japp in *Industrial Curiosities* (1880):

> We still see sturdy men slowly stitching away like so many women; and on inquiry we find it asserted that the machine cannot produce sufficiently strong work. Now that wax-thread machines are common this is a peculiar excuse. All the harness used in the United States us machine-made, even that employed in the artillery, consequently it cannot be said that it will not stand wear and tear. Saddlers and harness-makers are, as a trade, conservative, and obtain very high prices for their present work, and what keeps the machine at arm's length is the fear of strikes and the lowering of prices.[136]

Boot and shoemaking, though much less aristocratic than saddlery (London saddlers liked to refer to themselves as 'gentlemen stitchers'), was also, at mid-century, entirely a hand-sewn trade, with vast numbers of men, women, and children engaged at it, mostly as domestic outworkers. The industry was revolutionised not by machinery (which did not begin to appear until the 1860s), but by the increasingly elaborate sub-division of labour, and by the rise of wholesale manufacturing. In Northampton, the first great centre of the wholesale trade, the 'factories' of the 1840s and 1850s were little more than putting-out stations – warehouses in which the skins were cut, and the finished parts received on the various stages of their progress through production.[137] Not until the 1870s did anything like a modern factory system begin to appear, and not until the great strike of 1895 was its predominance ratified.

H. Woodworkers

In wood, as in leather, the variability of the raw material, and the delicacy, in many cases, of the finished product, made mechanisation problematical, and, as in the case of shoemaking, there was a superabundance of labour ready to take up new openings on the basis of handicraft skill. Economic growth took place almost independently of the machine. Steam-power was applied at the saw mills, turning timber into deals, or slicing them up thinly as veneers. And in the 1860s and 1870s steam joineries began to appear, supplying ready-made mouldings and parts. But woodworkers themselves, with the exception of the sawyers, were only indirectly affected by these changes.

In country districts, remote from the steam-powered saw mills, timber still came to the workshops rough from the woodman's axe; and down to the end of the century the saw-pit remained an inescapable adjunct of the work at the wheelwright's shop or the carpenter and joiner's. At Haddenham, in Buckinghamshire, the village carpenter in the 1880s purchased standing trees, cut them down, and stored them in the yard for twelve months. 'Then the sides of the logs were trimmed with the axe and afterwards rolled on the saw-pit to be sawn by hand into boards or planks.' At Codnor, Derbyshire, in the carpenter's shop where Joseph Severn began his apprenticeship in 1877, there was a circular saw 'ginned by a horse', but all the rest of the work was done by hand. 'The first thing … was to learn to plane and saw well … to sharpen planes, saws and chisels, and … to saw straightly long planks nine or eleven by three into spars and scantling.' The wheelwright's shop at Farnham, Surrey, where George Sturt began work some seven years later, had even less in the way of plant:

> The want of machinery was most evident in the daily task of cutting up plank or board for other work, and of planing and mortising afterwards. We had neither band-saw nor circular saw. Most of the felloes were shaped by adze or axe; the pieces for barrow-wheel felloes were clamped to a woodman's bench (they were too short and smell for an axe), and sawed out there by a boy with a frame-saw. (I hated the job – it was at once lonely and labourious); the heavy boards were cut out (and edged up) with a hand-saw,

being held down on the trestles with your knee (it was no joke to cut a set of one-inch elm boards – for a waggon-bottom – your arm knew about it), but all the timbers for framework of waggon or can, or harrow or plough or wheelbarrow, were cut out by two men on a saw-pit.[138]

The influence of machinery was greater than this in the towns, but the 'Mechanical Joiner', exhibited at the Crystal Palace in 1851, proved as phantasmagoric in real life as that later creature of the capitalist imagination, hopefully publicised in the *Builders' Trade Circular* for 1862, 'the self-acting Trowel'. Saw mills did not abolish the need for the hand-saw (the Sheffield manufacture of them was never more flourishing than in mid-Victorian times, when the grinders held the masters in their thrall), nor planing-machines the plane. They could supply the rougher classes of deal, such as flooring boards, railway sleepers, and ships' timbers. But their action was too crude for many hard woods and too indiscriminate for the different lengths, breadths, and thicknesses required in, say, the making of a writing desk, the framing of a roof, or the fitting of a steam-ship cabin. What such machinery did do was to provide a much broader base for handicraft activity by cheapening the raw materials of the trade. The case of machine-cut veneers, one of the earliest and most brilliant successes of nineteenth-century timber technology, is particularly striking. It robbed the sawyers of what had been by far the most skilled and paying branch of their trade. But at the same time it helped to produce a vast proliferation of activity in furniture making, especially at the 'slop' or lower-priced end of the trade. It encouraged the wholesalers and dealers – the 'slaughterhouse' men who bought the cabinet-makers' work – to extend the influence of novelty and fashion to new, more plebeian markets, and brought highly polished furniture within the reach of the comparatively impecunious (by the early 1870s, there were numerous complaints in the capitalist press of miners buying pianos). The process was already apparent in Mayhew's time, though it was not perhaps until the closing years of the century that its effects were universally felt. 'I think that machinery has been a benefit to us', a fancy cabinet-maker told Mayhew, 'it increases the material for our work. If there wasn't so much veneering, there wouldn't be so much fancy cabinet-work.'[139]

In the third quarter of the nineteenth century a number of machine tools were introduced into the woodworking trades, but though they speeded up portions of the work, they did not dispense with the need for either hand tools or handicraft skills. The application of steam power to the turner's lathe, for instance, enabled a man to produce double the quantity of work in the same time as when the lathe had been turned by hand, but it was still the turner who guided the lathe rather than vice-versa: 'Steam ... is only used ... as the motive power, for a man must still be employed to "turn".'[140] Similarly in the case of the band-saw, a treadle-worked machine which was very widely adopted in the East End cabinet-making trade, the work of cutting out depended on the versatility of man rather than of the machine which served his purposes – indeed the machine was so constructed that it could be handled almost as dextrously as if it had been a chisel or a plane.

The secular shift from wood to iron represented a more serious threat to the woodworkers' position, but in mid-Victorian times its effects were masked by the growth in the overall volume of work. In factory industry woodworkers found a place as coach-makers and body-builders in the railway works, patternmakers in the foundries, and coopers in the chemical works and breweries.[141] In the shipyards, in spite of the coming of the iron steamship – or because of it – the number of shipwrights recorded in the census increased from 27,805 in 1851 to 70,517 in 1891.[142] In furniture-making the third quarter of the century saw the advent of cheap mass production, though on the basis of hand labour rather than the machine. Windsor chairs, the new staple trade of High Wycombe, were being turned out in the 1860s at the rate of one a minute 'all the year round'; Kentish Town pianos serviced the musical needs of both shabby-genteel and the newly respectable; while in the East End of London there was a whole new industry of one-room cabinet-makers, using ramshackle materials and highly polished veneers.[143]

One sign of their handicraft status was that so many wood-workers owned their own means of production. The coopers, in Mayhew's time, found all their tools themselves – 'a kit for a general workman being worth £12' – except for the jointers to weld the staves.[144] A London cooper, who started work in 1912, remembers that those who went on tramp to take part in the cider-malting in the Vale of Evesham, or the herring harvest at Great Yarmouth, would leave the heavier tools in the shop, and travel with a hammer and driver, 'a knife or two', and an adze.[145] The value of a good cabinet-maker's chest of tools was reckoned at between £10 and £20 in 1853 Edinburgh.[146] In London at the same time it was stated by Mayhew to be about £10, but less in the more specialist branches of the trade, where the tools were lighter: a buhl-cutter's tools ('very small and niggling') cost £5 to assemble, the wood-carver's about the same. The garretmakers in the slop end of the trade would make their kit up second-hand, and Mayhew has a fine account of the makeshift way it would be assembled:

> The tools are generally collected by degrees, and often in the last year of apprenticeship, out of the boy's earnings. They are seldom bought 'first-hand', but at the marine store shops, or at the second-hand furniture broker's, in such pieces as the New Cut. The purchaser grinds and sharpens them at any friendly workmen's, where he can meet with the loan of a grindstone, and puts new handles to them himself, out of pieces of waste wood; 10s., or even 5s., thus invested has started a men with tools; while 20s. has accomplished it in what was considered 'good style'. Old chisels may be bought from 1d. or 1½d. to 2d., to 5d.; planing irons from 1d or 1½d. to 3d.; hammer heads from 1d. to 3d.; saws, from 1s. to 2s 6d., and rules and other tools equally low.[147]

The carpenter and joiner's tools – inscribed with his name – served him as a very title to employment, when he moved from job to job, and also as his means of production when he was forced to set up on his own. They cost a great deal to assemble, and their loss through theft or fire was a personal tragedy.[148] 'Tool benefit' was one of the chief provisions of the Amalgamated Society of Carpenters and Joiners, as it was of other trade unions in the woodworking trade; and the detection of tool-stealing offences seems to have been a recurring preoccupation of the local branches, to judge by the notices they sent up for printing in the Society's monthly report.

In factory industry, too, woodworkers characteristically owned their own means of production. A patternmaker's tools cost (in 1884) between £8 and £16 to assemble, and about 6d. a week to keep in repair.[149] They would be insured with the trade union and jealously guarded against misuse.[150] The young apprentice was advised to respect them. 'A patternmaker's tools are idols', wrote a Liverpool engineer in 1878, 'and one of the first duties the tyro must learn is, to return all tools to their owners properly sharpened and ready for immediate use, and above all things, he should be careful not to leave them kicking about his bench after having made use of them …'[151]

I. Metallurgy

In metallurgy steam power was massively harnessed to the primary processes of production, notably in puddling and rolling; but at the same time new fields were opened up for handicraft skills. In foundry work, machine moulding was introduced in the 1850s (during the lock-out of 1852 some engineering employers fondly believed that it would deliver them from their men); but it remained confined to the most inferior branches of the trade, such as the making of cast-iron drain-pipes.[152] Moulders – 'the wildest, the most grimy, the most independent, and, unfortunately, the most drunken and troublesome of any English workmen who have any claim to the title of "skilled"' – were virtually untouched by it and for the most part worked with the very simplest of tools, whilst their brethren, the dressers, smoothed the rough castings with hand-files.[153] The Friendly Society of Iron-moulders was composed uniquely of handicraft workers right down to the 1900s and (as employers complained) maintained a high rate of wages, restrictive shop practices, and unsleeping hostility to the machine-based class of worker.[154]

Engineering, though less severe than foundry work, was a heavier kind of labour than it is today, as well as one which demanded much more versatile skills. To begin with it involved working very largely with iron, which was much more difficult to shape than the high-speed steel and light alloys of twentieth-century engineering. The smith who had the forging of it was engaged in a muscle-hardening work, and one that was no less pivotal to production than it was at a country blacksmiths. Fitting was almost entirely done by hand. It involved the making of parts rather than the mere assembly of them – a protracted process of chipping and smoothing at the bench with no more sophisticated mechanical aid than a sharp-edged chisel and file.[155] In the 1860s production engineering was still in its infancy, and the system of manufacture by interchangeable parts, introduced from the United States at the time of the Crimean War, was for the most part confined to the making of sewing machines and small arms. Engineering firms, large and small, went in for a variety of different products rather than limiting themselves to standardised lines, and much of their work was 'bespoke' – carried out according to customer specifications and requirements. In the heavier classes of work, steam power was applied to the coarse, preparatory stages of production – rolling, stamping and cutting out – but most of the precision work was still hand-tooled, whether by smiths, fitters, or turners. At the St Pancras Ironworks where Wal Hennington worked as a boy, making spiral staircases, the iron handrails were bent in a rolling mill, but the shaping of the finished curvature depended on hand-hammered work of an exceedingly laborious kind:

> Joe Hands was a working foreman and I worked with him when he was fitting a hand-rail I suffered physically and mentally. I had to hold the rail with both hands across a heavy V-block fitted to an anvil, whilst he held the form block in one hand against the nut and struck it with a weighty club-hammer to get the required bend. It was a crude, old-fashioned trial-and-error method, requiring much hammering before the correct shape was obtained. Holding the curved rail ... on the V-block was not as supple as it would appear to be. The correct position was for it to rest evenly on both crowns of the block at the moment the hammer struck it. But if I moved slightly and the rail was a fraction of an inch off one crown the amount of error would be multiplied by the length at which I was holding it and I would get the shock of the hammer blow in

my hands and arms. I was always in fear of that happening and when it did I suffered. But my distress never evoked any sympathy from the foremen, on the contrary, he always abused me with the foulest language.[156]

The mid-Victorian engineer was still characteristically a crafts-man, an 'artisan' or a 'mechanic' rather than an 'operative' or 'hand'. He was engaged for the most part in speciality work, in which precision was more important than rapidity. He moved freely about the work-place – too freely, according to his critics, who would have preferred to tie him down in one place. He was expected to find his own tools (often he made them), and keep them in good fettle by grinding and sharpening them himself.[157] In a small workshop, the most frequent form of enterprise in the 1850s and 1860s, he would turn his hand to a variety of dif-ferent tasks, working sometimes at the forge, sometimes at the bench, sometimes on outside jobs.[158] Even in a larger works he would often have to improvise the materials for a job, cutting extra tools and accessories, finding additional jigs, and acting as his own draughtsman and designer.[159] He would also regulate, in some degree, his own work pace (opposition to piecework was a cardinal tenet of the Amalgamated Society of Engineers, defended in some notable strikes). Machine tools were increas-ingly introduced from the 1840s, but they were very far from automatic, and did not dispense with the need for a keen eye, a steady hand, and an ability to work to fine limits. Fitters, the most numerous class of engineer, were largely unaffected by them.[160] In turners' work, steam power was applied to the lathe, at least in the larger works, and Nasmyth slide-rests attached to them, but it was still the worker who guided the tool rather than the other way round – accuracy and speed depended on personal judgement rather than pre-set chucks or jigs.[161] Not until the technical innovations of the 1890s did the 'machine question' (bitterly fought out in the lock-out of 1896–7) begin to pose a fundamental threat to craftsmanly skills.

Machinery, the chief object of mid-Victorian engineering activ-ity, was built up very largely from hand-made components, all of them requiring individual attention, whether at the foundry where components were cast, at the smithy where they were forged, or at the bench where they were chipped and filed into serviceable parts. It was all precision work, much of it being undertaken to order, and mounted or fitted up on site.[162] A first-class reputation was much more important than cheapness, whether for the 'general' engineer or 'jobbing' foundry, servicing local customers, or the manufacturer of specialist machinery exported to the markets of the world. The majority of workers at a machinebuilders were artisans, though with a complement of boy labourers and apprentices to take on the more routine drudgeries.[163] Messrs Platt Brothers, Oldham, the leading manufacturers of textile machinery, were employing some 10,000 workers in the 1890s, and almost every one of them, according to Paul de Rousiers, was skilled:

> The work done there is of an extremely delicate and technical kind, and the mounting of the looms in particular requires great care and the most exact finish in all the component parts. Every workman is a specialist. A significant fact in proof of this is that not a single woman is employed by the firm ... There is no room for occasional hands or casuals, who take up any sort of work to-day to drop it for something else tomorrow. Every workman must be a master of his business. Except the porters, who are suspended as far as possible by lifts and locomotives, almost every individual employed by the firm is a skilled workman.[164]

Locomotive engineering, like machine building, was precision work which was simultaneously delicate and exacting. A single locomotive was said in 1852 to contain no fewer than 5,416 separate components, 'and it will readily be conceived that nothing short of the utmost completeness and accuracy, in the finish of these parts, could enable the workmen to combine them in one harmonious and efficient unity ... The failure of one screw or bolt, or the bending of one rod, may hereafter involve, not only the costly fabric itself in ruin, but occasion the destruction of property and life to a terrible extent.'[165] Hand tools were an indispensable condition of production. The worker would own a chest of them himself; and he would also have access to the 'shop tools' provided by the management.[166] At the G.W.R. works,

Swindon, in 1852, there were two Nasmyth steam hammers to shape the heavier metals, but no fewer than 176 smith's hearths where the smaller components were forged – axles, piston-rods 'and other pieces too numerous to mention'.[167] At Crewe in 1894 – the locomotive engine works of the London and North Western Railway – the smaller parts of the engines were forged at 120 smith's hearths. At the Wolverton works of the London and Birmingham railway there was practically no machinery at all when Hugh Stowell Brown went to work there in the 1840s. All the forging was done by hand ('it was a fine sight to see seven or eight stalwart strikers, at the forging of a crank-axle, plant their huge hammers in rapid succession upon the spot indicated by the smith with a piece of rivet rod iron'). There was no travelling drill ('all keyways had to be first drilled in round holes, and then cut out with a cross-cut chisel, and finished with the file'), and no shaping machine of any account save a machine for cutting nuts:

> Every surface that could not be formed by the plating-machine had to be chipped and filed ... Yet there were men who could do wonderfully true work. I have seen a fitter take two rough pieces of wrought iron of more than one pound weight each. I have seen him chip them to a surface almost perfectly smooth, and then with files so perfect the surface that when placed one upon the other the lower piece would hang to the upper by the force of molecular attraction, as if glued to it.[168]

In marine engineering – one of the foundations of Britain's trading supremacy, as well as an important focus for mid-Victorian capital investment – skill was no less at a premium than it was in a railway factory. In a highly competitive market, the reputation of a firm depended not on speed but on quality workmanship and attention to customer needs. Bespoke work was the norm, since every ship had to be individually suited, and it seems to have affected the manufacturers of components in much the same way as the marine engineers themselves. Lockwood and Carlisle of Sheffield, for instance, whose patent piston rings were adopted by some of the leading Clyde shipbuilders, met all their orders in the 1880s with a work force of about a dozen craftsmen: they would work up to seventy-five hours a week when a new order came in. 'Most of the orders ... reflected the views of designers of ships' engines ... Each had to be made individually.'[169] As in other classes of heavy engineering, the work was both laborious and skilled. Here is an account of it by one who served his apprenticeship on Clydeside in the 1880s, working for a firm which he describes as 'the greatest marine engine works in the world':

> The most powerful engines which have ever been made were then under construction in the works ... They were enormous things, and they stood fifty-four feet high when they were finished. Machine tools were not nearly so accurate then as they are now, and nearly everything had to be finished by hand. Bolts weighing over a hundredweight were not uncommon, and these were all fitted in place. It was hard work lifting these monsters all day long and driving them in and then driving them back and scraping them until they fitted perfectly. My wrists used to ache at night and my ribs were sore with swinging the big hammer. These hammers were known as 'mondays' and they weighed forty-two pounds. There was a certain amount of skill required to get in the full force of the blow, and unfortunately for me it was discovered that I had the knack. At first I was flattered when the foreman took me away from my work to knock out a bolt with a monday hammer, but it was a dearly bought pleasure and very exhausting.[170]

Steam boilers – the high-pressure engines which gave life to machinery and put railway trains and steamships on the move – were in the 1850s almost entirely hand-made. Some of the work, such as plating, remained beyond machinery's reach because of the intricacy or peculiarity of the parts; other parts resisted it because hand labour was more adaptable and precise.[171] The plates which gave the boilers their jackets were punched out by machinery, but they bad to be forged and welded at the hearth and they were then subjected to a tremendous hammering to make them both ductile and strong, to bend them to the right shape and to bring them to the right density. The joints were made steam-tight by a succession of blows with the sledge-hammer. Hydraulic riveting was introduced in the 1850s, but it made slow progress because it was considered much less trustworthy than hand-hammered work.[172] In the G.W.R. factory at Swindon, the premier locomotive plant in the kingdom, the preference for hand-hammered work continued right down to 1914: 'very little is left to the chance work of the machine, which is often faulty and unreliable. Rivets put in by hand are far more trustworthy.'[173]

There was a great deal of hand riveting in iron shipbuilding too, despite the massive concentration of capital and ownership. In 1884, according to Pollock's Modern Shipbuilding published in that year, hydraulic riveting was general in interior work, but shell plating – i.e. the ship's water-tight covering – was still riveted by hand. In 1905, according to a later work by the same writer, the situation had not changed: 'Probably a complete solution of the shell-riveting problem is not now far distant, but meantime the binding of the shell to the ship's framework is mostly accomplished by the old and laborious way by the "hand-and-hammer" of the craftsman.' Hand riveting was also widely employed in constructional engineering, and indeed in every class of wrought-iron work where there were metal plates to be joined. The Britannia Tubular Bridge (1850), one of the mechanical wonders of the age at the time of the Great Exhibition, was riveted entirely by hand, with some 2 million holes to be seamed and jointed.[174]

Ironmaking itself – i.e. the production of pigs and bars from iron ores – was very much a sweat-and-muscle job, as well as one requiring great vigilance to stave off injuries. Despite the vast mobilisation of steam power, all of the strategic operations were performed by hand: the preparation of the ores, which were broken up by sledge-hammers; the loading and tapping of the blast furnaces; the puddling of the iron; the shingling and rolling of the bars. In blast furnace work, the first stage of production, steam power was applied to the bellows, magnifying the blast a thousandfold compared to the old-time bloomeries. Everything else depended on men, working with heavy weights at almost inhuman temperatures. As Lady Bell wrote of Middlesbrough in At the Works (1908): 'From the moment when the ironstone is lifted off the trucks, then dropped into the kilns, afterwards taken to the furnace, and then drawn out of it, it has not been handled by any other means than the arms of powerful men, whose strength and vigilance are constantly strained almost to breaking-point.'[175]

Technology in the rolling mills, the second great department of production, was more sophisticated, with steam-powered hammers to pound the metal and steam-powered rollers to squeeze it into shape. But all the strategic operations were performed by men. Cort's puddling furnace, which revolutionised the work, was chemical rather than mechanical in its action. It cheapened the production process and made possible an enormous increase in output, but it made labour itself a great deal more severe. The puddler, who had the key role in the new process, was given a task that was simultaneously highly skilled and exhausting, turning a viscous mass of liquid into metal. He worked in conditions of tremendous heat, violently agitating the metal as it boiled, rab-bling it from side to side in the furnace, and then gathering it at the end of a rod while the molten liquid thickened and the super-charge of carbon burnt out. The men had to relieve each other every few minutes, so great was the exertion and so intense the heat, but even so it was said that every ounce of excess fat was drained from them and that cataracts 'induced by the intensely bright light of the furnaces' were a frequent complaint. Few puddlers, it was said, lived beyond the age of fifty. 'Shingling', the next stage of the process, was also very physical, a kind of blacksmith's work in which heavy balls of red-hot metal had to be heaved into place for the steam-hammer (shinglers wore iron masks to protect themselves from the raging heat).[176] Sir George Head, visiting the Low Moor ironworks at Wibsey Slack in 1835, likened the working conditions to those of an inferno:

Athletic men, bathed in perspiration, naked from the waist upwards, exposed to severe alterations of temperature, some, with long bars, stirring the fused metal through the door of the furnace, whose flaming concavity presented to the view a glowing lake of fire – were working like Cyclopes. By continued and violent applications of strength, visible in writhing changes of attitude and contortions of the body, raking backwards and forwards, and stirring round and about the yielding metal, they contrived to weld together a shapeless mass gradually increasing in size till

it became about an hundred pounds weight; thus, by a simultaneous effort of two men with massive tongs, was dragged out of the
furnace, radiant with white heat ... Now subjected to the blow
of a ponderous hammer, it was wonderful to mark the vigour and
dexterity with which the men contrived to heave the mass round
and round at every rise of the hammer ... while the fiery ball was
now turned one side, again the other side uppermost, with the same
facility apparently to the operators as if it had been a horseshoe.[177]

The rolling mills were also fearsome places to work in, with
giant plates to be drawn from the furnaces and positioned for
'Demon Crusher' hammers. At the Atlas Works of John Brown's,
Sheffield, the men who had the job of rolling armour plate would
gather some forty strong at the furnace mouth, dragging the plate
by main force to subject it to the rollers: 31 tons was an average
weight to drag. The men wore thin steel leggings, aprons of steel,
and a thin curtain of steel 'dropping over their faces like a large,
long vizor'. All the rest of their bodies were muffled in thick, wet
sacking, to keep out the infernal heat. 'In spite, however, of every
precaution that the best workmen can employ, they cannot always
escape splashes of melted iron.'[178]

The predominance of hand technology was yet more pronounced
in the so-called light metal trades, such as the manufacture of
domestic hardware. In the third quarter of the nineteenth century
an increasing number of mechanical aids were being brought
into use, such as fly wheels for polishing, and treadle lathes for
turning parts; but the vast growth of output was mainly due to
new alloys, cheaper iron, and skilled workmen. In the Wolverhampton tinware trade, stamping machinery was very common
in the 1860s, though operated by treadle or crank rather than by
steam. But workers in the trade depended on a galaxy of small
hand tools for the body of the work, with hammer and mallet as
the 'old indispensables' for finishing – 'polished hammers on polished anvils' in the case of quality goods, such as the better class
of saucepan, 'hammered ... till they acquire a beautifully smooth
and silvery surface'.[179] In the Sheffield cutlery trades steam power
was applied to the grinding and polishing wheels, but it provided
motive power only, leaving the grinder's work intact, while the

actual work of forging remained a purely manual process, with a hearth of fine coke 'forced into intermittent activity by a hand bellows', and frequent beatings with a hammer, to give the blade temper and tact.[180] In the Birmingham brass trades, which in the third quarter of the nineteenth century emerged as the town's leading employment, steam power was sometimes rented for polishing, but fittings were turned on a treadle-worked lathe with the guiding power as the worker's. ('In the turner's hand the tool must never be allowed to rest, but must have a proper rotation and a correct inclination to avoid furrowing the work.') Burnishing and decoration – a major feature in a trade wedded to ornamentation – was largely a work of hand-files. 'Any man who can use a hammer and file can be a bedstead maker', wrote Edward Peyton in 1866. Brass founding, a mainly Birmingham trade, carried on in ramshackle premises and open-fronted sheds, was largely in the hands of small masters: the 'plant' consisted for the most part of small moulding tubs where fittings and components were cast.[181]

Combined and Uneven Development

The foregoing epitome, though necessarily abbreviated, may be enough to suggest that in speaking of the primacy of labour power one is referring not to single instances, nor to curious survivals, but to a dominant pattern of growth. In manufacture, as in agriculture and mineral work, a vast amount of capitalist enterprise was organised on the basis of hand rather than steam-powered technologies. In Marxist terms, the labour process was dependent on the strength, skill, quickness, and sureness of touch of the individual worker, rather than upon the simultaneous and repetitive operations of the machine. The restraints 'inseparable from human labour power' had not yet been cast aside.[182] On the contrary, a great deal of entrepreneurial ingenuity was employed in turning them to advantage. Commercial progress depended quite largely on the physical adaptability of the worker, whether it involved crawling on all fours to gather the woad harvest, climbing up and down perpendicular ladders (in a Cornish tin mine the ascent would take an hour or more each day), or working, like boilermakers on repair jobs, upside down in tanks.[183] The lungs of the glassblower, working as bellows, or those of the gas-fitter, soldering pipes, were not the least of the forces of production which nineteenth-century capitalism summoned to its aid, nor were there any more important in the clothing trades than the needlewoman's fingers and thumbs. In the Potteries, dinner plates were shaped by dextrous jerks of the flat-presser's wrists, and surfaces varnished with the dipper's bare arms in a glaze tub (in 1861 Dr Greenhow estimated they were immersed for eight of a twelve-hour day). Ironmaking depended on violent muscular exertion, and an ability to withstand white heat, engineering on precision of judgement and touch. In the metal-working trades no action was more highly valued than the ability to deliver well-directed blows with the hammer, while those engaged in press-work were in almost perpetual motion with their arms and wrists: 'practiced workers' in the metal button trade were said to make from 14,000 to 20,000 strokes a day, 'the whole strength of a woman' being needed on the heavier class of press.[184]

Human beings were quite often used instead of horses for haulage, not only on the canals, but also on the brickfields, where the children who acted as 'offbearers' or 'pushers-out', taking cart-loads of bricks from the moulder's table to the brick-setter's kiln, carried an average weight variously computed at between 12 and 25 tons a day.[185] They were used as lifts in the lead factories, and as shunters in the docks. In the workshop trades, delivery boys were strapped to the heavier loads very much in the manner of Volga boatmen; so were some of the bakers' boys who went on 'rounds'. Men were also used like this in heavy industry, when there were plates to be drawn from the furnaces, or castings from their beds. At J. G. Thomson's, Clydeside (Peter Taylor recalls) there were a hundred and fifty men at the ropes when there was a ship's engine to deliver – they started off at a canter, outside the factory gates.[186] Sturdy legs were essential for mould-runners in the potteries, carrying plates from the flatpressers' wheels to the drying rooms; they were also much in demand at a glassworks, where a whole army of juvenile runners were kept on their feet all day: in a glass bottle factory of the 1860s it was calculated that they travelled the equivalent of between 13 and 17 miles a day. 'The smaller the articles ... and the rougher the workmanship, the greater is the number of them turned out ... and the greater also is the demand on a boy's exertion.'[187]

Human beings were also used as balances and weights, whether to give motion to machinery, like the lathe-treaders, or to act as see-saws when there were heavy loads to hoist. In clay-treading they had to act as mangles, in baking as rotary knives. In the London fur trade grown men were employed in the 1890s to bring seal skins to plasticity by jumping on them. 'It is a curious sight, on entering a room, to see a row of ... tubs each with its Jack-in-the-box bobbing up and down', wrote one of Booth's investigators. 'Every man is naked except for a vest, and a rough cloth which is tied round his waist and attached to the rim of his barrel. With hands resting on either ledge up and down he treads, and earns 20s to 25s piece-work. Skins cured by this process are said to be softer and silkier.'[188]

In mid-Victorian England there were few parts of the economy which steam power and machinery had left untouched, but fewer still where it ruled unchallenged. At both top and bottom a mainly hand technology prevailed, at top because of the irreplaceability of human skill, at bottom because of the plentiful supply of drudges. High technology industry – what some Marxists call 'machinofacture' – was for the most part confined to the factories, but even here mechanisation was very far from complete. One might refer to the pot-makers at a steel-works, the rag-sorters at a paper-mill or to the bottle hands whom Dodd describes at Day and Martin's, Holborn, meting out blacking from vats.[189] In the Lancashire mills the 'self-acting mule' depended on the nimble fingers of the piecers, while power-loom weavers kept their machines at work by 'shuttlekissing', threading the weft with their lips.[190] In ironmaking the whole scale of enterprise was transformed by technical innovation, but labour remained absolutely primary at the point of production itself. As the *Morning Chronicle* commissioner wrote in 1850, after investigating the Monmouthshire iron works: 'Although capital is the motive power, it is upon the rude virtues of the workman that the entire system of manufacture ... rests.'[191]

Capitalist development in the nineteenth century depended on numbers as well as strength. In coal-mining, the labour force expanded from some 218,000 in 1841 to 1,202,000 in 1911, at the height of the industry's prosperity. In the building trades, over the same period, it more than trebled. British agriculture was prodigal in its use of hands, and the labour force in the 1850s was greater than at any other time before or since. Factories, too, despite the introduction of labour-saving machinery – and in some cases because of it – required a phenomenal number of hands, both to take charge of the preparatory processes, and to make good the deficiencies of the machine. In the Nottingham lace trade of the 1860s there were many more people employed as outworkers, mending and making up, than there were in the factories themselves.[192] In the workshop trades, employers could rely on the services of a whole army of job-hands and strappers, permanently under-employed, who were only taken on when trade was seasonally brisk.

The slow progress of mechanisation in mid-Victorian times had many different causes, but one of them was undoubtedly the relative abundance of labour, both skilled and unskilled. In striking contrast to the earlier years of the industrial revolution, every branch of employment was over-stocked. In agriculture there was a huge labour surplus, men, women, and children who never had full employment except in the harvest months. Railway building and construction sites depended upon a great army of freelance, tramping navvies, who took up employment only for the duration of a job. The reserve army of labour was no less a feature of the workshop trades. The supply of needlewomen was infinitely elastic – the number recorded in the census tripled between 1841 and 1861 – while that of carpenters and joiners, tailors and shoemakers, printers and bookbinders was always far greater than the number of regular berths. 'Tramping artisans' were very much a feature of the labour market in the new industrial crafts, such as boilermaking.[193] In iron shipbuilding, where most employment was on a job-and-finish basis, they constituted the bulk of the labour force: Samuel Kydd in 1858 described the Clydeside shipbuilders, restlessly scouring the riverside for work, as being more like 'wandering tinkers' than regular mechanics.[194] The trade union records of the mid-Victorian ironmoulders show that there were seldom less than 5 per cent of members out of work, and often more than 10 per cent.[195] In the Sheffield trades as many as a fifth of union members in the 1860s were 'on the box' (out of work, and supported from union funds), and indeed it was the strain of maintaining them at a fair level of benefit which seems to have been indirectly responsible for the notorious Sheffield 'outrages' (industrial terrorism against members in arrears with subscriptions). Amongst Yorkshire glass bottlemakers the mean level of unemployment seems to have been even higher, to judge by the figures reproduced in Table 2.[196]

This superabundance of labour was a pre-condition of Victorian economic expansion, and it also helped to determine its distinctive physiognomy and style. It encouraged capitalists to engage in capital-saving rather than labour-saving investment, to perpetuate low-intensity technologies, and to rely on workers' skills even when there was machinery ready, in principle, to replace them.

In the United States, by contrast – a new world, sparsely populated by immigrants – labour-saving improvements were a very condition of capitalist growth, and self-acting machinery, which in many cases the American invented, and in others they adopted as their own, made much more rapid strides than it did in mid-Victorian England.[197] The reaper-binder was transforming the harvest on the prairies while in England it was still being taken by the sickle or the scythe. In construction work the steam navvy was so extensively employed in America, and from such an early date, that the very word 'navvy' was attached not to the men (as it was in England, and as it is today) but to the machine; the steam-navvy was patented in America as early as 1841; it did not appear in England until the 1870s, when the manufacture was taken up by Ruston and Proctor of Lincoln; and its capabilities only began to be widely recognised in the 1890s, when it was employed on such big construction jobs as the Great Central Railway and the Manchester Ship Canal.[198] There was an equally pronounced disparity in lock-making, where, in the 1870s, machine-made, cast-iron locks from America were sweeping the markets of the world, while the Willenhall lock was still hand-made: it was widely attributed to the superabundance of cheap handicraft

Table 2 Unemployment among Yorkshire Glass Bottlemakers, 1867–97

Year	No. of Men Unemployed	% of Unemployed
1867	163	31.3
1868	53	11.3
1869	61	12.6
1870	94	17.3
1871	39	9.5
1872	10	4.2
1873	18	5.6
1874	39	9.5
1875	57	8.8
1876	188	22.7
1877	204	24.5
1878	353	40.2
1879	632	70.7
1880	247	32.2
1881	242	36.5
1882	171	25.8
1883	223	24.7
1884	305	28.0
1885	432	25.3
1886	796	63.9
1887	246	25.6
1888	380	32.5
1889	201	16.7
1890	210	16.9
1891	231	15.6
1892	545	32.6
1893	430	26.2
1894	950	49.3
1895	580	31.5
1896	528	30.6
1897	444	25.3

Source: Glass Bottlemakers of Yorkshire: Quarterly Reports, XXII, 12 June 1909, p. 76. London School of Economics, Webb Trade Union Collection.

labour, penniless small masters, 'and … the perpetuation of an ancient and wasteful garret system of working'.[199] Much the same was true in nailmaking, where machinery had entirely conquered production in America when the Committee on Machinery reported on it in 1854 (the first American machine had been patented as early as 1810); in England, down to the 1880s, the

great bulk of production was in the hands of Black Country outworkers, using hammers or treadle-worked 'Olivers'.[200] In boot
and shoemaking the slow adoption in England of the McKay and
Blake machines – patented in America during the Civil War – was
also related directly to the disparities in labour supply. 'In America
weekly wages were quite double those ruling in the English shoe
trade. Many machines which were profitable to use when they
displaced labour at a shilling an hour were hardly worth invest-
ing in when hand labour cost but sixpence. And this was about
the relative position in the two countries at the time the revolution of manufacturing methods was in its most active phase.'[201]
Similarly the slow progress in England of the Danks' puddling
furnace – an American innovation of the 1860s in ironmaking –
was attributed in 1898 (thirty years after the first patents had
been taken out) to the fact that 'good puddlers can be obtained
here at a lower price than is paid for even inferior workmen in
the United States'.[202]

The contrasting pace of English and American mechanisation
was already beginning to arouse notice at the time of the Great
Exhibition.[203] By the 1860s it was a commonplace and Marx
makes it the subject of a characteristically caustic comment in
Capital: 'The Yankees have invented a stone-breaking machine.
The English do not make use of it, because the "wretch" who
does this work gets paid for such a small portion of his labour,
that machinery would increase the cost of production to the
capitalist.' Elsewhere in *Capital* he drew attention to 'the invention now-a-days of machines in England that are employed only
in North America' – an observation admirably borne out by the
subsequent history of automatic looms and ring spinning.[204]

Another reason for the slow progress of mechanisation was the
possibility of increasing productivity within a hand technology,
either by the introduction of improved tools, or by a more systematic exploitation of labour, or both. Agriculture provides a prime
example, with the change from sickle to the scythe, the extension
of soil-improving crops and manures, and the mid-Victorian
improvements in field drainage. Coal-mining, too, advanced
on the basis of improved hand technology. Between 1850 and
1880 output in the industry doubled, and this was due not only

to the increase in the number of underground workers, but also to improved haulage methods, harder work, and improvements in the miner's pick, with the substitution of steel for iron.[205] At the same time better transport, both by sea and land, helped to end local monopolies, and brought down prices to the industrial and domestic consumer. Another striking example, to which Eric Hobsbawm drew attention some years ago, is that of gas-making, an industry which down to almost the end of the century was entirely dependent on the physical strength of the stokers. The amount of coal carbonised in the London gasworks rose by some 75 per cent between 1874 and 1888, while the labour force increased by under a third. The employers' gain may be attributed partly to severer labour discipline, partly to the replacement of the one by the three-man scoop (which gave a much greater charge to the firing though leaving its manual character untouched), and partly to the adoption of new chemical processes.[206] In outwork productivity was increased by 'sweating' – screwing down piece-rates so that earnings could only be made up on the basis of unpaid family labour. This was the very principle of expansion in the clothing trade, and it played a large role in such important domestic or semi-domestic industries as nailmaking, chainmaking, and the furniture trade. With rates of 2d. a gross, and children to work all hours as 'little human machines' – the basis on which Bryant and May's got their matchboxes made – the incentives to mechanisation must have been low, particularly when the domestic workers had to pay for their own paste, heat, and light.[207]

Cheap, labour-saving materials were another alternative to the machine. In tanning, for instance, the cost structure of the industry was transformed by the use of new tanning extracts imported from abroad. By the 1870s they had cut down the average time taken in treating the individual hide from a year to as little as four months, though the individual stages of production remained unchanged.[208] In bookbinding, the substitution of cloth for leather bindings (an innovation in the 1820s), and the introduction of 'case' work – the sub-division of work on covers – made hand labour much more productive while at the same time reducing raw material costs.[209] Mechanical aids, though bitterly contested by the journeymen bookbinders, were comparatively few, at least until the 1850s, and speeded up production only on the simplest classes of work, such as edge-cutting and flattening.[210] But the amount of hand tooling needed on each individual volume was drastically reduced. In the new cloth binderies, books were numbered in thousands rather than hundreds – tens of thousands in the case of the new cheap bibles – and they were produced with an open market rather than individual subscribers in view.[211] Employment increased rapidly and the 'mystery and art' of bookbinding was transformed into something approaching a mass production industry. Cheaper iron was the main basis for expansion in the metalworking trades, together with the invention of new alloys, such as Britannia metal and German silver. In the Wolverhampton holloware trade, one of the chief sources of mid-Victorian kitchenware, the processes of manufacture remained 'essentially the same' in the fifty years from 1810 to 1860, but costs were reduced by the introduction of enamel linings, and progressive falls in the price, or quality, of iron.

A third alternative to mechanisation – and another avenue to more rapid workmanship – was the division of labour and simplification of the individual task. In mid-Victorian times it was just as likely to take place off the master's premises as on them. A prime example is the introduction of 'riveting' in the boot and shoe trade, which brought a new and cheaper class of boot on to the market, and revolutionised the wholesale trade. Under the new system of work the soles were nailed to the uppers, instead of being stitched, and the work of 'making', previously performed by one man, was now divided between two – the riveters and the finishers.[212] Riveting was a spectacular commercial success, and Leicester, where the invention was patented in 1861, rapidly established itself as the largest producer of ready-made footwear.[213] Skill was reduced, labour costs fell, and there was a sharp increase in productivity. 'The old crafts would make about three boots or two pairs a day ... the riveter and finisher can produce ten pairs in the same time.'[214] The new labour, however, was unmistakably handicraft in character:

No machinery was used, the soles and uppers were cut by hand, then the upper was moulded round a last, with the edges pulled inwards. A 'nailer' or 'riveter', as he was variously called, would fill his mouth with 'sprigs', and taking them one by one would hammer on the sole and heel. When this had been done, the edges were trimmed with a sham knife. Finally, the sole and edges were ... polished with a hot iron and a heelball.[215]

Riveters often worked at home; finishers did so 'almost invariably'; and attempts to mechanise their work and put them into factories were for a long time unsuccessful. Indeed, so far from hand-riveting being displaced by machine, it seemed at one time as if the reverse was taking place. 'The English workman prefers to drive his rivet by hand, which he can do more quickly than the machine', wrote the *Shoe and Leather Trades Record* in 1878, '... thus the rivet machine has been entirely superseded in England'.[216]

In the Sheffield trades the division of labour was the primary axis of nineteenth-century growth, and as in the case of boot and shoemaking it was accompanied by a wide extension of outwork. Saw-making was distributed between seven different classes of work, each branching out as a little industry on its own – cutting and paring, hardening and tempering, grinding, glazing, toothing, handlemaking, finishing and polishing.[217] Similarly in the manufacture of tableknives, the work was dispersed into separate, sub-divided processes, with the cutler himself confined to the intermediate and final stages of fitting: 'Forging the blade is now one trade, grinding it another, and forging the scales and springs another ... besides ... several subsidiary branches, as the cutting up of stag and buffalo horns, and the working of hard wood, pearl or tortoiseshell.'[218] The work was passed backwards and forwards between these various specialists – in the best class of work a blade might travel three or four times between the grinders and forgers alone, quite apart from its journeyings to and from the cutler.[219]

The division of labour in needle-making – a manufacture for the million largely based in Redditch in Worcestershire – had more in common with Adam Smith's classic example of pin-making in *The Wealth of Nations*. Here the division of labour was associated with minutely sub-divided repetition work rather than with a proliferation of skills – the needle 'however unconsiderable its size' passing through the hands of 120 different workers. Despite the scale of production, there was little in the way of plant. The needle was cut from the wire with hammer or mallet; the points were ground on a stone; the eyes were pierced with a hand-lever press; the sorting was done by touch. Here is an account of it published in 1861:

> The little girl who performs this office places a rag or dolly upon the forefinger of her right hand, and with the left presses the needle against it; the points suck into the soft cotton, and are thus easily withdrawn and laid in the contrary direction. Little children 'rag' with inconceivable rapidity, and with equal speed the process of sorting, according to lengths, is performed, the human hand appreciating even the sixteenth of an inch in length, end separating the different sizes with a kind of instinct with which the reasoning power seems to have nothing to do.[220]

Technical Difficulties

Another obstacle to mechanisation was the gap between expectation and performance. In many cases the machines failed to perform the 'self-acting' miracles promised in the patents, and either needed a great deal of skilled attendance, or failed to execute their appointed tasks. Even if brought 'nearly ... to perfection' by its inventor, a machine would often prove difficult to operate.[221] Unexpected snags would be encountered, unintended effects would appear, and it was possible for patent to follow patent without anything like continuous flow production being achieved. Wright's pin machine of 1824, which, according to its promoters, 'during a single revolution ... produced a perfect pin', turned out to be so far from perfect that forty years later, despite thousands of pounds spent on costly experiments, the 'nobbing' or heading of the pin had still very often to be done by hand (in Gloucester this was a cottage industry, though the body of the pin was made in factories).[222] Wall's 1880 machine for manufacturing cheap pottery failed more quickly, though causing a brief sensation among the operatives: 'There was one defect in nearly all the ware independent of the want of polishing; air cracks almost invariably made their appearance in the backs of the ware after firing.'[223] The steam-powered 'Jolly', which bad caused such a panic in the Potteries thirty-five years earlier (the Potters' Union set up an Emigration Society, and planted a colony in America, as a way of escaping it) failed 'partly, it is supposed, through the desire of the employers not to come into conflict with the men', but chiefly 'owing to some defects in ... construction'.[224] (Later it resurfaced, and by the 1890s was in general use.)[225]

Often the action of machinery was too crude and indiscriminate for the tasks it was appointed to perform. Power-looms, for instance, were too rough in their action for the more delicate processes of weaving, or the finer classes of thread. In hosiery, intricate patterns defeated the steam-powered rotary frame, and 'fancy' hosiery (a rapidly expanding branch of the trade) remained the province of the hand-frame knitters long after the plainer classes of ware had gone to the machine. Steam threshers, though successful with wheat, were much too violent in their action for barley, which continued to be hand-flailed down to the end of the nineteenth century.[226] Mechanical potato-diggers were too clumsy and impetuous in their grasp: J. R. Wallace's model was a great success when it was put on trial at the Glasgow show of 1875, but trials under more difficult conditions showed that the potatoes were so badly damaged that they could not be stored in pits. Milking machines, despite numerous patents and improvements, were also much too rough: the siphon type injured the cow's udders and were troublesome to fit; the suction type was abandoned because it was liable to force out blood.[227] In manufacturing industry the difficulty often lay with the raw materials which were too delicate, or too variable, for machinery's harsh beat. No two skins were ever precisely the same in the leather-working trades, no two grains in furniture.[228] In the Birmingham trade of pearl-button making, where union members were fined £5 if they worked with steam, the 'brittle nature' of the raw material did not allow for a faster rate of working than a foot-lathe would accomplish.[229] In cutlery, the difficulty lay with the steel: 'Cutlery ... is not an article that lends itself to alteration', a Sheffield manufacturer said in 1903: 'High-class steel is so hard that attempts to manipulate it by machinery break the tools, and heating it to make it work easily would destroy its temper.'[230]

Even when such difficulties were overcome, machinery was rarely self-acting, but required skilled hands to guide and to complete its work. Nor, for the most part, could it be adapted to the finer and more delicate classes of work, where quality counted for more than yield. Machinery was thus used to do some sorts of things and not others, and many manufacturers settled for a mixed development, in which machinery was installed for the coarse, preparatory, stages of production, while the shaping and finishing was done by hand. This was notably the case in the Potteries, where pug-mills were used for mixing the flints and clay, but all of the actual making was done by hand. It was also the compromise reached in the Sheffield trade of saw-making, where the teeth were punched out by machinery, but bent into shape by hand, while the blade itself was tempered on the anvil by repeated hammer blows. 'The sharpening and setting of a saw requires considerable skill of hand and accuracy of eye; for if any one of the teeth projects either edgewise or sidewise beyond the true line, it renders the sawing harsh.'[231]

Profitability and Costs

Economic considerations also limned machinery's scope. In some cases the gains in productivity were comparatively modest, either because the intricacy of the process slowed down working pace (the case in full-fashioned hosiery, and in certain branches of lace-making, where the machine was subject to frequent stoppages), or – in the simpler classes of work – because hand labour could be worked at an almost machine-like pace.[232] In the linen industry of the 1850s the slow tempo of mechanisation in weaving as compared with that in spinning seems to have been due to this cause. A power-loom could produce four times the amount of a hand-loom weaver in any given day, but in spinning the differential was 320:1. 'The enormous saving of expense ... made the transition from ... hand-spinning ... an unavoidable necessity ... The saving by power-looms not being nearly so great, the transition state will ... be prolonged.'[233] Then again, the saving in labour might be counterbalanced by a greater wastage in raw materials (machinery was seldom employed where they were costly) or a need for higher quality inputs. In the galvanised iron trade, for instance, the new machinery of the 1850s and 1860s required a more costly material because the metal could not be 'humoured' as it could when it was shaped by hand; while in cork-cutting it was thought likely to fail because of lack of discrimination: 'a skilful cork-cutter will so manage his material as to lead to a minimum of waste'.[234] A further disincentive was the possibility of breakdown, which could be expensive to repair, as well as bringing production to a halt.[235]

In agriculture, mechanisation brought no overall gain in output. Steam cultivation might be more effective than horse tillage, and reaper-binders than harvesting by hand, but they did not increase the yield of a cornfield. The saving was principally on wages, but since these were screwed down to the barest minimum, farmers had no great incentive to invest in plant. 'In other arts machinery not only renders operations formerly done by hand more effective, but multiplies results to an almost infinite extent, while from the very nature of agriculture such an effect is not to be looked for.'[236] In metallurgy the gain in yield was offset by the loss in quality. Machine-riveting, for instance, was credited with performing the work at ten times the rate of hand-riveting, but even Fairbairn, a great advocate of hydraulic riveting, had to admit that the machine-made joints were not as strong as those which had been hammered by hand, 'though the faults would not appear in a comparatively small experiment'.[237] In the making of ship's chains even speed was not on machinery's side. In 1860 the welding of links was still being done at small forge fires with a top tool and hammer to fasten the stay. A recent attempt to abridge the work by introducing mechanical compressors had been abandoned on grounds of both quality and speed. 'However completely this and other machines may do the work, hand labour does the work quicker and better, almost beyond comparison.'[238]

Another set of difficulties presented themselves on the question of fixed and variable costs. A machine had to be kept running all the time to justify the expense of outlay, but even so the rise in output might not be sufficient to offset the running charges, depreciation costs, and investment. For the small producer, engaged in a week-by-week struggle for survival, the cost of installing machinery made it, quite simply, unthinkable – 'economy in time, energy and manpower was ... less important than economy in cash outlay'.[239] But even for a large and well-established firm it could be daunting. Mechanisation involved not merely the substitution of a machine for a tool, but an entire revolution in the production process. It involved exchanging well-established and familiar routines for new and untried methods, either with a brand-new work force, which would have to be trained to perform new tasks, or with an old one determined to protect their jobs (workers at Waterlow's, the Finsbury papermakers, held a party when the 'striker', a new-fangled American machine of 1874, broke down, taking the day off to celebrate and going to Epping for a swim).[240] In the workshop trades, with their cramped, overcrowded premises, want of space made it difficult to accommodate more than a modicum of plant.[241] Even in a large firm want of space could present an intractable problem. A potteries, for instance, was a rambling maze of small work-rooms, and machinery could only be installed if the entire premises were rebuilt.[242] Layout could be difficult elsewhere. At the Saltley gasworks, Birmingham, in 1895, two of the three retort-houses, with 960 mouthpieces to feed, depended on manual labour entirely because: 'These houses being too narrow for ... machinery of any kind, the retorts are still drawn and charged by hand, and the coal is delivered ... and the coke removed ... by barrows.'[243] Extra fuel costs also militated against the introduction of machinery, especially in districts which were remote from the coalfields. A steam saw consumed a ton of coal and a quart of machine oil a day – ginned by a horse it would be as cheap as the local grass or hay.[244] All the big concentrations of mid-Victorian steam-power were to be found in close proximity to the coalfields, while in southern England, where coal prices were about double those in the manufacturing districts of the north, it was comparatively sparse. Nevertheless fuel costs do not seem to have acted as an independent force: the production census of 1871 shows that the variations within the coal districts were almost as steep as those which separated the coal districts from manufacturing industries further south. In Staffordshire, for instance, 66,425 horse-power were concentrated in the blast furnaces and iron mills, 2.09 h.p. per worker, while in the whole of the Staffordshire Potteries there was only 3,101 h.p. (0.09 h.p. per worker). Birmingham, despite the proximity of the Staffordshire coalfield, had only 11,272 h.p.; Oldham, in the cotton district of East Lancashire, had 31,025 h.p.[245]

Market Uncertainties

Another obstacle to mechanisation was the irregular nature of demand, and its often limited character. Steam power and machinery were only profitable if they were geared to large-scale production. But in the workshop trades short production runs were endemic, and output fluctuated sharply not only with the trade cycle, but also from season to season and in many cases from week to week. 'Little makers', like the Willenhall locksmiths, the Sheffield cutlers, or the cabinet-makers of Bethnal Green, could only afford to make up goods in small quantities at a time, because they had to meet wages and costs out of weekly earnings. Warehousemen and buyers-up, for their part, were niggardly in their purchases, and preferred, as a matter of policy, to trade from week to week rather than to run the risk of carrying unsold stock on their hands. Consumer demand also tended to favour limited production runs, alternating between periods of heavy pressure, when there was a helter-skelter rush of work (as in the 'bull' weeks immediately preceding Christmas) and others when trade was dead.[246] In conditions like these it was easier, when faced with a rush of orders, to take on extra hands, or sub-contract the work, than to install expensive machinery and plant: less risky in the long run, and in the short run at least a great deal more profitable.

The position was not necessarily different in heavy industry, despite the vast scale of many works. Tinplates – the most recent historian of the South Wales industry tells us – 'were not manufactured ahead of demand but were rolled to order'.[247] According to Menelaus, the manager of the Dowlais Works, this was also very frequently the case in heavy iron. 'When rolled iron is wanted either in large masses, or of difficult sections and ... lengths', he told the South Wales Institute of Engineers in 1860, 'the quantities generally are so small that even if you have suitable machinery, before you get properly to work ... the order is finished.'[248] In shipbuilding and engineering, a great deal of work was done to order rather than for stock, while the willingness of British engineering firms to make large numbers of products in small quantities – and to fit them up, if necessary, on site – was the very basis of the world-wide reputation for excellence they enjoyed.[249] Ransome's of Ipswich, the East Anglian manufacturers of agricultural machinery, maintained some 700 models in their catalogues, and any of these might be modified on the job at the pattern stage.[250] Much the same was true of many of the machine-tool makers discussed by Roderick Floud in his recent book.[251]

Limited production runs were also a feature of the hardware trades, partly because of market uncertainties, but also because demand was highly specific, and new lines were being continually pioneered to meet particular customer requirements. No fewer than three hundred different classes of nail were being manufac-tured in the 1860s, for instance, with at least ten different sizes to each sort, so that in all upwards of three thousand different kinds of nail were on the market.[252] 'Machine-made nails of certain kinds have largely invaded the market, but there seems no likelihood of machine nails superseding the general varieties now made by hand', runs a trade report from the Black Country in August 1878, 'for, considering the demand, it would not pay anyone to make these particular classes of nails by machinery'. The Willenhall lockmakers were even more individualistic: at Messrs Carpen-ter's, the oldest works in the town, there were not less than five hundred distinct patterns, 'and when it is remembered that each pattern is made in various sizes ranging inch by inch from five to twelve inches an idea may be formed of the bewildering array'.[253]

'Specialty' was also rife in the manufacture of workmen's tools. In 1850s Birmingham, for instance, forty-five different kinds of axe were being made – fourteen of them specifically directed at the American market; there were upwards of seventy different types of hoe, and no fewer than five hundred varieties of hammer: 'not only is each adapted to one particular purpose, but several varieties often serve exclusively for the different operations in one and the same process'.[254] The larger firms in toolmaking added complications of their own. Wilkinson, the Grimesthorpe saw-makers, with a world-wide market for their hand-made saws, were making them to some 200 different patterns in 1880, and constantly adding improvements to their design; Messrs Elwell and Co. at Wednesbury Forge showed some 1,200 different patterns in their catalogue, 'including mattocks, plantation hoes, pickaxes, axes, adzes, spades, shovels, and forks'.[255]

Short production runs were also encouraged by the continuing vitality of local markets. Baskets, for instance, took on quite different shapes and sizes according to the district in which they were made, and the specific purposes to which they were directed. In Furness they had to serve as corves for the local coal and iron pits, in Nottingham as skips for the dyers and bleachers, in Southport as hampers for the shrimps.[256] Much the same was true of other commodities which were locally manufactured to meet specific local needs, coopers' ware, for instance, fancy boxes and containers, hay wagons, carts, and barrows.[257]

Consumer Preference

In many cases hand labour retained favour against machinery because of better performance. In paper-staining, for instance – i.e. the manufacture of wallpapers – block-printers held their own against machine-made competitors because the colours (which they mixed themselves) were less liable to fade.[258] 'Cheap machine-made papers quickly lose their colour', an architect advised potential clients in 1872, 'and as the process of manufacture does not permit of their being properly "set", the tints rub off and the patterns fade.'[259]

In edge-tool making, hand-made planes were preferred on grounds of their greater accuracy, and the superior smoothness of their cut. 'Machinery has been employed for the manufacture of hand-planes, but with little success', wrote a commentator in 1866. 'The irregularity in the thickness of the irons requires the exercise of considerable skill in "bedding" them upon the wood, and hand-labour is indispensable to effect this … properly. Unless this point is attended to, the tool jumps over the wood it has to plane, and makes it rougher instead of smoother.'[260] Hand-cut files held their own, notwithstanding numerous attempts by Sheffield manufacturers to market a cheap, machine-made alternative.[261] 'The wonderful sympathy of the eye and hand of the file-cutter are as yet totally unapproached by any machinery', wrote *The Ironmonger* in August 1878: 'The machine will certainly cut the teeth in the forged shape, but it does not give them that peculiar feather which is the essential feature of the file-cutter's craft.'[262]

In consumer durables there was a well-established preference for hand-made goods, not only because of their better quality, but also because of their superior finish, and of those additional embellishments which manufacturers were apt to call 'artistic'. The preference for hand-made goods was particularly marked in mid-Victorian times, when the bourgeoisie, in one or other of its manifestations, not only dominated public taste, but very often constituted the bulk of effective demand. A very common commercial practice of the 1870s and 1880s was for manufacturers and merchants to send machine-made goods to the Colonies and America, while marketing higher-class, hand-made goods at home.[263] In domestic hardware and the cutlery trades, the preference for hand-hammered goods was virtually unchallenged, and continued until the end of the century. When, for instance, about 1900, the Bilston manufacturers began to go over to machine-stamped frying pans, they took good care to do so in disguise. 'The knowing housewife still looks for the marks of the hammer, so they are added afterwards, just as a little sand is added to sponges.'[264] Hand-made locks held their own in the home market, not only because of their cheapness, but also because they were more cumbersome than their streamlined American competitors and might therefore be more formidable to burglars. They also possessed that priceless quality of individuality which bourgeois householders have always sought after so eagerly, and held in such esteem. 'American locks are, it must be granted, marvels of cheapness', *The Ironmonger* wrote disparagingly in October 1877,

> and the expenditure of manual labour in their production is almost nil ... But in thus practically dispensing with manual and patient labour; in thus turning out a gross of locks faster than English makers turn out a dozen ... certain features of the article – which used to be thought indispensable – have necessarily to be sacrificed. The ordinary American cast doorlock has ... no wards, the only security being in the 'fancy' or shape of the keyhole. A few strokes

with a file will of course modify this ... and then all 'security' is destroyed ... Machine-made keys, however ingenious ... do not, and cannot in the nature of thing, sufficiently 'differ'.[265]

Industrial design – which will be discussed in a second article – served to reinforce the role of speciality, and the extension of fashion to a new and cheaper range of commodities brought a feverish search for new styles. In boot and shoemaking patterns changed regularly two or three times a year, quite apart from being subject to short-lived crazes such as glazed heels. Wallpaper manufacturers were continually bringing out new lines, with dazzling new tints and a bewildering variety of motifs. Carriage-makers, too, were subject to continual changes of taste, and this seems to have been one of the reasons why, even in the largest works, so little machinery was used. 'As a class of manufacturers, we labour under many disadvantages in adopting machinery', a Bath capitalist told the Institute of Carriage Manufacturers in 1890: 'Owing to the numerous sizes and great variety of design, even the very largest establishments can only place a limited number of any one carriage in hand at one time.'[266] In Birmingham, with its multiplicity of small producers, marginal differentiation of the product was a very principle of growth, and responsiveness to changes in public taste a condition of business survival. Patterns were constantly going out of date, and manufacturers continually experimenting with new lines – 'in Birmingham the different varieties and sizes and patterns of article are so numerous, that the adjustment of the steam-engine to do the work would be almost unpracticable, and unprofitable if practicable', wrote Charles Knight in 1846, spelling out some of the technological consequences. 'The adjustments required by the ever-varying tastes and wants of the age can be effected only by men's fingers: the steam-engine being appealed to for that kind of service which may be common to all the works required.'[267]

Combined and Uneven Development
Steam power and hand technology may represent different principles of industrial organisation, and to the historian they may well appear as belonging to different epochs, the one innovatory,

the other 'traditional' and unchanging in its ways. But from the point of view of nineteenth-century capitalist development they were two sides of the same coin, and it is fitting that the Great Exhibition of 1851 – 'the authentic voice of British capitalism in the hour of its greatest triumph' – should have given symbolic representation to them both.[268] 'Steam power', an admiring commentator noted, 'wholly turned the mahogany which runs round the galleries of the Crystal Palace'.[269] But the 300,000 panes of glass which covered it were blown by hand, and so was the Crystal Fountain which formed the centre-piece of the transept, 'glittering in all the colours of the rainbow'.[270] The promoters were intoxicated with the idea of 'self-acting machinery', and the technological miracles it might perform. But they devoted a great deal of their space to – among other things – needlework; and in demonstrating the competitive capabilities of British industry they were heavily dependent on artisan skills. Most of the manufactures on display were handicraft products, and even in the Machinery Court many of the exhibits were assembled from hand-made components. 'Few objects' excited more attention among foreigners than the displays of Sheffield cutlery and edge-tools (the Sheffield Court was one of the most extensive in the building), while domestic visitors, it seems, were no less enraptured by the impenetrable Jocks, 'myriopermutation' keys and incombustible safes of Messrs Chubb, Bramah, and Mordan.[271] Superimposed on the idea of mechanical progress there was also a nascent commercial aesthetic which the Exhibition's promoters rather grandly labelled 'the marriage of industry and art'. In subsequent years it was to make 'taste' a very principle of production and the marginal differentiation of products a primary axis of growth.

The balance of advantage between steam power and hand technology was, in mid-Victorian times, very far from settled, and many manufacturers, though experimental in marketing new products and multiplying novelties of design, remained wedded to conservative production routines. Human beings, the main alternative to machinery, were, from a commercial point of view, often a much more attractive proposition. They were a great deal cheaper to install than a power house, and much more adaptable in their action than a self-acting stamp or press. When they broke down, the master did not have to pay for repairs; when they made a mistake, he could fine them; when there was no work for them to do he could give them the sack. Skills too were cheaper than machinery to come by. A steam sawing machine, in 1850, cost £700 to install; a pair of travelling sawyers could be hired to do a job for five shillings, while a circular saw – such as the one used at Joseph Severn's shop in Codnor – could be ginned by a horse for free.[272] Machinery was thus often adopted as a last resort, when every alternative means of extracting surplus value had failed to yield an adequate return, and it is no accident that manufacturers – like the Sheffield file makers of 1866 – so often turned their eyes to it when they were faced with demands for higher wages.

The orthodox account of the industrial revolution concentrates on the rise of steam power and machinery, and the spread of the factory system. It has much less to say about alternative forms of capitalist enterprise (such as those to be found in mining and quarrying), about the rise of sweating, or the spread of back-yard industries and trades. Nor does it tell us much about the repercussions of technology on work. Landes's picture has the compelling power of paradigm, with mechanisation on an 'ever-widening front' and steam power – 'rapid, regular, precise' – effortlessly performing labour's tasks. But if one looks at the economy as a whole rather than at its most novel and striking features, a less orderly canvas might be drawn – one bearing more resemblance to a Bruegel or even a Hieronymus Bosch than to the geometrical regularities of a modern abstract. The industrial landscape would be seen to be full of diggings and pits, as well as of tall factory chimneys. Smithies would sprout in the shadows of the furnaces, sweatshops in those of the looms. Agricultural labourers might take up the foreground, armed with sickle or scythe, while behind them troops of women and children would be bent double over the ripening crops in the field, pulling charlock, hoeing nettles, or cleaning the furrows of stones. In the middle distance there might be navvies digging sewers and paviours laying flags. On the building sites there would be a bustle of man-powered activity, with housepainters on ladders, and slaters nailing roofs. Carters would be loading and unloading horses, market women carrying baskets of produce on their heads; dockers balancing weights. The factories would be hot and steamy, with men stripped to the singlet, and juvenile runners in bare feet. At the lead works women would be carrying pots of poisonous metal on their heads, in the bleachers' shed they would be stitching yards of chlorined cloth, at a shoddy mill sorting rags. Instead of calling his picture 'machinery' the artist might prefer to name it 'toil'.

Skill was as important as toil (the two often went hand in hand) and in mid-Victorian times it was plentifully available. The domestic housebuilder could draw on a vast substratum of carpentering skills: so could such booming industries as Kentish Town pianos and High Wycombe chairs. The new iron shipyards were quickly filled with artisans and mechanics drawn from a dozen different trades; by the 1870s they were already a very cockpit of sectarian craft rivalries. Engineering employers recruited their labour from those who had served their apprenticeships in the 'country' branches of the trade, with wheelwrights, blacksmiths, and in the small-town foundries; and it was a matter of real anxiety in the industry when, towards the end of the century, this source of recruitment began to dry up. 'There is no evidence that labour supply impeded any of the machine tool firms', writes Roderick Floud in his recent book: 'Even as early as the 1830s, Nasmyth was able to break a strike in his works, aimed at forcing him to employ only men who had served an apprenticeship, by importing sixty-four Scottish mechanics and he remarked ... that "we might easily have obtained three times the number ..." No other machine tool maker appears to have had difficulties in securing labour, or, indeed, ... in dismissing it when times were bad, in the confident expectation that the men could be re-employed if trade improved.'[273]

It was not only in craft industry that capitalism drew on reservoirs of skill, but in every branch of economic activity where a mainly hand technology prevailed. Tunnel bricklayers on the railway works were in their own way as skilled as stonemasons; so were the coal heavers and timber porters in the docks, the carters and wagoners in road haulage, the ploughmen and rick-builders on the farms, the shot-firers and hewers in the pits. As well as the 'aristocracy of labour', on whom British historians have lavished such continuous attention, there was also a whole army of rural mechanics and small-town artisans, like the 'ragged trousered philanthropists' of Mugsborough, who still await their chronicler. So do the poor artisans of Shoreditch and Bethnal Green, in East London, who at the time of the 1891 census constituted no less than 60 per cent of the local working population.

Nineteenth-century capitalism created many more skills than it destroyed, though they were different in kind from those of the all-round craftsmen, and subject to a wholly new level of exploitation. The change from sail to steam in shipping led to the rise of a whole number of new industrial crafts, as well as providing a wider arena for the exercise of old ones. The same may be said of the shift from wood to iron in vehicle building, and of horse to steam in transport. In the woodworking trades a comparatively small amount of machinery supported a vast proliferation of handicraft activities, while in metallurgy the cheapening of manufacturing raw materials led to a multiplication of journeymen-masters. The mid-Victorian engineer was a tool-bearer rather than a machine minder; the boilermaker was an artisan rather than a factory hand. In coal-mining, activity increased by the recruitment of a vast new class of workers who were neither exactly labourers, nor yet artisans, but who very soon laid claim to hereditary craft skills. Much the same was true of workers in the tinplate mills and ironworks. The number of craftsmen in the building trade increased by leaps and bounds, though the rise of new specialities led to a narrowing of all-round skills.

In juxtaposing hand and steam-powered technologies one is speaking of a combined as well as of an uneven development. In mid-Victorian times, as earlier in the nineteenth century, they represented concurrent phases of capitalist growth, feeding on one another's achievements, endorsing one another's effects. Both were exposed to the same market forces; both depended for their progress upon the mobilisation of wage labour on a hitherto unprecedented scale, and both were equally subject to the new work discipline, though it affected them in different ways. The industrial revolution rested on a broad handicraft basis, which was at once a condition of its development and a restraint on its further growth. In mid-Victorian times – as I shall attempt to show in a second article – the handicraft sector of the economy was quite as dynamic as high technology industry, and just as much subject to technical development and change. It was indeed in the first rather than the second that mass production methods in many cases were pioneered; that new classes of commodity were created; and that modern capitalist methods of exploitation – both of producers and consumers – were most clearly prefigured and explored.

A Spiritual Elect?

Robert Tressell and the Early Socialists

The lecture that I am going to give today is quite an uncomfortable one for people here who are socialists because it is about the apartness, or minority character, of socialists and how that is imprinted in Tressell's novel.[1] There was a fine lecture in this series by Raymond Williams talking about the particular quality of Tressell's work as somebody who lived on the edge or at the margin of working-class life rather than within it.[2] I want to pursue that line today, not so much by looking at Tressell's text in detail – I assume that people here will know it – but rather through some contexts.

I should say that I do believe that this is one of the great texts of our literature. It's to be compared with *Pilgrim's Progress*, and I find it moving that this book has survived through the minority enthusiasm of individual workers, of whom Fred Ball is an outstanding example.[3] Tressell's book was published almost on the eve of the First World War and not under socialist auspices, and it could very well have been buried along with a great mass of social and socially minded literature of that time. There are numbers of now forgotten novels, for example, by Allen Clarke the Lancashire novelist, which are unknown in literature or in working-class reading. There were great numbers of communist and socialist novels between the wars; some of them are currently being reprinted by Lawrence and Wishart.

But there are only two texts which have survived as major works of literature, one is *The Ragged Trousered Philanthropists* and the other is Lewis Grassic Gibbon's *A Scot's Quair*. Both those books have an increasing following, and I think it is interesting to speculate on why that should be so. One of the qualities in Tressell's, which differentiates it from almost all other socialist imaginative literature, is that it is a deeply pessimistic work. It has the hope of socialism at the end, but Tressell had a thoroughgoing realism about the obstacles that socialist advocacy had to face and, above all, the ways in which socialism came up against the working-class conservatism of the time.

It is very much like a *Pilgrim's Progress* of our time, in which the lonely seeker after salvation finds himself beset by weakness and temptation on all sides. The language used by the building workers in the Cave is language that those of us who have had occasion to advocate socialism or communism today will recognise. All those arguments about human nature, all those arguments – about which Owen is so sarcastic – about how God ought not to have invented foreigners, are ones that we encountered, alas! only a year and a half ago at the time of the Falklands expedition. It's this absolute truthfulness to the isolation of socialists which, I think, accounts in part for the great appeal which Tressell's book has in the labour and trade union movement today, because in some sense Owen's position in Mugsborough corresponds to the often lonely, isolated, embattled position in which individual socialists, especially working-class socialists, find themselves.

Socialism, as an idea, is committed to equality and the democratisation of power and the self-determination of working people. And yet typically, socialists – at whatever time you choose to look at the history of the socialist movement, whether in the 1830s or in Tressell's period or I think today – have seen themselves as a minority elect. In one version – very much that of people like the Hastings members of the SDF [Social Democratic Federation] – they were salvationists bringing light into dark places, redemptionists carrying out rescue work among the masses. Or, like the early Fabians, they were a clerisy, representing the advanced and progressive thought of the day, the bearers of enlightenment. The more revolutionary socialists have typically constituted themselves as a vanguard. That's most familiar in the case of the Communist parties but it is also true of the syndicalist movement of the 1910s and 1920s, and I think it's also true of many constituency activists in the Labour Party and the new kind of Labour councillor today. The whole idea of Leninism, of Russian Communism, was of the Party, whether conceived of as an intelligentsia or as a cadre of professional revolutionaries, bringing understanding from the outside to the people. I think there are real affinities between vanguardism and the very English idea of Sidney and Beatrice Webb and the Fabians in which it was the professional classes, devoted to the public service and the public service ethic, who would administer to the common good. The will to lead is one which has been very strong both in reformist and in revolutionary versions of socialism.

The sources of this apartness, of this vanguardism, are multiple, I think. They come in part from socialism's inheritance from the French Revolution, from Jacobinism, and from those secret societies and revolutionary conspiracies in which the socialist idea was born in France, and in Germany in the 1830s and 1840s, or in groups like the Owenites in England. Marx and Engels drafted *The Communist Manifesto* for one such a group – a German tailors' club in London – and one of the organisations which Marx took part in in 1850 was a head committee for the world revolution. It was also the leading idea of Blanqui, the great revolutionist. The idea of the professional revolutionary, the person who lived for the revolution, is something which descends from the French Revolution of 1789 and goes on through the Paris Commune and continues in the world Communist movement that issues from 1917. So, one source of vanguardism or socialists as a people apart comes from the Jacobin idea of revolutionary virtue, of the Incorruptibles like Robespierre in the French Revolution, and those who would withstand the temptations of worldliness and bring about a reign of virtue.

Another quite different source of socialist vanguardism, I think, is Christianity – socialism born as a new Christianity (this is what Saint-Simon calls it). Socialism's working-class adherents in particular have often come from a deep religious culture and one of the ways in which socialists then conceptualised themselves was as spiritual leaders and guides. Now, Tressell is perhaps different from other English socialists of his time – if I recall from Fred

Ball's biography – in that his family origin may have been Catholic on his mother's side, rather than Protestant. In fact, it was a very deep Protestantism and above all Nonconformity which is the formative culture, the moral capital, on which English social-ism draws. So there are many affinities, indeed in my opinion, homologies, analogies, likenesses, between the socialist mission of the 1880s and 1890s and the Salvation Army. Frank Smith, who was General Booth's right-hand man in the Salvation Army, joins the socialist movement of the time and becomes Keir Hardie's closest friend. If you think of the salvationist orator going to the street corner with his or her words of blood and fire and think of the socialist orators of the same period, you are inhabiting a very similar mental universe. I think you cannot overestimate both the closeness of socialism's relation to Christianity and also the way in which socialists conceptualised themselves very much, as late Victorians did, as making war against an evil, contaminating world, as in the wonderful passage of Tawney's *Religion and the Rise of Capitalism* where seventeenth-century Puritans are seen as soldiers in hostile territory surrounded by manifest terrors and evil, even the forces of the devil.

A third source of this apartness of socialists, or of socialists as an elect or as a vanguard, comes from an idea in art which was born in the 1850s and 1860s: the idea of art as representing the forces of beauty and truth against the vulgarity and degradation of a commercial society. It was an idea which had an eloquent advocate in John Ruskin, who was one of the principal intel-lectual influences on the socialist movement in this country. (In France, in Baudelaire, in the symbolist poets, and the Parnassians, the writer or poet might be seen as representing the values of art against the materialism and corruption of the bourgeoisie.) This was very important for Tressell, and indeed for working-class socialists, because the typical working man (and I'm afraid it was mostly working men rather than working women, though there were many women in the early socialist movement, but they weren't characteristically from the working class) who joined the socialist movement of the 1880s and 1890s is the 'artistic' kind of workman – of whom Tressell is the very type (as you know from his mural that was rescued).[4]

One of our colleagues interviewed Fenner Brockway. He was talking about the Kentish Town branch of the SDF when he joined it. They weren't exactly intellectuals; they were more kind of 'artistic'. They were people who craved beauty in their lives. There is a wonderful description of a man called Anderson, the Finsbury Park Impossibilist who held forth at Finsbury Park night after night in the 1900s, and somebody who was recruited to socialism by him, Ralph Fox, says he listened to him month after month and suddenly he realised that this man didn't want to change anything.[5] What he wanted to do was to produce beautiful words – word-pictures – of a wonderful future of absolute harmony. It was a kind of compensation for the misery of his work by day in a motorcycle factory, and that was sufficient unto itself. An awful lot of socialist energy in the 1890s and 1900s was spent preaching and offering beautiful word-pictures of the socialist future or even more beautiful pictures of the medieval or primitive communist past, as Tressell does through Owen in *The Ragged Trousered Philanthropists* when he talks about the fifteenth century, the golden age of the artisan.

A lot of socialism could be seen as a kind of displaced artistic activity. I think there is some example of that in the current miners' strike, with the enormous upsurge of creativity normally thwarted in the pit villages and the huge outpouring of poetry which is one of the ways in which the miners, if you go to pit villages, have expressed what their strike is about. Socialism provided one kind of outlet for all that normally buried artistic impulse within the working class. But together with that, I think, went a profound sense – which you get in *The Ragged Trousered Philanthropists* – that if art is beautiful, surrounding life is ugly. And working-class life is sordid, and so a sense of carrying the values of art is something that sets you off against those surroundings rather than making you sympathetic to them. The idea of destroying, the idea of being in a living hell – I mean hell because of its denial of art as much as because of its poverty – I think, is one of the driving forces for working-class people who become socialists in that time.

This character of socialists as a people apart is also something that you come upon in the Labour Party between the wars. The kind of people who became Labour councillors in the 1920s and 1930s thought of themselves as being stewards for people who were too weak to help themselves. So the Labour Party built itself as a kind of paternalism in the localities. There are some very interesting films that were discovered recently by the Bermondsey, South East London Labour Party in the 1920s; they were campaigning pictures for public health. Among other things, they showed the hop pickers in their huts, in their insanitary conditions and in their enjoyment of the September holiday, and then you saw the Labour councillors coming down to help them in their wage demands and to make their conditions a bit more sanitary. And they are a different race; they're in suits and ties, they are well intentioned and benevolent, but definitely of a different species-being.

Again, if you think of the women of the Co-operative Women's Guild, part of the force of the Labour Party between the wars in working-class areas was that of the woman who joined the Guild (which was a mass organisation at the time), who was a kind of missionary of enlightenment. She was the person who had the knowledge – above all, the knowledge – of birth control and the new labour-saving devices which could rescue working-class women from endless child-rearing and from the drudgery of the kitchen. She represented in herself a principle of hope. I remember talking to somebody who joined the Labour theatre group in Hackney in East London and she recalled Kath Duncan, an elementary school teacher who was there and had mauve curtains – sixty years later there was still a note of wonder in her voice that someone could have something so daring as mauve curtains, in contrast to the drabness of working-class or lower middle-class respectability. Kath represented, as it were, modern living. Marion Philips, the National Women's Secretary of the Labour Party, wrote a book in 1921 on the labour-saving home.[6] So again it's a sense of being outsiders, helping people, bringing light into dark places. Within a poor street would be the Labour family that could manage, who had ambitions for their children to have some education; they were people of the community but also in some way apart from it, different. And one could go into the ways in which socialists today, even more strikingly, whether in the trade union movement or in the Labour Party, are in some way different from the people whom they can see themselves as serving.

I want to talk about the particular historical period of English socialism in which Tressell joins the Hastings Branch of the SDF and *The Ragged Trousered Philanthropists* is written. There was enormous social distance between socialists and the people that they were serving and in whose interests they were agitating. It is spectacular in the case of a gentleman turned agitator, like Henry Hyndman, the leader of the SDF, and in those patricians who joined the Fabian Society in the 1880s or people like Bernard Shaw and Sidney and Beatrice Webb. Just to give you an example of this social distance: in 1886 there was a spontaneous camp-out of the unemployed in Trafalgar Square – thousands of unemployed in a bad winter congregating there. The Socialist League, which was the most revolutionary socialist organisation of that time, founded by William Morris, Eleanor and Edward Marx-Aveling, and patronised by Friedrich Engels, for a month couldn't decide whether they should actually send a speaker down to the unemployed because this was a class below the level at which respectable, even revolutionary, politics was possible – this was called the 'lumpenproletariat'. The social distance between the artisan on the one hand and the poor on the other was so immense that even leading socialists whose mission it was to agitate amongst them drew back. It was in fact a matter of pride amongst socialists of all stripes, revolutionists or reformists, right up to 1920, that the person who supported the socialists or who voted for the Independent Labour Party was the artisan, not the slum poor. The slum poor, like the half-drunks in Tressell's book, are the people who are Tories. The working man who votes Tory doesn't think. It was the thinking working man who supported the Labour cause. Right up to and including the elections in which the slums actually began to return Labour councillors, for example, in the Gorbals in Glasgow, the local Labour Party wouldn't actually recognise it was having support from the lower depths. Labour's ideal constituency was the thinking working class, the artisan.

So there was a tremendous sense of distance between socialists and the poor. This was true not only of the early socialist political movement but also of the New Unionism, the organisation of unskilled workers. The matchgirls' strike, one of the historic events in English trade unionism, was organised by Annie Besant, a woman who had the courage to desert her clergyman husband and live independently, and Herbert Burroughs, who was a civil servant. Then, think of the London Dock Strike of 1889. That was led by two quintessential Victorian artisans: Tom Mann, whose political apprenticeship was served as a Shakespearean (he formed the Shakespearean Mutual Improvement Society of Chiswick), who had travelled to Paris, a man of great respectability, a vegetarian – very different from an East London docker; and John Burns, who would take his wife on a Saturday night to the opera, a very cultivated engineer and artisan. Or think of the gasworkers, who were indeed led by a gasworker, Will Thorne, but whose advisor was Eleanor Marx-Aveling, Karl Marx's daughter; or the famous Manningham Mills strike in Bradford in 1890 or thereabouts where it was Isabella Ford, an elementary school teacher, and Tom Maguire, a photographer's assistant (and, like Tressell, another consumptive working-class writer) who were the original leaders. So trade unionism at this time, in so far as it was beginning to become a mass trade unionism, also came from people who weren't the same as those whom they were leading.

Not only was there a social difference between socialists and the people whom they led and appealed to, but the very fact of their socialist activity made them socially further apart. Annie Besant was a pariah to respectable society because she had abandoned her husband, but to the workgirls of Bryant & May in Bow Common, East London, she was a great lady. And one of the things that her participation in the socialist movement did was to actually elevate her status, not with that intention, but because that was the effect of the enormous social gulfs of that time. There was a whole process of cultural upgrading which participation in the socialist movement involved, above all for working-class recruits. It was the historic character of socialist and later on of communist movements that they were workers' universities. People might join the socialist movement for the most instrumental of reasons, because of a strike or because of poverty or whatever, but the fact is that political activity is an intensely intellectual activity. It involved continuous argument; it involved inevitably and immediately arguments of a kind wonderfully rehearsed in *The Ragged Trousered Philanthropists* about human nature; it involved, for those who are free thinkers, giving testimony against God; it involved knowing the Bible better than those whom you had to combat.

The socialist inevitably became a bookish kind of person, so socialism partly appeals to the bookworms amongst the working class. But even if you are not a bookworm, you become one by nature of the political activity itself and all that intellectual practice which was the very stuff of socialism, which was mainly advocacy. So to become debater, to become a speaker was required of you, even if you didn't get up on the platform. That would be so in the workplace. Inevitably the socialist working man becomes, as Owen in *The Ragged Trousered Philanthropists* was referred to sarcastically, the 'Professor'. A little while ago, a very far left organisation indeed, the Revolutionary Workers' Party, a Trotskyist organisation, expelled one of their members, a shop steward in Oxford, from their ranks, and they wrote a pamphlet to denounce him and the main error that he was condemned for was 'neo-Kantianism'.[7] In other words, he was perpetrating a German philosophical heresy of the 1900s. So this whole way in which many people complain about socialists, that they speak a language which other people can't understand, comes from this kind of intellectuality which is a part of the ordinary practice of the socialist movement. It means both that the socialist movement of that time reproduced the existing social divisions of society, that is, it was recreated mainly from the kind of working person who could cope, who had some education, but also that it then set up divisions of its own. The very fact of becoming a socialist set socialists apart from their fellow workers.

Now, I think Tressell unconsciously and unintendedly structures his own book around that. Owen is the one working man in *The Ragged Trousered Philanthropists* who speaks standard English. Owen doesn't speak a dialect, a Sussex version of cockney. He speaks the English of any literature of the day. The other workers speak in wonderfully memorable language, a language so idiomatic and so close to the heart of popular feeling that you could reproduce much of the dialogue without embarrassment today for its contemporary form. The only words that are outdated are Owen's, and, though you may agree as I do with the sentiment, the actual way in which they are phrased is very literary. So in other words, what I am suggesting is that implicitly Tressell is recognising the gulf linguistically between the socialists and other people. Owen is a propagandist. But there were socialists of the time who seem to be concerned less with persuading others than in showing the banner, people who nursed their socialism as a private passion, who weren't actually concerned to spread the word or to convert as much as to display their own moral or intellectual superiority.

Then there is the very deep sense of artistic outrage that Tressell as a craftsman felt about 'slosh' work. Some of the finest passages in the book are about 'scamping', the interest only in profit, the fact that pumice stone, he said, is something that painters will no longer use because you no longer rub down the surfaces – you are just told to 'slosh', he says, to 'slosh the stuff on'. Remember the many passages where, when he has a chance to exercise his own suppressed artistic talent when for Rushton and the others this is simply a means to make a profit, Owen's indignation as a craftsman – which is, I think, exactly Tressell's own – at what the building trade was and what it ought to be whenever there was a chance to employ Moorish decorative work. Tressell had a lovely conceit about this; he erected an imaginary memorial of pumice stone, formerly used by house-painters. He was himself, you remember, apprenticed to one of the old-style builders who had a sense of craftsmanship, before sweating and the like.

So I think you can see the particular appeal of socialism to the sense of artistic outrage at the ugliness of capitalism, which is common to both working-class socialists of that time and also to middle and upper-class socialists. It's the very basis of William Morris's socialism: capitalism is ugly. I think one of the difficulties we have now in relating to socialists of that time is their wholesale condemnation of the urban environment. Morris, embarrassingly for those of us who are campaigning to defend the Greater London Council, wanted to destroy London physically. He wanted there to be a great annual festival to observe the destruction of East London and its replacement by forests – something which seems to be more a vision of the Conservative Party today than of those on the left. Morris takes it for granted that city life and all the artefacts of capitalism are ugly. So does Owen in *The Ragged Trousered Philanthropists*. This sense that everything commercial is equally ugly, that there are artistic values which are minority ones that are being overwhelmed by commerce was, I think, a very important part of the socialist imagination until very recently.

The socialist mission of the 1880s and 1890s had very close affinities to what was called at the time 'rescue work'. We know it best through the Salvation Army and through General Booth's *In Darkest England*. General Booth has a most dramatic picture at the front of his book showing the drunks, the out-of-works, people being pulled down into a slough of despond, and then the helping hand of the Salvation Army and its labour colonies. I think that idea of the life of the poor as a pit of both oppression and of infamy is one which socialists share. And indeed the socialist idea was born at the same time as the modern word 'slum'. The idea of 'slumming' was born in 1883, at the same time as Oxford and Belgravia were swept by a craze for slumming – people going down to the lower depths in places like East London.

Socialism also has affinities to the imperialist idea of the 'white man's burden'. Imperialism itself at the time wore a moral garb. The empire-builders weren't going to India or to Suez or Africa or Sudan or South Africa for profit. They were going out in the way that missionaries believed themselves to be going out, in order to help those who were incapable of helping themselves. I think that socialists in their own way, working class as much as middle class or upper class, conceived of themselves as bearing the burden of the world. The kind of working man who becomes a socialist in this period, like Tressell or like Fred Jowett of Bradford, would not be the person who would be himself in the lowest depths but a person who would be aware that there were people around the corner who had children who had no shoes on their feet, a family at the end of the street who couldn't cope because the husband was always drinking. So it was very much a kind of rescue work, going, as it were, from the strong to help the weak, very much in the way in which the Salvation Army went out. And again, Owen – it isn't that he is materially better off than his fellows, but culturally he is an aristocrat, isn't he, in *The Ragged Trousered Philanthropists*, an aristocrat who's giving his life to helping to enlighten them in their darkness?

A great deal of early socialist activity was, in fact though not in name, philanthropic. One of the main activities of the Clarion League – which was the mass organisation of young men and women who went cycling every weekend, when they weren't romantically preaching the word of socialism on the village green which is what they did on Sundays, or subversively brandishing their knapsacks and their flasks in front of the respectable churchgoers on church parade – was what were called Cinderella Clubs. Cinderella Clubs used to hold Christmas and other parties for the slum children, very much like the kind of effort that local Labour parties gave for miners' children this last Christmas. That was the main activity of the Clarion League Cinderella Clubs. And the Marxist Social Democratic Federation, when it wasn't preaching the inevitability and necessity of revolution, was setting up soup kitchens in poor districts and agitating for work for the unemployed. There was a lot of charitable work, though not in name, that entered into the practice in the socialist mission.

Socialism got rooted in this country because socialists took up the cause of the most helpless. The socialists who were elected to the Board of Guardians campaigned for the orphan children not to have the stigma of wearing the workhouse uniform, for them to have cottage homes, for them to have toys. Or like Graham Wallas, who was on a School Board, socialists campaigned for there to be flowers in the elementary schools to bring some beauty into the lives of the poor. The earliest campaign was on school milk and school feeding – a great plank of socialist agitation in the 1900s – which was bitterly opposed on the grounds that if the schools provided the children with meals, it would undermine parental responsibility – very similar arguments to the ones used by critics of welfare today. There were all kinds of very practical ways in which socialists presented themselves as bringing help and protection to the needy, to those unable to help themselves.

Socialists saw themselves, whatever their social position – working class, bourgeois, aristocratic – during these years, as spokesmen for the most helpless poor. They had a chivalresque idea of themselves, and indeed the language of chivalry, of knight errantry, of crusading, is one that you find in socialist oratory of the period. Shaw's Major Barbara is a Salvationist, but really she could equally have been a socialist of that period, for the way in which she sees her mission. Industrially, also, the socialists and trade unionists of the period are concerned above all with the more helpless industrial worker, with the sweated trades, with the dangerous trades, the trades where people would die after a few years because of poisoning, as in the white lead trade in East London or phosphorus work and the match trade, the sweated shopworker, the laundrywoman, the un-unionised, the casual labourer and above all the unemployed. It was a matter of the strong helping the weak – a trade union principle, as well as an aristocratic one of *noblesse oblige*.

The socialist support for the suffragettes and the women's movement – the suffragette movement, it's worth recalling, was formed within the Independent Labour Party – all had some of that character of chivalry. For Keir Hardie, who was an ardent supporter of women's suffrage, or George Lansbury, women were seen as the weaker, the victim of society, being helped by the men who took up the women's cause.

I think the socialist movement of the 1880s also had very strong affinities with the social purity movement of the time, with the crusades against moral corruption, of the kind that Josephine Butler had pioneered in the campaign on the Contagious Diseases Act in the 1870s. There was a very strong temperance component in socialism and indeed in early communism. There was a temperance group of Labour MPs right down to the end of the 1920s. There were dry housing estates, Labour housing estates, continuing right to the end of the 1950s, and bitter divisions within Labour parties between the temperance advocates and others. But in many ways socialism was conceived of as a kind of moral cleansing of society. Capitalism was a corrupt and contaminating society, and I'd remind you that some of the most powerful passages in *The Ragged Trousered Philanthropists* are the accounts of the besotted, of the drunken: the Cricketers' Arms as one absolute pit of human weakness and depravity. It's because his writing transcends as well as represents his politics that he can actually convey those music hall songs that he does wonderfully, in ways that you can actually (if you feel sympathetic to music hall, as probably most of us would nowadays) still respond to. But recall that he is giving this as an example of human stupidity, that these are absurd ditties on which people are regaling themselves and stopping themselves seeing the truth. *The Ragged Trousered Philanthropists* obviously isn't written as the book of a temperance advocate, and we have the character of Slyme to show how partial and hypocritical the merely Christian or the merely temperant would be. But the fact is that, in Tressell's own way, it is a very powerful advocacy against drink, and in that he's of the socialism of his time.

I want to end by saying something about mysticism, because I think this also has a bearing on Tressell and on the socialism of that time. It is arguable that socialism in all its different versions, among other things, represents a kind of displaced religious longing. It's a common accusation against socialism (or communism) that it is a kind of religion. I don't want to enter into that now, but to say about this particular period that whether they were evolutionists or revolutionists, Fabians or SDFers or ILPers, those who came to socialism in these years embraced it with the rapture of a newfound faith. Socialism was not only historically inevitable, it was also, in Annie Besant's expressive phrase, 'ethically beautiful'. It offered not only a more equitable mode of economic organisation, but also a philosophy of life: 'a noble practical religion, a true solidarity of interests, a morality of the higher self'. It called on men and women to transcend the immediate necessities of existence and take on larger views. Quite interestingly, in socialist feminism of the period and in socialist support for feminism and the emancipation of women, there was an ideal of transcending sexuality, that sexuality degraded, an idea which you could often find in the socialist marriages of the period, a true spiritual, platonic companionship, very often of childless marriages, like those of Sidney and Beatrice Webb and other Fabians; the idea that the only way of rescuing a woman from her degradation was to rescue her from her sex – that was also shared by many suffragettes – and that it was by rising to a higher plane of spiritual being that people could find real freedom and real companionship.

And a part of that was also – and this was a working-class idea as well as an upper or middle-class idea – the appeal of the simple life: that what was wrong with society was that there was too much luxury, too many goods, too much busy-ness and that the route to social salvation was by a radical simplification of life. The first class in sociology at Ruskin College in 1899 was of the kind that must have been captivating to impecunious, young working-class bachelors trying to persuade potential mothers and fathers-in-law that they were a good match. It divided human needs into two kinds: the first kind is companionship, warmth, love, art – that was primary; things like crockery, tablecloths, household furniture were contingent and secondary. In other words, it was the things of the spirit that mattered. That was the kind of ideal that was being put before young working-class students at Ruskin at that time.

There was also a middle and upper-class version of that, of those who, like Charlotte Wilson, abandoned life in stockbroker Hampstead and went to live in the simplicity of a farm on the edge of Hampstead Heath, or those who built the first garden city at Letchworth. Much of the Fabian mission to the middle class in the 1890s was to tell them that they didn't need so many domestic servants – you could get by with one domestic servant or, if you were really revolutionary like Edward Carpenter, none at all. This is one of the ways in which socialists were pioneers of modern living because if you simplified life, you didn't need domestic servants, you didn't need that kind of inequality. With this went a very strong religion of nature, which came partly from Walt Whitman, from American transcendentalism. It can be seen in the huge social enthusiasm for rambling and cycling which went on until quite recent times.

Although socialists of the period were very often in revolt against orthodox Christianity, one way of describing them is that they were spiritual vagrants. Quite often conversion to the social-ist movement involved a kind of born-again religious practice.

The socialism of the 1890s and 1900s was mixed up with various forms of secularist religion and materialist mysticism. Tom Mann was a Swedenborgean; Keir Hardie, whom people remember for his deepset, sunken, visionary look, was a practising spiritualist who communed with the spirits of the departed, as did his friend, Frank Smith; Herbert Burroughs, the Marxist co-organiser of the matchgirl strike, was a Theosophist; and the Fabians were honeycombed with Theosophists. Beyond those who were actually members of cults, there was also a kind of diffused 'ethical' socialism. Labour churches of the time constructed a kind of socialist alternative to, but also reproduction of, ceremonial religious practice and set up socialist Sunday schools as a kind of nursery of socialism.

Apart from such explicitly proto-religious and semi-religious practices, there were also some very deep mystical impulses in the socialism of that time. There was the idea, for example, that in becoming a socialist you transcended yourself, you ceased to be a person of the middle class or for that matter of the working class and you became transfigured and made anew. Stephen Yeo has written a very fine article in the *History Workshop Journal* called 'Socialism and the New Life: the Religion of Socialism in the 1880s and 1890s'. In autobiography after autobiography, you can read about the sense of personal salvation that becoming a socialist entailed. But apart from that, there were also the ways which socialists conceived of history, the idea of there being invisible powers, invisible forces at work making for a socialist future – for Marxists the succession of modes of production; for Fabians, the inevitability of collectivism. But the whole idea (which is a wonderful idea) that history is on your side was the basis of the socialist idea until about fifteen or twenty years ago. It gave tremendous confidence, even in the worst of conditions. History pointed in one way only – forwards. The idea that you were being carried as if you were on history's back and that you were realising a historical mission seems to me to be in essence a mystical idea.

In the ideas that socialists had of what the socialist state would be, there is also I think something which is very close indeed to a Christian idea of paradise. If you read William Morris's *News from Nowhere*, his socialist utopia set in the Thames Valley, it is a vision (it is one of the difficulties for us because our own imagination doesn't work like that in the late twentieth century) of absolute peace. The railways, which Morris hated almost as much as Mrs Thatcher, have disappeared, while people travel on donkeys. The figures are of a dream; there are young maidens and patriarchal figures with grey beards. Everybody is at rest; there is complete amity and happiness. It's a picture of heaven and, like Milton's heaven, it's rather dull. But it is one where all contradiction has been resolved. Now I think one of the real difficulties that we have is understanding (for those people who are socialists) how it was that an idea of absolute peace could be as appealing as that. What I think is beyond question is that, in the first place, it is a mystic vision. It isn't a development of things as they were. It was the world turned upside down; as there was energy, bustle – in the salesmen's term of the period, 'push' – and commercialism, so under socialism you have the end of that.

I would like to end by quoting from the last paragraphs in *The Ragged Trousered Philanthropists*:

> The gloomy shadows enshrouding the streets, concealing for the time their grey and mournful air of poverty and hidden suffering, and the black masses of cloud gathering so menacingly in the tempestuous sky, seemed typical of the Nemesis which was overtaking the Capitalist System. That atrocious system which, having attained to the fullest measure of detestable injustice and cruelty, was now fast crumbling into ruin ...

And then there is Owen's vision of the co-operative commonwealth, this being striking because it's in such contrast, I think, to the social realism of the novel heretofore:

> But from these ruins was surely growing the glorious fabric of the Co-operative Commonwealth. Mankind, awakening from the long night of bondage and mourning and arising from the dust wherein they had lain prone so long, were at last looking upwards to the light that was riving asunder and dissolving the dark clouds which had so long concealed from them the face of heaven. The light that

will shine upon the world wide Fatherland and illumine the gilded domes and glittering pinnacles of the beautiful cities of the future, where men shall dwell together in true brotherhood and goodwill and joy. The Golden Light that will be diffused throughout all the happy world from the rays of the risen sun of Socialism.

That's the vision splendid of a Marxist, revolutionary socialist of the 1900s. And it is a mystical vision.

The Roman Catholic Church and the Irish Poor

Father Sheridan, a priest at St Patrick's, Sutton Street, Soho Square in the 1880s appears to have shared with the Irishwomen of his congregation – those at any rate gathered together in the meetings of St Bridget's Confraternity – a familiar relationship which social anthropology may explain – the changing balance of intimacy and unease – but which the historian, for want of supporting evidence, can do little more than record.[1] It seems worth recording at some length, if only because it suggests the peculiar flavour of the subject, and the kind of reality, a context of community, which a merely ecclesiastical history of religion is likely to neglect.

The women of the Confraternity held their meetings on Monday evenings in a room at St Joseph's, Prince's Row, an infant school maintained by St Patrick's for the children of the poor Irish in and about Newport Market – 'this miserable outcast locality', as it had been called in 1875, inhabited by 'the poorest of God's poor'.[2] Father Sheridan, who compiled a register of the Confraternity's activities, had come to St Patrick's in August 1880; he introduced himself to the women for the first time on 27 September, and thereafter attended their meetings 'as regularly as circumstances allowed'.[3] It was his custom, when he addressed them, to read a selection of anecdotes and stories about Irish life, readings uninhibitedly selected, as the register makes clear, to excite the 'risible qualities' among the listeners, and he seems to have been content when his efforts were rewarded with an appreciative response. More serious questions were mainly reserved for a communal devotion in church observed by the members on the third Monday of every month, and a directly sacred emphasis appears sometimes to have been confined to the recitation of the Rosary, with which the evening's proceedings were invariably closed. Individual entries in the register begin in January 1881. The following is a selection:

Monday 31.1.81. – Medals and cards procured of Sisters. Feast of St Bridget for February 1st to be observed. Read story of the pranks of Irish fairies Carleton's Poor Sch and other tales com. p.214. Said Rosary; but did not speak on any religious topic. Present about 60.

Monday 7.2.81. – Read ... the story of Fin Mac Coul, and a giant from Carleton. They were amused, but did not laugh to my satisfaction, for, I fear, their tastes had been vitiated by the excruciatingly (from Miss Ruffe's collection of words), funny tales read to them at other sittings ... We said the Rosary & asked the assistance of our dear Saint Bridget. Very good attendance, notwithstanding the heavy downpour. Dispersed at 9.30.

Monday 28.2.81. – Read to them a chapter from A. M. Sullivan's 'New Ireland' about F. Mathew which seemingly pleased.[4] *Mem.* Always read beforehand for subject for evening: withdraw the jambreakers & skip French and other quotations. Then said Rosary.

Monday 3.10.81. – This evening fair attendance filling hall. Read for them a few anecdotes concerning Newfoundland dogs taken from Lamp followed by a laughable & entertaining Irish skit entitled Nell Hegarty's visit to Cork from October ('80) no of Lamp. Rosary... N.B. the *bête noire* of our meeting Mrs. Mahoney was present with her snuff, coughing & disturbance.

Monday 24.10.81. – This evening we read one of Lover's comic sketches – the Curse of Roshogue. There was a great deal of laughing and would have been much more had I carefully prepared the reading of the piece. The attendance was extremely large and I believe the largest yet. Rosary as usual.

Monday 7.11.81. – This evening having previously read the account of Guy Fawkes Day in the Clifton Tract series I chatted to those present about it. It took, I fancy, pretty well. As large a number as usual were present though I noticed strange faces which were their proprietors to bring them often might add a little respectability to proceedings.

Monday 14.11.81. – This evening very large attendance so much so that the babies gallery was taken possession by benign matres who couldn't sit elsewhere. Reading was choice as the new 'Irish Pleasantry & Fun' furnish some excellent pieces. 'Shemus O'Brien' & 'The Donnybrook Spree' seemed to excite the risible qualities wonderfully.

Monday 12.12.81. – The evening being cold & wet and having been disappointed the two previous evenings the number of people did not exceed forty. Was not up to much myself but as proceeded reading the 'Waiver of Duleck Gate' [?] (Irish Pleasantry and Fun) our spirits rose and we had a few good roaring laughs. Rosary & a few words wishing a happy Xmas.

Monday 2.1.82. – Our first meeting of 1882 was not brilliantly attended. Something like 56 put in an appearance & all of them listened with apparent satisfaction to the veracious narration of 'Puss in Brogues' (Irish Pleasantry and Fun, p. 3). Rosary & a few words wishing them a happy New Year.

The last entry is for Monday 5 June 1882.

This evening read the skit by Lover (From Handy Andy) in Father Phil's collection. It took very well, but yet I fancy things can be made to take as well as twenty times better if I were to study them beforehand and read them acting partly the while – giving a romantic recital. Attendance very good something like 70 I fancy.

The meetings evidently prospered under this benign direction – the comic Irish stories, in particular, 'seemed to take them' – and attendance, which had been no more than 'about a dozen' when Father Sheridan began his work, was brought up within a few months to eighty. The association had originally been designated and held as a 'Mother's Meeting': but Father Sheridan objected to the name as too 'Proddy', and in December 1880, at the suggestion of Father Barge, Missionary Rector of the parish, it was raised to the status of a religious fraternity and given a Catholic

and Irish dedicatory name. (Father Sheridan wrote to the Arch-
bishop of Dublin 'to know if it were possible to procure a relic
of St. Bridget in Ireland'). Rules were drawn up setting out the
women's religious obligations ('above all not to neglect their
monthly confession and communion'), medals were struck to
wear as insignia at Mass ('pleasing to saints P and B to see the
green'), and collecting cards distributed.[5] By October 1881 Father
Sheridan was hopefully anticipating a banner:

> Monday 3.10.81. – I had a few words with them about our pros-
> pects and hopes. First I proposed getting a banner of St. Bridget
> and expect to make by collecting cards and concerts £15 ... Sec-
> ondly I said that we should have our monthly mass on the fourth
> Sunday and day of general communion, and lastly I informed them
> that on procession evenings they should take part in our Church
> procession wearing their regalia (l can easily fancy how proud
> they'll be) ... *an idea* occurring to me is that should I be able to
> have some money over banners cost could get new medals of St.
> Bridget with name of conf. attached.

The climax of these activities, as they are recorded in the brief
period covered by the register (1880–2), occurs on the Sunday
evening when a solemn enrolment of members takes place, and
the new members come to the altar rails, 'with candles alight',
and form themselves in to a procession – 'the first procession in
which the women of St. Patrick's ever took part'.

> Sunday evening the 23rd April (1882) was a gala day ... For on that
> evening took place our second solemn enrolment of members, the
> blessing of the Banner & the first procession in which the women
> of St. Patrick's ever took part. We had first the devotions to Jesus
> Risen, beautiful ... prayers which accompanied with the apostles'
> creed, said by people standing, seemed to take immensely well.
> Then F. Roche preached an eloquent ... discourse with which I
> am sure the people were delighted & tears testified the sincerity of
> the feelings of many. Text was concerning the brazen serpent put
> up as a sign. Thence he came to speak of the similarity in many
> points between the chosen people of ancient days & the chosen

ones of today – Jews and Irish. He exhorted all to keep pure and unblemished amongst them their holy religion, many points of which were brought to their minds by the emblems on Banner. Then I received the new members who with candles alight came to rails & received their medals. The procession was then formed in this wise: 1st small boys, 2 Brothers, 3 women of the Conf. 4 girls. Incensation of relic followed then procession & afterwards blessing of Relic of St. P & Benediction. The church was indeed full, & many testified as to not having seen such a sight for many years in our church.

It would not be difficult to explain these extracts by reference to the conventional emotional religious practice of the time, and there is no reason to insist upon a peculiarly Catholic inspiration. The Irish of St Patrick's were not the only congregation to be commended by their pastor as a 'peculiar' people, chosen of God; the interleaving of religious and colloquial effects is often met with in nineteenth-century popular religion – it was a powerful ingredient in Spurgeon's religious oratory, while among the vernacular preachers of the provinces (whose 'vulgarity' fastidious men deplored) it was sometimes rampant; and in the last years of the century, Nonconformist deacons promoted Pleasant Sunday Afternoons.[6] No doubt Father Sheridan's Irish sketches share something of this character, but the 'roaring laughs', whose very decibels he makes the subject of retrospective calculation, do seem at some distance removed from the self–proclaimed 'joyousness' of the revivalist hymn or the religious and moral address.[7] One has only to think of Octavia Hill, little more than a mile away in her Marylebone courts, harassing the lives of her tenantry, or of the Scripture Reader, as he was fondly pictured, at the sinner's bedside, to see that, among the ragged communities of the poor at least, the relationship has a certain individual quality. The priest may be irritated by a particular member of his congregation ('Mrs Mahoney... with her snuff, coughing and disturbance') but the hostility seems almost neighbourly in character; he may crave for 'a little respectability' to be added to the proceedings but it is scarcely an active hope, and he appears well satisfied if attendance has been good and the membership entertained. The setting is gregarious and familiar, and the moral atmosphere characteristic of the congregations of the Irish poor in England during the second half of the nineteenth century.

The great wave of Irish immigration coincided in years with the Romeward movement among the Tractarians, and the Catholic revival to which Newman gave the name of 'Second Spring'. Indeed, it may be said to have engulfed it, and never more obviously so than during the cholera of 1849, when Newman and St John were sent to administer the last sacraments to the cholera victims at Walsall and Bilston – 'everyone crying as if we were going to be killed' – while the London house of the Oratory was employed on a similar mission among the poor Irish hop-pickers in Kent.[8] Between, on the one hand, the Catholic yeomen and the farmers of Broughton in the Fylde, whose annual festivities at the Whitsuntide dinner of their Friendly Society in 1843 included the collective rendering of a glee bearing the eloquently hybrid title 'St. Patrick Was a Gentleman', or so distinguished a figure among the Catholic laity of England as Lord Arundel, 'the representative of the Mowbrays and the Howards, whose nobility extended beyond that even of Rodolph of Hapsburgh', who at the Oratorians' first celebration of the Quarant'ore in 1850 was so alarmed at the number of candles displayed that he brought down a fire engine 'which at his request was kept ready charged in the sacristy', and, on the other, the Irish Catholic poor – market people, washerwomen, labourers – congregating together in belligerent fidelity, the contrast in religious sensibility, as in nationality and social station, was not easy to ignore, and Catholicity in England during the second half of the nineteenth century may be said to bear the character of a plural church.[9] It pursued simultaneously a double mission. It reached out in its proselytising work of conversion to the well-born and the rich – those especially who had come within the Puseyite orbit. At the same time, it served as a national church of the Irish poor, planting its chapels and schoolrooms in the close quarters and the narrow streets, seeking out the Irish in the workhouse, the children's orphanage and the reformatory, ministering to the Irish soldier in his barracks, and the Irish prisoner in his cell.[10]

The new missions reflected the line and cluster of Irish settlement, following isolated groups of labourers at distant points – like the Franciscan mission in the Monmouthshire hills – or planting themselves in the midst of the densely crowded pent-up rookeries of the towns, as at Holy Cross, Liverpool, where 'not a house' in the district was more than seven minutes' walk from the church.[11] The 'churches' in the newly founded missions were sometimes no more than temporary chapels, improvised in wood and iron; sometimes merely a hired shop or 'rooms'. The Church of the Sacred Heart, Camberwell, founded as a temporary chapel in 1863, and built upon a site of tumbledown premises – 'comprising a rag-shop with a pig-sty in the rear'– illustrates the characteristically plebeian setting.[12] The mission was deliberately established among the poorest inhabitants, 'so that shabby clothes shall not hinder them from coming to Mass'. It stood on the edge of the Sultan Street area, whose moral and social condition was some years later to invite the anxious investigations of Charles Booth, and it served an Irish colony in densely-crowded conditions – 'seven or eight different surnames and up to twenty inhabitants … under one roof'.[13]

The establishment of a new mission was liable to provoke in the local community an outburst of Protestant indignation. Mission rooms were difficult to hire (above all in Wales), obstacles were placed in the way of a purchase of land, and the chapels, as they were building, had sometimes to face the threat of malicious damage: at Carmarthen, 'it was necessary to enlist the help of voluntary watchmen, for otherwise what was being built in the day would have been pulled down in the night by the hands of the unfriendly Protestants'.[14] The arrival of a Catholic priest was in some places an historic event. At Pontypool, where a Franciscan mission was established in 1860, the appearance of Father Elzear in their midst ('a real live monk') provoked among the native Welsh inhabitants an animated curiosity which they were not at pains to hide. 'Every time Father Elzear went out … he was surrounded by crowds of eager faces, and his progress through the streets caused as much excitements as though he had been the Pope in person.'[15] At distinct points, where Protestant feeling was strong, the early congregations met under conditions of menace or even siege. At Colne, where a missioner from Burnley attempted to gather a congregation in 1851, the Catholic worshippers, meeting above a stable in the Angel inn yard were surrounded by a No Popery crowd 'sometimes five times as numerous', a factory manager leading his people to demonstrate against the services, and a Protestant agitator haranguing the priest from below.[16] At Wallasey, where a priest from Liverpool crossed the river to celebrate Mass, the congregation had filled their pockets with the local stones before setting out for the service, 'it being almost certain that the local Orangemen would assail them either coming or going'.[17] At Cwmbran, in Monmouthshire, where the Irish were employed about the furnaces and iron-works, 'it was for some time no unusual occurrence for stones to be hurled against the windows during Mass or Benedictions'; the Catholic chapel, 'an iron building capable of accommodating 250 peoples', was surrounded by five hostile chapels, in which, 'Sunday after Sunday', Dissenting ministers hurled their anathemas at the stranger in their midst – 'our meek-looking chapel', a Franciscan chronicler wrote, 'standing as a little Goschen amidst the Egyptian darkness'.[18]

The religious orders provoked an especially great reflexive national hostility, and against convents in particular a campaign waged for many years. The appearance of a religious habit in the street, so far from protecting the wearer by announcement of a religious status, might service rather as an excitement to insulting personal remarks.[19] Even in the relative seclusion of Woodchester, Gloucestershire, Father Tom Burke, the Irish Dominican, and his novices, found themselves exposed to the 'unbecoming jibes' of factory girls on the way to work.[20] During the Protestant hysteria of 1850–1, Father Ignatius Spencer, clothed in the coarse black habit of Passionist Order, was attacked by roughs in Liverpool as he was passing from St Patrick's chapel, and in a near street was 'hustled and … thrown down into a cellar full of people'; near Charterhouse Square in London he was mobbed 'and almost killed' by an infuriated crowd.[21] So strong was the popular feeling that, independently of the hostile parliamentary moves in the same direction, the more timid among the English Catholics were urging the abandonment of religious dress 'on the public road'.[22] An attempt to establish the Sisters of Charity in Salford provoked such violent persecution that they were withdrawn by their superior to Paris:

At first ... the labours of the three sisters whom Father had sent ... promised to be conducive to good. They visited the sick unmolested in the daytime, and held classes for factory girls and others in the evening ... hundreds were prepared for the sacraments ... (But) the bulk of the people became more and more anti-Catholic. The Sisters were insulted wherever they appeared, and one of them was thrown down, and returned home covered with blood; and, on another occasion, while the Sisters were at church, their house was set on fire. The violent treatment frightened Sister de Missy, the Superioress, and led her to relate everything Father Etienne, who considered it his duty to recall the Sisters.[23]

Some years later, in 1859, when they were installed at York Street, Westminster – 'a very old house ... In the midst of a swarming population of the poorer people' – the 'cries' and 'shouts' of derision 'once more sounded on all sides'.[24]

On the evening of the Sisters' arrival a young teacher in the catholic school, attached to the Church of St. Peter and St. Edward, offered to take them there to Benediction, but no sooner did they appear in the street than they were surrounded by an unfriendly mob. Cries and shouts of derision sounded on all sides; mud and even stones were thrown at the Sisters, and the consequences might have been serious had not some tall Guardsmen from the neighbouring barracks come forward and constituted themselves their protectors, giving them their escort as far as the Church, and even remaining there to see them back to their poor little dwelling in York Street ... For some time a number of them took it in turns to protect them whenever they went into the streets; but sometimes even their presence was not sufficient to keep the boys, and even men and women, from attacking them, and then the aid of the law had to be evoked, so that it was by no means unusual to see the Sisters walking along with a soldier on one side of them and a policeman on the other.[25]

The native disposition was not kindly, yet these were the streets in which popular Catholicism sought to find a sanctuary and, like the Irish immigrants themselves, to create the familiar surroundings of home.

The Catholic 'Poor Schools', to which the Church devoted so remarkable an effort in the third quarter of the century, were planted in the very midst of the poor, quite without regard to the reputation of the 'low' Irish neighbourhoods. London Prentice Street, where in 1849 St Chad's Cathedral set up its poor schools in the seven back rooms of a court, was reputedly the most dangerous street in Birmingham;[26] it carried the stigma of a particularly brutal murder in 1853 and was the centre of rookery, 'notoriously infested with bad characters of every description'.[27] Park Street nearby, where in 1845 the Sisters of Mercy established their Sunday School in a loft, was another very poor street; it had received an early influx of Irish, and in 1867 when 'the ragged Catholic children who squat among the dust-heaps and gutter' were recited as a commonplace feature of the street, they had grown so numerous that it provided a natural focus, as the most Irish street in town, for racial and religious riot.[28] The early schools were in no way cloistered. One at Liverpool was 'a large room or loft above a cow-house, in a dirty, back, ill-ventilated lane;' another – rented by Father Parker of St Patrick's when Protestant bigotry turned the Catholic children out of the Council schools – was a converted Penny Gaff.[29] At Cardiff the Council school in 1847 was a loft above a cooper's workshop; at Barnsley 'only a cellar'.[30] In the second half of the century, despite the intense efforts of the Catholic Poor Schools Committee, many of the children continued to be taught in very primitive conditions. The Catholic school in Lincoln, as Joseph O'Connor remembered it in the early 1880s – 'a long walk down the hill ... through a maze of streets' – was 'a makeshift of corrugated iron attached to a makeshift chapel of the same depressing material ... almost hidden on a waste spot in the poorest slum'.[31] At Kilburn, in 1871,

> the chief school room where the elder children are taught is the upper room of a shopkeeper's house ill-suited for a school room ... The infants are taught in a dark kitchen used after the children are dismissed for culinary purposes.[32]

In a crowded part of Westminster where the Catholic school was housed in a converted theatre, 'formerly ... very popular among the poor', the children had to make their way at the beginning of the day through a milling crowd of costers.

> There was a very long covered passage leading from the street to the school; to this all the costermongers of the neighbourhood laid claim as having a prescriptive right to deposit there their barrows for the night; so that. what with the children in the morning fighting to get in, and the costers struggle to get out, we may leave the reader to imagine the confusion.[33]

'Child hunting', as Father Vere described it in a memoir of his early days in Soho, was a frequent addition to the ordinary duties of the priest.[34] The children of the Irish poor were apt to be irregular in their attendance at school, more especially in the great cities, and a great deal depended on the pressure which could be brought to bear on 'negligent' parents.[35] Even those – they seem in general to have been a small minority – whom the priest found it otherwise 'difficult to touch' might nevertheless be persuaded on this single point to yield.[36] At Tarry Town, Hackney Wick, 'a poor and woebegone spot at the Junction of Hackney Cut and Duckett's canal', the Servants of the Sacred Heart went out to hunt up the children of a little colony of lapsed Irish Catholics, and bring them to the Catholic school.[37] At a private 'adventure' school in Periwinkle Street, Tower Hamlets, where upwards of one hundred boys and girls, 'the children of very poor parents', were accommodated in the space of a 'wretched hovel', the local Catholic priest was said to treat the children as though they were his own: 'the school being almost wholly composed of the children of Irish Rom. Catholics, the priest periodically, *but unasked*, visits in order to take the pupils to their religious duties'.[38] At St Francis Xavier's, Liverpool, the Jesuit Fathers gathered together a host of street urchins on Sunday mornings, provided them with breakfast, and marched them off to Mass, some 'almost "sansculotte"' in appearance, 'most of them shoeless'.[39] Moreover, Protestant aggression – 'the obvious danger of proselytism' – represented in places as potent a danger as apathy or negligence, and the Poor Schools themselves served in places less as educational establishments than as an improved arm of confessional war. St Joseph's infant school in Princes Row, Soho, 'that little school with its close atmosphere and dirty children', as Father Vere affectionately recalled it – housed above the parlours of an itinerant Irish shellfish dealer, who cooked his whelks and winkles in the yard, and sent his own little girls to the school – was set up to counter the rival persuasions of the Puseyite mission which had its headquarters nearby in Crown Street.[40] A scribbled entry in the 'log book' for 1868 (a few tattered pages are all of the school's existence to survive) records an early triumph,

> May 11th until this date 36 children have left the Puseyite schools to come to St. Joseph's only 6 of them have gone back again
> 3 Griffins Newport Market
> 2 Connolly's Princes Court
> M.A. Morgan Princes Court
> 10 June Anna Griffin again returned having previously been at the Puseyite school[41]

A mile away to the north, at the far end of Charlotte Street, off Fitzroy Square, the Catholic children of another infant school named St Joseph's – crammed into the space of a single ground-floor room – faced the Protestant children of a rival school on opposite sides of the same narrow court. The hectic situation may be imagined. 'Some panes of glass have been removed to ensure ventilation', an inspector commented, 'but the noise from outside makes satisfactory teaching impossible'.[42]

The priest, in the Irish mission, lived in close vicinity with his flock, having no society other than that of his parishioners: 'no rich to interfere … no invitations to ruin the clergy', nor any round save that of the close quarters and the narrow streets.[43] His daily transactions were conducted as those of a familiar, and yet one who at the same time enjoyed a peculiar and esoteric power, a figure at once accessible and remote. His entire life was devoted to his ministry. He might be called out at any hour to visit the sick, to bring the sacraments to the dying or to act as arbiter in a family quarrel. His life was intimately associated with that of the community, even though he was assigned an exalted role in it. As the 'man of God' his blessing was eagerly sought, as the leader of the flock he was looked to for the kindness of a friendly recognition or a brief exchange of words. Mayhew, who accompanied a priest on his round among the street-Irish of London, described how his mere presence brought the people crowding to their doors.

> Everywhere the people ran out to meet him. He had just returned to them I found, and the news spread round, and women crowded to their door-steps and came creeping up from the callers through the trap-doors, merely to curtsey to him. One old crone, as he passed, cried 'You're a good father. Heaven comfort you', and the boys playing about stood stiff to watch him. A lad, in a man's tall coat and a shirt-collar that nearly covered in head – like the paper round a bouquet – was fortunate enough to be noticed, and his eyes sparkled, as he touched his hair at each word he spoke in answer. At a conversation that took place between the priest and a woman who kept a dry fish-stall, the dame excused herself for not having been up to take tea 'with his rivirince's mother lately, for thrade had been so busy, and night was the fullest time.' Even as the priest walked along the street, boys running at full speed would pull up to touch their hair, and the stall-women would rise from their baskets; while all noise – even a quarrel – ceased until he had passed by. Still there was no look of fear in the people. He called them all by their names, and asked after their families, and once or twice the 'father' was taken aside and held by the button while some point that required his advice was whispered in his ear.[44]

The priest's house – no more than a humble workman's cottage in some of the poorest missions – was barely separated from the work of his ministry, but served rather as a second focal point.[45] In earlier years, before the placing of the confessional in church had been made obligatory, it was sometimes used for the reception of penitents: at St Patrick's, Soho, when the clergy lived in Dean Street, 'a long line of penitents knelt all up the stairs' on confessional nights, and took their turns for admission to the priest's room'.[46] It was a recipient for 'American' and 'foreign' letters which arrived for members of the congregation ('for James Hogan ... from Australia', 'from John Dolan, Royal Marine, for his sister', 'Mr David Magee for Mr P. O'Brien').[47] It was a natural point of call when trouble broke out in any part of the community. Above all the priest was perpetually on call for visits to the sick. Each day there was a lengthy list of the sick to be visited; calls continued to come in through the day ('We generally had to look in at the presbytery about midday, to see if any new … calls had been sent in'), and the sick bell might be rung even in the dark hours of night.[48] At St Peter's, Birmingham, ministering to a very poor community of Irish, the notices suggest that the parishioners were not reticent in calling upon the services of the priest.

> 23 November 1862 – At the approach of winter when sick calls are more numerous, we beg to give notice that such calls must be left at the Chapel house before 10 in the morning.
> January 1863 – *Once more* we beg to remind the congregation that sick calls must be sent to the Chapel house before ten o'clock in the morning, except in very urgent cases which seldom happen as those which are *called* urgent are nearly always nothing of the kind.[49]

Sneyd-Kynnersley's summary of such calls, though highly coloured, has the authority of one who had many years of professional association, as an inspector of Schools, with the priests of the Irish mission in the north-west:

> The heavy work undoubtedly comes at night. The door bells seem to get no rest; sometimes it is a drunken woman, who comes to take the pledge, just as a wealthier drunkard might ask for a bottle of seltzer; sometimes, and many times, an urgent demand for a speedy visit to Biddy, who is 'dyin' entirely', but turns out to be dismally drunk. The whole force of the mission is sometimes called out …
> In the small hours of the morning the flock break out afresh. Patsey is brought home helpless at 2 a.m. Michael has his head cut open at 3; Molly upsets the lamp, and sets the baby on fire at 4. In each and every case his reverence is brought down to give the last rites to the afflicted person, and in each and every case he finds he might as well have gone on with his sleep.[50]

The priest's relationship to the individual believer was different in kind from that of the Anglican clergyman or the conscientious 'visitor to the poor'. In Irish missions the period of a ministry often extended to an adult lifetime, and he might know his penitents through two or more generations. He heard the believer's confession from early childhood, preparing him for first communion as for the later crises of life.[51] Preparation for marriage was liable to involve the priest in a far more detailed moral supervision than it did his Protestant counterpart among the poor, and there was nothing of that desultory relationship exemplified, at the opposite extreme, by the notorious 'Red Church' of Bethnal Green.[52]

The priest was the secular as well as the religious leader of his flock, and his authority was recognised not only by the devout, but by some at least who had virtually lapsed from the practice of the Church: 'They rarely deny their own faith ... and when confronted by it they still accept the authority of the priest.'[53] His personal intervention might bring the most obstinate sinner penitently to his knees, as could 'that champion converter' Father Flynn of St Vincent's; a single visit could put a stop to Evangelical attack.[54] His Jurisdiction extended over the entire range of the community's affairs, and the power which he expressed sacramentally at the altar rail might be no less compelling when exercised in the informal surroundings of the street. Serving a people among whom fighting, as Booth remarked, was 'almost a recreation', and whose drinking was apt to become 'riotous', the pacification of communal disorder was not the least of the extempore duties he was called upon to perform.[55] Family rows, when they exploded into the street, seem to have been an especial care, and the priest was credited with a power of restoring tranquillity in neighbourhoods where the policeman ventured at his peril: 'if in some domestic quarrel the priest interferes, they submit, but let a policeman attempt it, and he may be kicked to death'.[56] In *The Brandons* John Denvir presents the same setting in more sentimental terms, but the role of Father Peter MacMahon – 'as fine a specimen of the good old Irish *soggarth* as you would see in a day's work' – is substantially the same as that described by Booth.

Often when there was a real row, and No.9, aided by all the constables from the surrounding beats could no cope with the disturbance, as a last resource the cry would be – 'Run for Father MacMahon', and when the well-known face appear fiercest storm or strife would be quelled, and peace would again reign in Homer's Garden.[57]

And yet. If the priest's influence among his people was, in Faucher's phrase, 'absolute', it was also tempered by a realistic appreciation of the nature of the flock, their hereditary weaknesses and strengths.[58] The moral lessons which he taught might be impeccably orthodox, and indistinguishable at times from the conventional homilies of self-help – 'detachment', 'watchfulness', 'peace with our neighbourhood'.[59] But the community context remained obstinately perverse, and offered few points of departure for the improving social career. The administration of the pledge was apt to involve not one but frequent and recurring interventions by the priest. For some, at least, like those who took the pledge from Father Mathew in 1843 'whilst in a state of intoxication', it may have represented less a decision for life – 'to cut off at once and for ever this insidious and devastating temptation', – than an interlude of remorse between compulsive bouts of drink, as in Mayhew's story of old Norah.[60]

One may suggest the same of fighting as of drink. The priest's interventions were frequent, and urgently renewed, but they seem to have carried no expectation of permanent moral reform. Booth describes them as 'lenient judges of the frailties that are not sins, and of the disorder that is not crime', and suggests a resigned acceptance of the unchangeable necessities of life.

This kindly gentleness is after the event; at the same time no one could be more uncompromising in denunciation or more prompt in interference. It is said that the voice of the priest or the presence of the Sister will quell any disorder; but the trouble recurs. I do not go so far as to say that the same quarrel breaks out again as soon as the priest or Sister has gone, but it may be so; at any rate the occasions repeat themselves. Savagery is checked, but there is no sign of permanent improvement. Drinking and fighting are the ordinary conditions of life among many of their flock, and the streets in which they dwell show it.[61]

This is a kind of negative capability, extending to every question save those which threatened the fundamentals of the faith.

> As a rule the better Catholic the better Irishman, and the better Irishman the better Catholic: their priests, being often of Irish blood, are at one with the people, and in sentiment are even more Irish than they are Catholic. Amongst the Irish, rebellious blood turns not against both Church and State as in Italy, but against the State alone. With the poor Irish the police are recognised enemies, against whom the whole street is ready to unite … Quarrelsome and violent, unrestrained as children, and brutal when their passions are loosed, they are yet full of natural piety, and the priest, who live with them and love them 'can find no harm in them'.[62]

The Roman Catholic Church of the second half of the nineteenth century thus occupied a singular position.[63] In districts 'too poor for Dissent' and where the Anglican Church preached its message as to the heathen, amid a people whom rival denominations found it even dangerous to touch, Irish congregations flourished.[64] They supported the 'round' of the Church's house-to-house collectors; they crowded the chapels at Sunday Mass; and they gave to the Church, in the neighbourhoods of their settlement, an unmistakably proletarian complexion: 'A Catholic chapel', complained an estate agent in 1849, 'crowds the streets with the lower classes and deteriorates surrounding property.'[65]

The Irish poor were for half a century the great support of the Church, and it was the increase in their numbers, especially in the decades following the Famine, which was responsible for the multiplication of Catholic missions and schools. So close, indeed, was the association that the Church, which gratefully acknowledged their role as 'eminent propagandists of the faith', sometimes treated 'Catholic' and 'Irish' as interchangeable terms:[66] workhouse registers were diligently scrutinised for children who might be recognised as Catholics 'from their names only'; parishes were occasionally credited with 'Catholic' neighbourhoods and

'Catholic' streets; while the appearance of a settled body of Irish in any place was generally a signal for the planting of a Catholic mission.[67] Protestant missionaries, who suffered their persecutions in the street, were accustomed to classify the Irish indiscriminately as 'Romanists', whose 'superstition' and 'ignorance' it was one of their painful duties to meet – one missionary even complained of 'Papist charwomen' at a London hospital biasing the patients against the influence of 'Bible instructions'.[68] For working people too, like the colliers at Airdrie who struck work in 1854 'until the Catholic miners were dismissed', the religion of the newly arrived immigrants might appear as distinctive a peculiarity as their race; the Roman Catholic Church, a London street sweeper told Mayhew, was 'a Irish religion' which, as he explained, he 'wasn't to be expected to understand'.[69] The Irish, for their part, rejoiced in the equation and seem to have sought occasions on which it might be displayed.[70] During the taking of the 1871 Census in Ancoats, a batch of returns was found to have been completed at a local public house – 'the House of Commons for Ireland' – in which religion and social status were interestingly confused: 'Numbers of papers were found filled up in the same handwriting, and the occupation of almost all of them returned as Catholic.'[71]

The Irish stood in a hereditary relationship to their religion. Faith and nationality, hallowed by persecution, reciprocated one another's claims, and in the harsh conditions of their exile, stigmatised alike by religion and by race, the partnership was persistently renewed. Samuel Bamford describes the scene in 1819 when the Rochdale and Middleton people, on their way to Peterloo, stopped their procession at Newtown, just outside Manchester:

> We were welcomed with open arms by the poor Irish weavers, who came out in their best drapery, and uttered blessings and words of endearment, many of which were not understood by our rural patriots. Some of them danced and others stood with clasped hands and tearful eyes, adoring almost, that banner whose colour was often their national one, and the emblem of their green island home. We thanked them by the band striking up 'Saint Patrick's day

in the morning'. They were electrified; and we passed on, leaving these warm-hearted suburbans capering and whooping like mad.[72]

The nearby community at Wigan displayed an early combativity.[73] Religious spirit among the street folk whom Mayhew wrote about ran high, and they entered keenly into the subject of their faith. 'I don't go much among the English street-dealers', said one. 'They talk like haythens': and he went on to say that he was 'almost glad' to have no 'childer' because of the way that in England they were allowed to run wild: 'They haven't the fear of God or the saints. They'd hang a praste – glory to be to God they would.'[74] Another, who crossed himself repeatedly as he spoke, claimed to be more tolerant. He had 'nothing to say' against 'Protistints' ('I've heard it said "it's best to pray for them"'), and he observed that the 'Protistint gintlemen and ladies' among his customers 'sometimes ... talk to me kindly about religion'. But he referred with contempt to the spiritual state of his fellow-costers among the English ('the street-people that call themselves Protistants are no riligion at all'), and as for the Protestant 'gintlemen and ladies', he mused upon the possible fate awaiting them 'in another worruld': 'I can't say what their lot may be ... for not being of the true faith. No, sir, I'll give no opinions – none.'[75]

The Irish in England defended the Church when under attack with something of that primitive violence which made it dangerous, in the more inflammatory parts of rural Ireland, for a bailiff to serve his writ or for a landlord to reside. The 'rough' elements in the congregation were ready, and indeed eager, to avenge whatever insults were offered to their priests or to the honour of the Church – 'the roughest the readiest', a London priest told Booth.[76] At times like these, the primal solidarities of the community were engaged. The children of the immigrant poor – 'chiefly noisy, unwashed young Hibernian' in the unenthusiastic description of a Schools Inspector, 'very rough and obstreperous', as even their own priests sometimes felt constrained to complain – seem to have shared the combativity of their parents.[77] They might be called upon to defend their very homes against attack, as at Barrack Yard, Wigan, where on the third night of the De Camin rioting in 1859 a mob of English workmen and colliers was 'gallantly resisted by a handful of boys and girls, who showered stones won the attacking party' and were compelled for a time to retreat: and they seem to have been no less ready to take part in the tumults of the street, as at Failsworth in 1868, and Tredegar in 1882.[78] The turbulent Irishwoman, with her sleeves tucked up, and her apron full of stones, or flourishing her rolling pin in battle, was as distinguished a presence in the Irish mob as the labourer with his shillelagh.[79] And when the chapel bells pealed their alarms, and the narrow streets echoed to the No Popery cry, the Irishman was ready, with a stone in his hand, an iron stick or cudgel – indeed as at Ashton-under-Lyne and Stalybridge fortified by pistols – to defend his church, as he was wont to do his street, with an impulsive belligerence which the clergy themselves found impossible to restrain.[80]

However lowly and inferior their position in English society, the Irish maintained an exalted notion of their own religion, and a sovereign contempt for the 'haythen' with whom they were surrounded. Town missionaries, seeking to enlighten their darkness, found them 'warm antagonists of truth': 'Generally they refuse to take a tract, or to listen to any remarks that may be made for their benefit'; the 'pleasing testimonies' which they were able occasionally able to record, where an isolated believer has been persuaded to accept a tract or to listen to a reading of the Bible, were apt to collapse under the intervention of a religious member of the family or a visit from the priest.[81] Distrust of Protestantism was, like the faith itself, inveterate, and might survive even a formal separation from the Church. An Irish tinker girl, who admitted to George Borrow that she was 'clane unsettled about religion', and who family had discarded the Catholic symbols of faith, was nevertheless indignant at the suggestion that she might join the Methodists:

I have been at their chapels at nights and have listened to their screaming prayers, and have seen what's been going on outside the chapel after their services, as they call them, were over – I never saw the like going on outside Father Toban's chapel, yere hanner![82]

The sorrowing note of a Birmingham town missionary suggests that even among those whom the Evangelical found seemingly complaisant, there remained still a loyalty, furtive but persistent, to the ancient faith:

> In one house that I entered a man & his wife were sitting opposite each other with short pipes in their mouths smoking & playing at cards, the woman was very much ashamed to see me & shuffled the cards up to hide them. The man seeing he was detected in his hypocrisy for he remembered as well as I did the conversation we had together the week before, and the way in which he had spoken of the religion of the Bible, speaking of it in the highest terms. He said 'I won't deceive you. I am not a Protestant, I am a Roman Catholic and if you should run a spear into me I will not change the religion I believe, I said I had a good tract which would suit him if he would promise to read it. He said he would and I left with him a tract on the Wrath of the Soul. I asked the woman if she would not be happier reading some good book than playing at cards. She confessed she should, but when I proposed burning the cards she said they were borrowed.[83]

It seems that rush-bearing at Manchester was brought to an end in the 1820s because the Irish, 'taking offence at some orange-coloured lilies adorning a rush-cart', fell upon the hapless dancers accompanying the carts from the outlying townships and dispersed them, a process which was repeated until the visits of the rush-carts ceased.[84] This extreme case illustrates a general truth. For the merest symptom of Protestant activity seems to have been treated by the Irish as a national affront, and to have provoked them, individually and collectively – and often with a reckless disregard of the consequences – to riot. The Anglo-Catholic Father Charles Lowder in St George's in the East, attempting to open a mission at Lower Wall Walk, where a population of indigenous Irish 'swarmed', was no more immune from their hostile attention, though Catholic in his theology, than was the Hallelujah Band of Accrington, whom a drunken Irishman cursed in the streets, the Temperance Seminary at Oldham, whose Sunday afternoon proceedings were interrupted by a disorderly Irishman calling for 'beer', or Mr Finnigan, an Irish-speaking Scripture reader, seized by the waistcoat in a Birmingham court.[85] The Irish did not abstain from the early persecutions of the Salvation Army. 'Romanists' ranged themselves with 'infidels' and 'drunkards' at Canning Town, 'set on and backed up by the devil himself', to attempt to drive the Christian Missionary from the field.[86] At Croydon, where the missioner had the misfortune to set up his preaching stand directly opposite an Irish street, the meetings were the subject of their tireless abuse – 'an alley ... full of Roman Catholics who are bitter opposers to the truth'; while a brother labouring in the vineyard of Stratford Marshes, and asking at each of the houses he canvassed 'if there was anyone there on the way to Heaven', recorded only one, 'a Roman Catholic and a tinker', who was ready to make profession of a faith, 'and when he discovered who I was, he threatened to burn me with his soldering-iron ... if I did not leave the place'.[87] Gipsy Smith, who in his later years as an independent evangelist was to suffer the 'loud and unseemly noises' and 'foul parodies' of the Catholic children of the Liverpool slums, was in his Salvation Army years faced with 'one of those wild Irish Catholic yells', issuing from the throats of the Bolton Irish – an excited swaying crowd in the Market Square, who took the uttering of Benediction as a signal for attack.[88]

The second and third generations of the immigrants seem to have shared a good deal of the belligerent fidelity of the first. The walls of the Irish home continued to be adorned by a free intermixture of sacred and patriotic subjects, as they had been when Mayhew described them in the middle of the century.[89] 'Often', Joe Toole recalls of the Salford Irish homes of his child-hood, 'did I see a picture of the Saviour on one wall and one of J. L. Sullivan, the bare-knuckle fighter, opposite.'[90] For the Home Rule canvasser, indeed, they served indiscriminately as insignia of national support: 'If they see a picture of St. Patrick, or the Pope, or Robert Emmet, they assume they are in an Irish house of the right sort.'[91] On St Patrick's day itself, religion and nationality continued to meet in explosive combination with the drink, as a missionary in the East End of London prudently acknowledged:

Tuesday (St. Patrick's Day). The Irish dock labourer is rampant to-day, and anyone who wishes to be involved in a serious row could not do better than broach the subject of Evangelical religion. I wisely refrain to-day and confine my efforts to railway men at Millwall.[92]

The spiritual inheritance of the children included a vivid recollection of national wrong. James Sexton, growing up in St Helens, where his parents kept a stall in the open market, served his political apprenticeship when, as a boy, he accompanied his father and grandfather in their 'missionary' activity among the Irish navvies at work on a nearby railway, to whom they administered the Fenian oath. His mother had been born in Warrington, but her parents had experienced the terrible aftermath of the Irish rebellion of 1798 – 'the days when the pitch-cap and gibbet were the certain fate of any priest caught celebrating Mass, as they were of the peasant who dared to take up arms against injustice': for a young boy of the second generation, to whom the memory was handed down, it still served as a family inheritance:

The story of those days of terror was handed on to the children of all who endured their agony; it spread all over the world, and engendered in the mind of every Irishman and Irishwoman who heard it hatred – bitter and boundless hatred – of everything connected with the Briton and the British. That, so far as my mind was concerned, was my principal political and spiritual inheritance. Even to-day … my mind goes back at times, to the stories of my maternal grandparents – of men being hanged, drawn and quartered … of an ancestor, hanged from the shafts of his own cart, and the gruesome story of Donald dun O'Byrne. Who, driven mad by the bayoneting of his wife and child, waylaid individual members of the British yeomanry whom he thought responsible for the outrage, and killed them with the primitive flail he used when threshing the wheat, cutting a notch on the hand for every one he slew.[93]

Tom Barclay, recalling a Leicester Irish childhood of the 1860s, describes the militant religion which he took with him to the workshop – 'Protestant hymns disgusted me, and I actually used to spit out to cleanse my mouth it if I thoughtlessly had been singing a strain caught from some pious shop-mates.' As a child he had been made familiar with the heritage of national struggle. 'My father was a Limerick man, and we were often hearing of the hero Patrick Sarsfield, and the women of Limerick who fought and repelled the English during the siege of that city.' A quite ordinary scuffle with the children at the other end of the yard took on for him the epic quality of an historical national drama:

> One day the kids from the other end of the court, or 'yard' as we called it, attacked us under Bill, their leader, and broke a pane of glass and thrust a rod through: unable to get out, or fearful of a spanking if we did, we scuttled upstairs and threw cinders from the chamber window on Billy and his pals: they battered the door, and we retaliated as we could. My imagination went to work: Billy was King William and we were the Irish: it was the siege of Limerick being in some mysterious manner enacted over again.[94]

George Lansbury remembered the Irish boys at his school in Bethnal Green as being 'all "Fenians"':

> Consequently, when the wall of Clerkenwell prison was blown down and three Irish martyrs executed in Manchester because a police officer was accidentally killed, very great excitement prevailed in our classes and playground. The teachers tried to make us understand how wicked the Irishmen had been on both occasions but my Irish friends would have none of it, and when a few months later T.D. Sullivan's song God Save Ireland came out, we boys were shouting it at the tops of our voices every playtime.[95]

In Clerkenwell, where the Irish and Italians occupied adjacent quarters, and fought between each other, the name 'Garibaldi' was perpetuated as a ritual challenge in the children's games of the street.[96] 'Faith and fatherland', in short, found their defenders in the tenement streets of East and Central London, and in the back streets of Bradford and the Scholes, as well as in Ireland itself.

Conditions of worship in England were characteristically more restrained than in Ireland, and in the pent-up rookeries where the immigrants made a home, popular Catholicism enjoyed for its arena a less exuberant space. But Father Mathew's reception among the Irish poor of St Giles, when portraits and medals were on sale in the streets, and the rookery 'poured forth its thousands' ('The windows and even the roofs of many of the surrounding houses ... crowded with people'), suggests that, however different the material circumstance and setting of life, the new communities shared strong cultural affinities with the old and reproduced some, at least, of their religious and national characteristics.[97]

There is some scattered though strongly suggestive evidence for the survival of folk religious practices among the immigrants. Father Mathew's crusade served as a magnet to the afflicted and diseased, and although it is not possible to pronounce with any confidence upon the motives of those who fell upon their knees before the hustings (many seem to have been anxious to take the pledge not once but repeatedly). It seems clear that the belief in supernatural agency – an important element in his success in Ireland itself – played a part.[98] The pledge was administered to vast assemblies of the Irish poor, and the benediction by which it was accompanied – the sign of the cross which Father Mathew made over the kneeling figure of the postulant, 'descending from the platform and placing his hands upon each persons head', and the temperance medal which he hung with ribbons about the neck – seem to have been credited by some, at least, with a physically healing power.[99] At Glasgow, where 'crowds of diseased persons' were taken to the cattle market, and where the impetuous rush of people was such that 'many who ardently longed for an opportunity of kneeling before the great Apostle of Temperance ... could not even get a sight of his face, Father Mathew felt obliged specifically to disclaim a supernatural power, 'the power of performing miracles belonging alone to the Supreme Being'.[100] At Kennington common, where women and children were especially numerous among those who came forward to take the pledge – a feature remarked upon elsewhere – 'several curious evidences of the spirit of superstition which pervades the lower orders of Irish Roman Catholics were said to have been exhibited: 'On one occasion a woman having a cancerous deformity in the face and on another a mother with a child afflicted with scrofula, implored the rev. gentleman to place his hand on the part affected.'[101] John Denvir, who took the pledge as a little boy in Liverpool, suggests one explanation for the particular anxiety shown by Irish women to take the pledge:

> My mother took the whole family, and, wherever he was – at St. Patrick's, or in a great field on one side of Crown Street or at St. Anthony's – there she was with her family. She was a woman with the strong Irish faith in the supernatural, and in the power of God and His Church, that can 'move mountains'. A younger brother of mine had a running sore in his foot which the doctors could not cure. She determined to take Bernard to Father Mathew and get him to lay his hands on her boy.
>
> At St. Patrick's with her children kneeling around her, she asked the good Father to touch her son. He, no doubt thinking it would be presumptuous on his part to claim any supernatural gift, passed on without complying with her request.

When Father Mathew came to Crown Street

> my mother was there again with her afflicted boy and the rest of her children, and again she pleaded in vain. She was a courageous woman, with great force of character – and a *third* time she went to Father Mathew's gathering. This was in St. Anthony's chapel yard, and amongst the thousands there to hear him take the pledge she awaited her turn. Again she besought him to touch the boy's foot. He knew her again, and, deeply moved by her importunity and great faith, he, at length to her great joy, put his hand on my brother's foot and gave him his blessing. My mother's faith in the power of through his minister, was rewarded for the foot was healed.[102]

The Irish brought with them into the country a complex of popular devotional practices, whose warmth and externality were often contrasted with the more reserved tradition of worship which prevailed among English Catholics. The Irish might carry the signs of religious privilege about their person – the scapular, the crucifix, the picture of Mary, blessed by the priest for members of the congregation and worn close to the heart; they crossed themselves devoutly at the mention of each holy name.[103] The 'rude representation of the Crucifixion' and the show of sacred pictures upon the wall made the mysteries of the faith a commonplace feature of the immigrant family home – 'the adoration of the shepherds', as Mayhew remarked in an Irish lodging house near Drury Lane, 'watched on the other side of the fireplace by a portrait of Daniel O'Connell'; 'the very staircase', as he writes of another he visited, 'having pictures fastened against the wooden partition'.[104] The Rosary served as a focus and discipline of prayer, an instrument of domestic piety by which the spiritual exercises of the Church were produced in a kindred ceremonial of the home:

> Before going to bed we all knelt down and after a supper of Indian meal, on the bare uneven brick floor recited the Rosary, father leading off: one Our Father to ten Hail Marys: one of the prayers spoken fifty times by the help of a string of beads: and we arose feeling good and comforted and strengthened for the tomorrow's work.[105]

Personal prayer seems to have provided a religious comfort and consolation of the simplest and most elemental kind, as it did for the Irish crossing-sweeper whom Mayhew records, 'a very melancholy-looking man, who could not understand the Mass, but who prayed every night "for a blissin", and to rise me out of my misery'; or the travelling packman who came to the Franciscans in Wales, an elderly man 'with a sad and weary-looking face' who 'thought he should like to learn a few prayers ... as he was getting old and did not feel very strong'.[106] Of the strong impression which might be produced upon the mind and imagination of the young, one has a record in Tom Barclay's account of the time when he was 'something like what the Irish call a voteen':

> Just now I am very religious. Every morning on awakening and dressing I make the sign of the Cross from forehead to breast and from shoulder to shoulder, uttering 'in the name of the Father, and

the Son, and of the Holy Ghost. Amen.' I say the Our Father, Hail
Mary, and Apostle's Creed, and invoke the Holy Family –

Jesus, Mary, Joseph, I offer my heart and life.

Jesus, Mary, Joseph, assist me in my last agony.

Jesus, Mary, Joseph, may I die in peace in your blessed company.
… I was very devout … I chalked an altar on the bare brown
wall of the chamber where six of us slept, father. mother, and four
children: I sketched candles, three each side of a tabernacle and a
crucifix above it in the centre, all in chalk.[107]

The Irish language, 'the tongue in which they both think and
pray', provided one continuing association.[108] Some of the immigrants from the West of Ireland knew no other, and for many,
especially among the women, it remained a primary cultural
resource.[109] When the new Catholic cemetery was opened at
Kensal Town, in 1858,

> A very large number of the poorer class of funerals at the time
> were those of emigrants from the West of Ireland, all speaking the
> Irish language … chattering among themselves and collecting the
> money for the payments of their relations funerals.[110]

Even those who had ceased to use the Irish in everyday life might
revert to it in moments of high feeling. 'When they began to get
elevated', a stonemason remarked of the Irish harvesters who
spent their Saturday nights at a public house in Mosston, Surrey,
'they always started to talk in their own native tongue, and I
noticed it was generally the women who commenced.'[111] Tom
Barclay's memoir indicates how it might serve as a common
bond of nationality and faith. His mother, whose people were
O'Reillys, and who had been brought up 'in the wilds of County
Mayo', could 'sing and recite a goodly number of old Irish songs
and poems', a solace amidst the hardship and penury of life in a
Leicester back court:

> She was not permitted, even had she the money and leisure, to
> indulge in beer and dominoes of an evening like my father; her
> the consolation was an old Irish lamentation or love song and

the contemplation of the sufferings of 'Our Blessed Lord' and his virgin mother.

She was held to be 'quite exceptional' among her fellow-countrywomen in that she could 'read Dr Gallacher's sermons in Irish', and it was her custom to read them aloud to her neighbours on Good Friday: 'It did them good to hear a ... sermon ... in the first language they ever spoke.'

> How she who read English with difficulty could read these sermons, though in Roman characters, with their transliteration nearly as bad as Welsh, is something I do not understand: but ... often have I seen the tears come into her eyes over the sermon on the Passion of Our Lord.[112]

The Church seems to have followed the practice of sending Irish priests to many of the newly founded missions, and one reads of Irish-speaking priests ministering in their own native tongue in places as removed from the principal centres of Irish settlement as Bilston, where Father Sherlock, who had been taught Irish in his infancy, 'was able to hear the confessions of his countrymen who could speak in no other tongue', York, where the Irish Vincentian Fathers from Sheffield were sent to organise the Irish part of the Catholic population into a separate parish, and Merthyr Tydfil, where Father Caroll contracted the Irish fever, and died in 1847.[113]

Sunday Mass provided a natural meeting point in the life of the community. Indeed Mayhew said that it was their 'consistent association' at chapel which kept the street Irish of London so distinct.[114]

For those who during the week suffered the servitude of the workhouse – or of an English lady's household – the privilege of attending Mass offered a solitary occasion of escape; indeed, it was so highly regarded by the inmates of the Birmingham workhouse that Protestant paupers were accused of passing themselves off as Catholic 'in order to get five days' holiday in the month instead of one'.[115] In country missions – remote from the ordinary track of Irish settlement – squads of harvesters, during the season, or contract labourers, when a railway was building or a

canal being cut, arrived to swell the numbers attending weekly
Mass, as at a Bollington, Cheshire where the navvies at work on
the Macclesfield and Stockport line walked over in a body from
Prestbury, 'and as they always knelt on one side of the church
this was known ... as the "Prestbury side"'.[116] At distant points,
Sunday brought together isolated groups of labourers to form
the nucleus of a congregation and provided at the same time, as
for the street Irish described by Mayhew, a focal point for social
gathering. At Abertillery, where Mass was celebrated in the room
of a public house – as in other part of Wales, the only kind of
room which could be hired – and where the congregation was
recruited from the Irish mine-workers employed about the pits at
Coomtillery, higher up the valley, a priest complained that it was
'with the greatest difficulty' that the congregation could be pre-
vented from 'hovering about' though the service had ended, and
'evincing their gratitude to the landlord' when the public-house
opened 'by an unlimited consumption of beer'.[117] At Wednesbury
in the Black Country, where an Irish community of iron-workers
had recently settled, the throng outside Father Montgomery's
church – described in a series of articles which appeared in *The
Nation* in June 1856 – recalled for A. M. Sullivan the crowded
informality of an Irish parish:

> Thronging the gateway, I was glad to perceive that infallible tes-
> timony of the presence of a good pastor among his flock – and to
> be seen at the door of many a soggarth aroon in Ireland, a crowd
> of poor people who each has need of him in one of the numerous
> capacities in which the truly good priest is always consulted by his
> people; arbitrator, magistrate or judge; benefactor, comforter, or
> friend. A father who had come to complain to him about a rebel-
> lious child; a son coming to give the priest some money to send
> to his poor mother in Ireland; an old man to get a letter which
> had come from him to the 'care' of the priest; a young girl to seek
> through him reconciliation with her mother ...[118]

There is evidence that the new communities retained strong
cultural affinities with the old. There were parishes whose congregations were almost exclusively Irish or of Irish extraction,

often served by their own fellow countrymen as priests, and where the national influence was so very strong that it was said to produce a linguistic mutation in the rare 'sprinkling' of English priests who found their way among them: 'by dint of living almost wholly with Irish co-religionists they nearly always have a noticeable brogue'.[119] The presence of large and increasing numbers of Irish priests during the second half of the century, 'in sentiment ... even more Irish than they are Catholic', preserved a line of communication with their native land; so, too, did the continuing arrival of fresh immigrants.[120] The chapel, a 'moral property' in Thomas and Znaniecki's excellent phrase, was a very emblem of the community's collective existence. Its building was in some cases the joint activity of parishioners and priests; its maintenance called forth a loyalty and devotion in singular contrast to the 'eleemosynary' character so often complained of in Evangelical missionary activity among the poor ('some of them would live a week on bread and water rather than be behindhand with their monthly contributions, or their subscription to the Altar Society'); its defence, when menaced by No Popery attacks, brought the impetuous violence of the Irish countryside into the heart of the English town.[121] The Church thus served as a nexus of communal solidarity, the very means by which, amidst the deprived conditions of their exile, a national identity among the Irish was preserved.

The Irish congregations of the second half of the nineteenth century may be said to have existed, to some degree, in the original condition of a sect. Their churches were characteristically plain and unadorned, and 'externals', for all the attention they received from Protestant controversialists, counted for very little. St Patrick's, Liverpool, appears in an early account as 'very large but very ugly, quite methodistick in its architecture' though 'nobly crowded with people'; the patronless church in Garstang is described in a Visitation return as 'a very plain square building ... No tower no bells ... the sanctuary ... plain'.[122] The smaller chapels seem to have borne a resemblance to those which George Eliot recorded as being thought characteristic of latter-day Methodism – 'low-pitched gables up dingy streets'.[123] Some in fact were Methodist chapels, or independent meeting-houses converted to

Catholic use. St Mary's, Ashton-under-Lyne, was Joseph Rayner Stephens's old chapel in Charlestown; St Bridget's, Liverpool, opened 'in a part of town ... where there was a large Irish Catholic population was a chapel formerly used by the Methodists; so too was the chapel at Westhoughton, which had also enjoyed a secular period of existence as a weaving shed.'[124] Others were commercial buildings, adapted for religious use. At Eldon Street, Liverpool, 'the centre of a most congested district', a warehouse capable of holding one thousand people was opened as a church, 'and in its gloomy and unattractive rooms was opened the mission of Our Lady of Reconciliation de la Salette'.[125] St Michael's, Stockport, sacked by the rioters in 1852 ('little else remaining than the four bare walls of the building, and the four bare steps to the altar'), had previously been a theatre, and then a Mechanics institute, before it was opened as a Catholic mission in 1851; at Whitworth, near Rochdale, the Catholic mission was opened in a room above the premises of the Co-operative stores; at Kensal New Town in an uninhabited corner building which had been intended for use as a baker's shop ('the inner room served as a sanctuary, the door being removed and the opening widened').[126]

When I was travelling the parishes and record offices of northern England preparing this paper in the summer of 1966, the old Irish districts had not yet succumbed to the bulldozer and the depredations of comprehensive clearance and re-development. The churches I visited often seemed to stand in half-deserted urban wastelands, but their original hinterland had not yet been effaced from the district map. At St Patrick's, Wigan, in the heart of the old Irish district of the Schooles, the priest was distinctively an Irishman, deeply 'reactionary' in his views (he was uncomfortable about Vatican II, and hostile to 'progressive' innovations within the Church), utterly devoted to his parishioners, and in his simple manner of life (we shared the dinner-table with his Irish-born housekeeper) – even in his tobacco-stained waistcoat – recalled pictures one might have had of the old-time soggarth, racy of the soil. Next door to the Catholic Church in Bradford, in the old Irish district around Silsbridge Lane, there was a fading notice which read 'J Walsh, undertaker', and a document in the lumber-room of the town hall (they have now been safely deposited in the public library) disclosed that in the late nineteenth century the church was faced by a pub called 'The Harp of Erin': a suggestive cluster for the complex of sociability and communal service which helped to bond together the Irish Catholic communities of later Victorian times. At the time I was looking for continuity, and conceptualising it in terms of a timeless tradition, and the traces of this will be evident in the foregoing pages. Subsequent research is more likely to be interested – quite legitimately – in the mutations which took place, even within an apparently unchanging framework, and more alert than I was to the 'Victorian' transformation of both Irish and English Catholicity. I no longer believe, as I believed in 1966, that the Irish Catholics of the end of the nineteenth century were the same as those of the 1840s and 1850s. But the tenacity of both parish organisation and settlement, not only over the second half of the nineteenth century, but at least in the northern towns, right down to the 1960s (at St Andrew's, Newcastle, one of the unofficial pastoral duties was still that of giving help to the wandering Irish beggars who came to the door) suggests that there is indeed here a confessional and social reality which historians – locally as well as nationally – should study, a study which could throw new light on one of the more substantial – and one of the more beleaguered – of those minority cultures of which (it could be argued) the 'majority' culture of modern Britain is composed.

Notes

Introduction

1   Bill Schwarz, Foreword to Raphael Samuel, *Theatres of Memory*, London: 2012, p. vii.
2   Ibid., p. 3.
3   Raphael Samuel, *The Lost World of British Communism*, London: 2006, p. 43.
4   Ibid., p. 13.
5   Ibid., p. 45.
6   Ibid., p. 14.
7   Raphael Samuel, *Workshop of the World: Essays in People's History*, London: 2023, p. 208.
8   Samuel, *Lost World of British Communism*, p. 14.
9   Alison Light, Preface to Samuel, *Lost World of British Communism*, pp. viii, ix.
10 Brian Harrison, 'Interview with Raphael Samuel', 23 October 1979. Thanks to Sophie Scott-Brown for providing me with the transcript of these interviews.
11 Eric Hobsbawm, *Interesting Times*, London: 2002, p. 206; John Callaghan, *Cold War, Crisis and Conflict: The CPGB 1951–68*, London: 2003, p. 17.
12 Andrew Whitehead, 'Interview with Charles "Chuck" Taylor', 9 February 2021, andrewwhitehead.net.
13 Alison Light, email to author, 5 October 2022.
14 Unpublished letter, undated. Copyright, Estate of Raphael Samuel. A selection of Samuel's letters is currently being planned for publication.
15 Sheila Rowbotham, 'Some Memories of Raphael, *NLR* I:221, January–February 1997, p. 128; Sheila Rowbotham, *Promise of a Dream*, London: 2000, p. 62.
16 Samuel, *Workshop of the World*, p. 218.
17 See A. D. Gilbert, *Religion and Society in Industrial England*, London: 1976.
18 Samuel, *Workshop of the World*, p. 226.

19 Ibid., p. 231.
20 Colm Kerrigan, 'Mathew, Theobald (1790–1856)', *Oxford Dictionary of National Biography*, Oxford: 2004.
21 Samuel, *Workshop of the World*, p. 228.
22 Unpublished letter, 28 August 1966. Copyright, Estate of Raphael Samuel.
23 Samuel, *Workshop of the World*, p. 68.
24 Keith Thomas, 'History and Anthropology', *Past & Present*, 24:1, April 1963, pp. 3–24.
25 Lise Butler, 'Michael Young, the Institute of Community Studies, and the Politics of Kinship', *Twentieth Century British History*, 26:2, 2015, pp. 203–24.
26 Sophie Scott-Brown, *The Histories of Raphael Samuel: A Portrait of a People's Historian*, Canberra: 2017, p. 86. Samuel's work on the Stevenage project has recently been studied: Jon Lawrence, *Me, Me, Me: The Search for Community in Post-war England*, Oxford: 2019.
27 Interview with Brian Harrison, 1979.
28 Unpublished letter, February 1966. Copyright, Estate of Raphael Samuel.
29 Poppy Sebag-Montefiore, 'Beyond "Misbehaviour": Sally Alexander in Conversation', *History Workshop Online*, 11 March 2020.
30 Robin Blackburn, 'Raphael Samuel: The Politics of Thick Description', *New Left Review*, I:221, January–February 1997, p. 133.
31 This method is discussed in greater detail in Alison Light, 'A Biographical Note on the Text', in Raphael Samuel, *Island Stories: Unravelling Britain*, London: 1998, pp. xix–xxi.
32 Raphael Samuel (ed.), 'Introduction to Raphael Samuel', in *Village Life and Labour*, London: 1975, p. xix.
33 Sophie Scott-Brown, *The Histories of Raphael Samuel*, p. 142; Sally Alexander, email to author, 9 October 2022.
34 Raphael Samuel, 'Quarry Roughs: Life and Labour in Headington Quarry, 1860–1920. An Essay in Oral History', in Raphael Samuel (ed.), *Village Life and Labour*, London: 1975, p. 142.
35 Samuel, 'Quarry Roughs', p. 144.
36 Samuel, *Workshop of the World*, p. 51.
37 Samuel, 'Quarry Roughs', p. 148.
38 There was also a second, much longer essay published in 1975 in the first volume in the History Workshop book series, *Village Life and Labour*. Unfortunately, due to space (it comes to over 55,000 words on its own) we are not able to include it here.
39 Samuel, *Workshop of the World*, p. 171.
40 Raphael Samuel, 'History and Theory', in Raphael Samuel (ed.), *People's History and Socialist Theory*, London: 1981, pp. l, xi.
41 Samuel, *Workshop of the World*, p. 34.

42 Samuel, *Workshop of the World*, p. 44.
43 Dennis Dworkin, *Cultural Marxism in Postwar Britain: History, the New Left, and the Origins of Cultural Studies*, Durham, NC: 1997, p. 239.
44 Samuel, *Workshop of the World*, p. 27.

People's History

1 Essay originally published in Samuel, *People's History and Socialist Theory*, pp. xiv–xl. Following the essay as it originally appeared was a list of 'further reading', as well as Bertolt Brecht's poem, 'A Worker Reads History', which we have decided to omit from this collection.
2 John Baxter (1794–1816), silversmith and founding member of the radical London Corresponding Society [ed.].
3 The collection for which this essay served as one of the two introductions, the other also by Samuel on 'History and Theory', contained an extraordinarily diverse set of contributions. If the Workshop is today thought of as a peculiarly English phenomena, one look at the table of contents – which includes some fifty essays on everything from 'Decolonising Africa History' and debates on the term 'patriarchy' in feminist thought, as well as significant contributions on origins of modern capitalism, observations on George V's Silver Jubilee as celebrated in Kenya, and contributions from French, German, Italian, Scandinavian, and American writers – gives the lie to that [ed.].
4 John Richard Green (1837–1883) was a historian and former clergyman. His most famous work, *Short History of the English People*, was widely influential in both Britain and America in the latter decades of the nineteenth century [ed.].
5 Augustin Thierry (1795–1856), pioneering French historian and former secretary of Henri de Saint-Simon [ed.].
6 Jules Michelet (1798–1874), French historian best known for his monumental *Histoire de France* (1833–67) [ed.].
7 Franz Carl Müller-Lyer (1857–1916) was a German psychologist and sociologist; Karl Gotthard Lamprecht (1856–1915) was a German historian and one of the first scholars to develop a systematic theory of psychological factors in history [ed.].
8 Mark Starr (1894–1985), author and educationist. Born into a Methodist family in Somerset, he abandoned all religious faith in his late teens, and soon after went to work in the coal-mining industry in both his home county and later in the south Wales coalfield. He soon became an active member of the South Wales Miners' Federation, and gained a scholarship to Central Labour

College in London. In 1917, the Plebs League published his first book, *A Worker Looks at History*, which became the standard textbook among classes of the Marxist-orientated independent working-class education (IWCE) movement. He later moved to America, where he worked as the educational organiser of the International Ladies' Garment Workers Union [ed.].

9 Wilhelm Maximilian Wundt (1832–1920) was a German physiologist and psychologist who founded a new branch of psychology known as *Völkerpsychologie*, distinct for its use of historical and comparative methods rather than simply laboratory experimentation [ed.].

10 Paul Vidal de La Blache (1845–1918), academic often considered the founder of modern French geography [ed.].

11 John Lothrop Motley (1814–1877), American author best known for his two popular histories *The Rise of the Dutch Republic* and *The United Netherlands*.

12 'The Class Struggle in Fourteenth-Century England', in *People's History and Socialist Theory*, on late medieval peasantry and its significance for contemporary peasant studies [ed.].

13 Quote from David Selbourne, 'On the Methods of the History Workshop', *History Workshop*, 9, Spring 1980, p. 153 [ed.]

14 Catherine Hall, 'Gender Divisions and Class Formation in the Birmingham Middle Class. 1780-1850', in *People's History and Socialist Theory*, London: 1981.

Headington Quarry

1 Essay originally published in *Oral History*, 1:4, 1972, pp. 107–22.
2 PP 1865, VVXI, 7th Report, Medical Officer of the Privy Council, Appendix 6, Dr Hunter's Report on Rural Housing.
3 Incorrectly written as 'Matfin murders' and 'Samfordham' in the original essay [ed.].

Comers and Goers

1 This essay was originally published in H. J. Dyos and Michael Wolf (eds), *The Victorian City: Images and Realities*, Volume 1, London: 1973, pp. 123–60; *A Plan for Preventing Destitution and Mendicancy in the British Metropolis*, London: 1850, p. 6.
2 Public Record Office (PRO), Home Office Papers (HO) 45/10499/117669/10.
3 *Household Words*, 6 December 185; Richard Rowe, *Jack Afloat and Ashore*, London: 1875, p. 74.

4 On the Settle-Carlisle railway, which was building in the early 1870s, more than 33,000 men found employment on a single section of the line, although the greatest number of men employed at any one time was never more than 2,000. F. S. Williams, *The Midland Railway*, London: 1876, p. 522.

5 R. T. Berthoff, *British Immigration in Industrial America*, Cambridge, MA: 1953, pp. 82–3. For a parallel migration of stone-cutters, see 50 Cong. 1, Misc. Doc. 572, part 11, Dip. and Consular Reps on Immigration, p. 10, and 51 Cong. 2, Rep. No. 3472, Select Committee (SC) on Immigration, pp. 301, 305, 352, 870.

6 James Greenwood, *On the Tramp*, 1872, p. 26.

7 Charity Organisation Society (COS), *Report on the Homeless Poor*, London: 1891, p. xx.

8 For an example, see Sir James Sexton, *Agitator: The Life of the Dockers' MP. An Autobiography*, London: 1936, pp. 21–2.

9 F. Groome, *In Gypsy Tents*, Edinburgh: 1880, p. 286; Charles Hindley (ed.), *Life and Adventures of a Cheap Jack*, London: 1881, passim.

10 Henry Mayhew, *London Labour and the London Poor*, Volume I, London: 1861, p. 339.

11 Charles Booth, *Life and Labour of the People in London*, 3rd series, V, London: 1902–4, p. 157.

12 Lancashire Record Office, RCLv, Visitation Records, 1865.

13 John Denvir, *The Irish in Britain*, 2nd edn, London: 1894, p. 411.

14 'St. Patrick's Church Sunderland', notes in the possession of the Rev. Vincent Smith. For a similar situation at Warrington, 'a large thoroughfare for Irish people', see PRO, HO 129/466: St Alban's, Warrington.

15 B. S. Rowntree, *Poverty: A Study of Town Life*, 2nd edn, London: n.d., pp. 31–2. For earlier references to the travels of the York Irish, see PP 1867–8, XVII, Royal Commission (RC) on Employment of Children, Young Persons, and Women in Agriculture, First Report: Appendix Pt II (4068-I), pp. 255, 258. See also Denvir, *Irish in Britain*, p. 400.

16 Lady Bell, *At the Works: Study of a Manufacturing Town, Middlesbrough*, London and New York: 1907, p. 8.

17 *The Word on the Waters*, I, December 1858, p. 258, and *The Word on the Waters*, April 1892, p. 332.

18 *Word on the Waters*, April 1892, p. 332.

19 J. Flanagan, *Scenes from My Life*, London: 1907, p. 36.

20 *Morning Chronicle*, 4 January 1850. Sixty years later, Angel Meadow still bore a 'peculiar reputation' on account of its common lodging-house. See PP 1909, XLIII, RC on the Poor Laws, Reports on the Relation of Industrial and Sanitary Conditions to Pauperism (Cd 4653), App. XVI, p. 102.

21 *Morning Chronicle*, 29 April 1850; PP 1847, XXVII, Pt 1, RC on Education in Wales, 1870, p. 304.
22 Greenwood, *On the Tramp*, pp. 27–8.
23 Booth, *Life and Labour*, 3rd series, V, p. 75; *cf.* London Mendicity Society, 76th Annual Report, 1894, p. xiii; Mayhew, *London Labour*, I, p. 337.
24 Booth, *Life and Labour*, 3rd series, VI, p. 136.
25 London School of Economics, Booth MSS, B. 267, pp. 145–9; Booth, *Life and Labour*, I, p. 138.
26 LSE, Booth MSS, B. 281, pp. 83–5; B.371, pp. 117–29, 143–61; John W. Horsley, *I Remember: Memories of a Sky Pilot in the Prison and the Slum*, London: 1911, pp. 125–31; Booth, *Life and Labour*, 3rd series, V, pp. 90–91.
27 Booth, *Life and Labour*, 3rd series, V, pp. 90–91.
28 Booth, *Life and Labour*, 3rd series, III, pp. 151–2.
39 Sam Shaw, *Guttersnipe*, London: 1946, p. 29.
30 PP 1842, XXVI, Report of the Poor Law Commissioners on an Inquiry into the Sanitary Condition of the Labouring Population of Great Britain: Appendix.
31 T. W. Rammell, *Report to the Board of Health: on a Preliminary Inquiry into the Sewerage, Drainage, and Supply of Water, and the Sanitary Condition of the Inhabitants of the Borough and Parish of Banbury and Township of Neithrop, in the Counties of Oxford and Northampton*, London: 1854, p. 11. There is an excellent description of Rag Row in Barrie S. Trinder, *Banbury's Poor in 1850*, Banbury: 1966.
32 PRO, HO 107, Census Returns; Huddersfield Ref. Lib., Lodging House Committee MB, 1 May 1854 and passim.
33 W. C. E. Ranger, *Report to the Board of Health: ... Doncaster*: 1850, p. 38.
34 Sanitary Condition of the Labouring Population, Local Reports, pp. 63–5, 78.
35 Sanitary Condition of the Labouring Population, Local Reports, p. 174; E. Cresy, *Report to the Board of Health: ... Derby*: 1849, pp. 13–15.
36 J. R. Coulthart, Report on Ashton-under-Lyne, in PP 1844, XVII, RC on the State of Large Towns and Populous Districts: First Report (572), Appendix, p. 84.
37 COS, *Report on the Homeless Poor*, p. xvi.
38 Coulthart, Report on Ashton-under-Lyne, pp. 36–7.
39 PRO: Metropolitan Police (Mepol.), 2/1490.
40 PP 1906, CIII, Departmental Committee on Vagrancy (Cd 2891), II, QQ 7768, 7947, and Report on Vagrancy (Cd 2892), III, App. XXXII; Mary Higgs, *Glimpses into the Abyss*, London: 1906,

p. 51; S. and B. Webb, *The Public Organisation of the Labour Market*, London: 1909, pp. 81, 83.

41 Bishopsgate Library, Mansion House Committee on the Unemployed in London, 1885, transcript of proceedings, fol. 10r.

42 John Fisher Murray, *The World of London*, London: 1844, I, p. 247.

43 Daniel Joseph Kirwan, *Palace and Hovel*, London and New York: 1963 edn, pp. 64–70.

44 Thomas Miller, *Picturesque Sketches of London*, London: 1852, p. 207. See also *London in the Sixties, by One of the Old Brigade*, London: 1914, pp. 61–2.

45 PRO, HO 45/10499/117669; Booth, *Life and Labour*, 1st series, I, p. 68, and 3rd series, II, p. 244; *The Times*, 28 August 1894.

46 *Liverpool Review*, 19 April 1890.

47 Booth MSS, B. 152, p. 104.

48 PRO, Mepol. 2/645, Mepol. 2/1068, Mepol. 2/1425, Mepol. 2/1490; HO 14571/ 20236; T. W. Wilkinson, 'London's Homes for the Homeless', in G. R. Sims (ed.), *Living London*, London: 1903, I, p. 337.

49 General Booth, *In Darkest England and the Way Out*, London: 1891, p. 25. PRO, Mepol. 2/1068.

50 Terry Coleman, *The Railway Navvies*, London: 1965, p. 49; John R. Kellett, *The Impact of Railways on Victorian Cities*, London: 1969, p. 346.

51 *Surrey Gazette*, 10 November 1863. PRO, HO 45/10499/117669; Mepol. 2/1490.

52 Stan Hugill, *Sailortown*, London: 1967, p. 112; Rowland Kenney, *Westering: An Autobiography*, London: 1938, p. 82.

53 *Porcupine*, XXI, 1879, p. 409; George Smith, *Incidents in a Gipsy's Life*, Liverpool: 1886, p. 11.

54 *Labour Press and Miners' and Workmen's Examiner*, 15 August 1874.

55 Booth MSS, B. 371, p. 55.

56 Ibid., p. 239.

57 *Illustrated London News*, LXXV, 1879, p. 503; Reginald Blunt, *Red Anchor Pieces*, London: 1928, p. 110.

58 *Illustrated London News*, LXXVI, 1880, p. 11; Booth MSS, B. 346, pp. 165, 231; George Smith, *Gipsy Life: Being an Account of our Gipsies and their Children with Suggestions for their Improvement*, London: 1880, p. 267; Booth MSS, B. 348, p. 97.

59 Henry Wilkinson, 'Van Dwelling London', *Living London*, III, pp. 321–2.

60 Henry Woodcock, *The Gipsies: Being a Brief Account of their Origin, Capabilities, Manners, and Customs, with Suggestions*

for the Reformation, London: 1865, pp. 144–7; V. Morwood, *Our Gipsies in City, Tent, and Van*, London: 1885, pp. 338–40; George Sims, *Off the Track in London*, London: 1911, pp. 36–7.

61 Booth, *Life and Labour*, 3rd series, V, p. 206.

62 J. J. Sexby, *The Municipal Parks, Gardens, and Open Spaces of London: Their History and Associations*, London: 1898, pp. 237–8; British Museum Leland Collection, newspaper cutting, 2 January 1879; Booth MSS, B. 298, pp. 91–7.

63 Booth, *Life and Labour*, 3rd series, V, p. 157; Booth MSS, B. 366, pp. 183–5, 190; *Building Trade News*, December 1894.

64 COS, *Report on the Homeless Poor*, QQ 1892–4.

65 'The Greenland Whale Fishery' and 'The Whale-Catchers', in R. Vaughan Williams and A. L. Lloyd (eds), *The Penguin Book of English Folk Songs*, Harmondsworth: 1968, pp. 50–1, 100, the date is 23 March. For the spring departure of the whalers at Dundee, see G. N. Barnes, *From Workshop to War Cabinet*, New York: 1924, pp. 14–15; for Hull, see *Autobiography of Thomas Wilkinson Wallis*, Louth: 1899, pp. 14–15.

66 COS, *Report on the Homeless Poor*, pp. xv–xvi.

67 Mayhew, *London Labour*, I, p. 88.

68 P. A. Whittle, *Blackburn as It Is*, Preston: 1852, pp. 31–2, Hindley, *Life and Adventures*, pp. 280–1.

69 James Lloyd, *My Circus Life: Being the Life and Adventures and World Travels and Experiences of an Artist and Circus Proprietory Now Aged 79 Years*, London: 1925.

70 Ben Tillett, *Memories and Reflections*, London: 1931, pp. 33, 37, 38.

71 David Prince Miller, *The Life of a Showman*, New York: 1849, pp. 65, 67, 83–4, 86; *Free Lance*, VIII, 1873, p. 125; Hindley, *Life and Adventures*, p. 149.

72 [C. Thomson], *The Autobiography of an Artisan*, London: 1847, pp. 240–1; Mayhew, I, p. 329.

73 'Lord' George Sanger, *Seventy Years a Showman*, London: 1952, pp. 42–4, 66.

74 COS, *Report on Unskilled Labour*, 1890, Q.885.

75 PP 1893–4, XX.XIV, RC on Labour: Minutes of Evidence (Group 'C') (C. 6894–IX), Q.26,435.

76 COS, *Unskilled Labour*, Q.282; cf. Frank Popplewell, 'The Gas Industry', in A. Freeman and S. Webb (eds), *The Seasonal Trades*, London: 1912, pp. 168–71; Booth MSS, A.3 fol. 209; Will Thorne, *My Life's Battles*, London: 1925, p. 36.

77 Mayhew, *London Labour*, II, p. 375.

78 G. Elson, *The Last of the Climbing Boys*, London: 1900, p. 199.

79 George Ewart Evans, *Where Beards Wag All: The Relevance of the Oral Tradition*, Newton Abbot: 1970, p. 266.

80 Mayhew, *London Labour*, II, ill. p. 399.

81 BM, Leland Coll., cutting, 16 May 1872; J. Crabb, *The Gipsies' Advocate*, London: 1831, pp. 136–7.

82 Sanger, *Seventy Years*, pp. 141, 147, 195.

83 George Smith, *I've Been a-Gipsying, or Rambles among our Gipsies and their Children in their Tents and Vans*, London: 1883, pp. 39–59.

84 PP 1868–9, XIII, RC on Children in Agriculture, 2nd Report (4202-I), App. II, A.i., p. 61.

85 PP 1893–4, XXXV, RC on Labour: Agricultural Labourer, Assistant Commissioners' District Reports (C. 6894-VI), B.-VI. [Holbeach], para. 12, and (C. 6894-V), B-VII [Godstone], para. 10.

86 *Seaman and Fisherman's Friendly Visitor*, III, 1860, pp. 111, 126.

87 *Labour News*, 13 July 1872.

88 *Jackson's Oxford Journal*, 3 August 1872 (I am grateful to David Morgan for this excellent reference).

89 PP 1880, XIV, Factory Inspectors' Report for 1879 (C. 2489), p. 54.

90 Booth, *Life and Labour*, 2nd series, II, p. 140.

91 Booth MSS, B. 93, fol. 88.

92 PP 1893–4, XVII, Departmental Committee on Conditions of Labour in Lead Industries (C. 7239-1), P ISL (I am grateful to Anna Davin for this excellent reference, also for the refugee London enameller).

93 PP 1893–4, XVII, Departmental Committee on Conditions of Labour in Lead Industries (C. 7239-1), Q.5216.

94 RC on Labour: Agricultural Labourer, Summary Report (C. 6894-VI), para. 20.

95 William Cobbett, *Rural Rides*, New York: 1957, I, p. 84.

96 Thor Fredur, *Sketches from Shady Places*: 1879, p. 24.

97 William A. Jevons, 'The Weavers' Strike at Padiham in 1859', *Trade Societies and Strikes* (National Association for the Promotion of Social Science), 1860, pp. 468–9.

98 B. S. Rowntree and B. Lasker, *Unemployment: A Social Study*, London: 1911, p. 63; *cf.* pp. 30, 99, 152, 160.

99 'The Irish in England, III', *Labour News*, 14 March 1874.

100 'Whitechapel Villagers' in [James Greenwood], *Toilers in London by One of the Crowd*, London: 1883, pp. 99–101; for some Essex evidence, see G. A. Cuttle, *The Legacy of the Rural Guardians*, Cambridge: 1934, pp. 267, 273; for Irish pea-pickers at Stoke Poges, PP 1867–8, XVII, RC on Children in Agriculture, First Report: App. Pt II, p. 539; for a Bloomsbury pea-picker, see PRO, NH 13/268, paper dated 2 April 1851.

101 Thomas Fayers, *Labour among the Navvies*, Kendal: 1862, p. 12.
102 Mayhew, *London Labour*, I, p. 478.
103 Thomas Wright, *The Great Unwashed*: 1868, pp. 261–2.
104 Booth MSS, B.210, pp. 1–3.
105 Booth MSS, A. 28.
106 Booth, *Life and Labour*, 2nd series, II, pp. 277–8.
107 Booth, *Life and Labour*, 2nd series, IV, App. B. 1.
108 Booth MSS, B. 152, p. 104.
109 Booth, *Life and Labour*, 2nd series, III, p. 411.
110 *Labour News*, 20 September 1873; A. M. Anderson, *Women in the Factory*, London: 1922, p. 38 (I am grateful to Anna Davin for this reference); *Labour News*, 20 September 1873.
111 Booth MSS, B. 93, fol. 69; Booth, *Life and Labour*, 1st series, IV, pp. 286, 313–14, 324, and 2nd series, I, p. 220.
112 A. T. Pask, *Eyes of the Thames*, 1889, pp. 148–9.
113 Mayhew, *London Labour*, II, p. 299.
114 'The Irish in England, II', *Labour News*, 28 February 1874.
115 Denvir, *Irish in Britain*, p. 400; PP 1906, CIII, Report on Vagrancy (2891) II, QQ. 5820–2; J. Ewing Ritchie, *Crying for the Light*, 1895, p. 123.
116 *Indoor Paupers, by One of Them*: 1885, pp. 54–5.
117 Denvir, *Irish in Britain*, p. 401.
118 'The Irish in England', *Dublin Review*, 1856, p. 508.
119 COS, *Homeless Poor*, Q. 398; PRO, Mepol. 2/1490, 1 August 1913.
120 Report on Vagrancy, II, Q. 4180.
121 RC on Children in Agriculture, 2nd Report, App. Pt II, p. 139.
122 *Runcorn Examiner*, 20 September 1893.
123 RC on Children in Agriculture, 2nd Report, App. Pt II Ai, p. 135; RC on Labour: Agricultural Labourer, District Reports (C. 6894–IV), B-V [Bromyard], para. 9; *cf. Stourbridge Observer*, 10 September 1881.
124 RC on Children in Agriculture, 2nd Report, App. Pt II, G, p. 43.
125 *Labour News*, September 1876; 'Three Weeks with the Hop-Pickers', *Fraser's Magazine*, n.s., xvi, 1877, p. 635.
126 George Sturt, *A Small Boy in the Sixties*, Cambridge: 1923, p. 76; RC on Children in Agriculture, 2nd Report. App. Pt. II, C, p. 4; William Marshall, *The Rural Economy of the Southern Counties*, London: 1798, II, p. 69.
127 Ellen Chase, *Tenant Friends in Deptford*, London: 1929, pp. 102–3; George Meek, *Bath Chair Man*, London: 1910, p. 55.
128 'Shelter for the Homeless', *Leisure Hour*, 1865, p. 11.
129 Mayhew, *London Labour*, III, pp. 405, 406.
130 Alexander Somerville, *The Autobiography of a Working Man*,

London: 1848, p. 56; PP, 1895, VIII, SC on Distress from Want of Employment, 2nd Report (253): App., p. 33; 'Trade Tramps', *Leisure Hour*, 1868, p. 358.

131 *London City Mission Magazine*, 2 December 1861.

132 George Sturt, *The Wheelwright's Shop*, Cambridge: 1963, p. 29.

133 Charles Manby Smith, *The Little World of London*, London: 1857, p. 143.

134 Mayhew, *London Labour*, I, p. 329; Hindley, *Life and Adventures*, p. 209.

135 Booth MSS, B. 50, p. 58, and B. 82, p. 14.

136 BM, Leland Collection, undated cutting [1879?].

137 Mayhew, *London Labour*, II, p. 335.

138 COS, *Homeless Poor*, Q. 1, p. 498; Sir Henry Smith, *From Constable to Commissione*: 1910, p. 165.

139 LNR [Mrs Ellen Ranyard], *The Missing Link, or Bible-Women in the Homes of the London Poor*, London: 1859, pp. 29–30, 51; PP 1833, XVI, SC on Irish Vagrants (394), pp. 175, 193; Mayhew, *London Labour*, IV, p. 297.

140 Holborn Board of Works MB, Report of Septimus Gibbon, 6 October 1856 (Holborn Reference Library).

141 *Labour News*, 10 October 1874.

142 Edward G. Howarth and Mona Wilson, *West Ham*, London: 1907, pp. 306–7; RC on Children in Agriculture, 2nd Report, Appendix.

143 Verbal communication from Charles Connor.

144 *Morning Chronicle*, 23 January 1851.

145 T. W. Wilkinson, 'Van Dwelling London', in Sims, *Off the Track*, III, pp. 319–20; according to J. Howard Swinstead, *A Parish on Wheels*, London: 1897, p. 194, the Drill Hall, Portsmouth, seems to have served a similar winter function.

146 John Hollingshead, *Ragged London in 1861*, London: 1861, pp. 81–2.

147 Sanger, *Seventy Years*, pp. 135–6, 175, 204–5.

148 *London City Mission Magazine*, 2 December 1861; Mayhew, *London Labour*, III, p. 407.

149 Report on Vagrancy, App. XXXII.

150 Mayhew, *London Labour*, III, p. 381.

151 26th Report of the Mendicity Society, 1844, pp. 13–14.

152 PP, 1846, VII, Report on District Asylums (368), Q. 1903.

153 PP, 1914–16, XXXII, XXXII, Report of the Metropolitan Poor Law Inspectors' Advisory Committee on the Homeless Poor (Cd 7840), p. 7.

154 COS, *Homeless Poor*, p. xiv; Report on District Asylums, Q. 1812; Mayhew, *London Labour*, III, p. 140.

155 For some venomous attacks, see C. E. Trevelyan, *Three Letters*

from Sir Charles Trevelyan to The Times *on London Pauperism*, London: 1870; COS, *Conference on Night Refuges Held at 15 Buckingham Street, Strand*, 1870.

156 Report on District Asylums, Q. 1909.
157 James Greenwood, *Low-Life Deeps: An Account of the Strange Fish To Be Found There*, London: 1876, p. 212.
158 *London City Mission Magazine*, 2 January 1860.
159 George Smith, *Our Canal, Gipsy Van and other Travelling Children*: 1883, pp. 17–18.
160 Chase, *Tenant Friends*, p. 96.
161 Mayhew, *London Labour*, III, p. 412.
162 COS, *Homeless Poor*, QQ.2, pp. 141–2.
163 Evans, *Where Beards Wag*, pp. 235–6.
164 RC on Labour: Agricultural Labourer, District Reports (C. 6894-IV), B–V [Bromyard], paras 8, 9; A. H. John, *The Industrial Revolution in South Wales*, Cardiff: 1950, p. 66.
165 SC on Distress from Want of Employment, 2nd Report, App., p. 53.
166 RC on the Poor Laws, Reports on Relation of Industrial and Sanitary Conditions to Pauperism, p. 364.
167 Evans, *Where Beards Wag*, p. 243; cf. Leone Levi, *Wages and Earnings*, London: 1885, pp. 112–13.
168 *Morning Chronicle*, 8 May 1850.
169 RC on Labour, Agricultural Labourer, District Reports (C. 6894-Vl), B–V, 62.
170 RC on Children in Agriculture, 2nd Report, Aj2, 33, 36b, 37a, 38.
171 Evans, *Where Beards Wag*, Appendix I.
172 *Labour News*, 19 October and 30 November 1872, and 18 January 1873.
173 COS, *Homeless Poor*, p. xxii.
174 N. B. Dearle, *Unemployment in the London Building Trades*, London: 1908, p. 80.
175 *Labour News*, 5 December 1874 and passim.
176 *Reminiscences of a Stonemason, by a Working Man*, London: 1908, p. 75; *51st Report of the Mendicity Society*, London: 1869, p. 11; *Labour News*, passim.
177 COS, *Unskilled, Labour*, QQ. 1722–3.
178 *Building and Engineering Times*, 7 January 1882.
179 *Fisherman's Friendly Visitor and Mariner's Companion*, March 1844, p. 27; cf. *Morning Chronicle*, 19 April 1850.
180 SC on Distress from Want of Employment, 2nd Report, App., p. 159; G. Holden Pike, *Among the Sailors*: 1897, p. 127; *The Word on the Waters*, III, 1860, p. 270.
181 *London Gazette*, 11 May 1894.

182 J. R. Bagshawe, *The Wooden Ships of Whitby*, Whitby: 1933, pp. 84–5.
183 *Labour News*, 14 October 1876.
184 Booth MSS, B. 122, fol. 63.
185 *Labour News*, 21 October 1876.
186 Webb, *Public Organisation*, p. 256.
187 *Labour News*, November 1873; Booth MSS, B. 84, fols 2, 9, 18, 26, 65.
188 Booth MSS, B. 84, passim, and B. 104, fols 12, 26, and B.101, fol. 75; PP, 1876, XXX, Factories and Workshops, Q. 4604.
189 R. Williams, *The Liverpool Docks Problem*, Liverpool: 1912, p. 42, and 'The First Year's Working of the Liverpool Docks Scheme', *Transactions of the Liverpool Economic and Statistical Society*, 1913–14, p. 99.
190 RC on Labour: Minutes of Evidence (C. 6894-IX), QQ. 31598, 31616, and 31501; *The Port of Hull*, Hull: 1907, p. 189.
191 Bagshawe, *Wooden Ships*, pp. 84–5.
192 *The Diaries of Sir Daniel Gooch, Baronet*, London: 1892, p. 78.
193 *Labour News*, 25 January 1873.
194 *My Story, by Patrick Gallagher ('Paddy the Cope')*, Dungloe: 1935, p. 61; RC on Labour, QQ. 31501, 31598, 31616; Booth MSS, B. 94, fols 5, 14, and B.117, fols 1, 18.
195 Webb, *Public Organisation*, pp. 256, 257.
196 RC on Labour, Q. 26439.
197 *Labour Standard*, 15 April 1882; 'The Irish in England', *Labour News*, 28 March 1874.
198 *Labour News*, 4 November 1876.
199 'The Irish in England', *Labour News*, 28 March 1874.
200 Thorne, *My Life's Battles*, pp. 49–50.
201 Hindley, *Life and Adventures*, pp. 188–9; Mayhew, *London Labour*, I, p. 338.
202 Mayhew, *London Labour*, I, pp. 104, 105, and III, p. 413.
203 Mayhew, *London Labour*, III, p. 94; *Labour News*, 8 January 1876; Booth, *Life and Labour*, 1st series, I, p. 211, and 2nd series, IV, p. 130; Webb, *Public Organisation*, p. 257.
204 COS, *Report on Soup Kitchens*, 1877, p. 13.
205 T. Camden Pratt, *Unknown London*, London: 1897, p. 32.
206 Booth MSS, A. 17, part A, fol. 82.
207 COS, *Homeless Poor*, Q. 1871.
208 Alsager Hay Hill, *The Unemployed in Great Cities with Suggestions for the Better Organisation of Labourers*: 1877, p. 15; Wilkinson, in Sims, *Off the Track*, I, p. 332; J. B. Booth, *London Town*, 1929, pp. 302–3, 232.
209 PRO, HO 45/10499/117669; Mepol. 2/1490.
210 COS, Exceptional Distress, 1886, and, for a hostile scrutiny,

Winter out-of-Work, 1892–3, 1893. Booth wrote that the vestries, were 'the principal extra source of casual employment during the winter': Booth, *Life and Labour*, 2nd series, IV, p. 40.

211 Mayhew, *London Labour*, III, p. 6.

212 Walter Besant and James Rice, *The Seamy Side*, 1880, p.10; *Labour News*, 8 November 1873; Booth, *Life and Labour*, 2nd series, I, pp. 94, 131.

213 Sanger, *Seventy Years*, pp. 128–9.

214 W. E. Adams, *Memoirs of a Social Atom*, London: 1893, I, pp. 304–7.

215 George Acorn, *One of the Multitude*, London: 1911, pp. 92–4.

216 David Morgan, 'The Place of Harvesters in Nineteenth-Century Village Life', in Raphael Samuel (ed.), *Work: Industrial Work Group and Workers' Control in Nineteenth-Century England* (forthcoming). [Ed. note: volume containing Morgan's essay was published in 1975 as Raphael Samuel (ed.), *Village Life and Labour*].

Workshop of the World

GUIDE TO ABBREVIATIONS AND REFERENCES

Booth MSS – London School of Economics, Charles Booth's MSS for *London Life and Labour*

Goldsmith Coll. – University of London, Goldsmith's collection of economic literature

Howell Coll. – Bishopsgate Institute, George Howell trade union collection

MB – Minute Book

MO – Medical Officer

MSS – manuscripts

PP – Parliamentary Papers

PRO – Public Record Office

RC – Royal Commission

SC – Select Committee

Webb Coll. – London School of Economics, Webb collection of trade union journals and MSS

Econ. H. R. – *Economic History Review*

Iron & Steel J. – *Journal of the Iron and Steel Institute*

Journ. Soc. Arts – *Journal of the Royal Society of Arts*

Newcomen Soc. – *Transactions of the Newcomen Society*

Royal Ag. Soc. J. – *Journal of the Royal Agricultural Society of England*

Stat. Soc. J. – *Journal of the Royal Statistical Society*

Bevan, *Manufacturing Industries* – *British Manufacturing Industries*, George Bevan (ed.), 14 unnumbered volumes, London: 1876.

Clapham, *Economic History* – J. H. Clapham, *An Economic History of Modern Britain*, 3 vols, Cambridge: 1926–38.

Cox, *British Industries* – Harold Cox (ed.), *British Industries under Free Trade*, London: 1903.

Labouring Men – E. J. Hobsbawm, *Labouring Men, Studies in the History of Labour*, London: 1964.

Marx, *Capital* – Karl Marx, *Capital*, Vol. I, ed. Dona Torr, London: 1949.

Mitchell and Deane – B. R. Mitchell and Phyllis Deane, *Abstract of British Historical Statistics*, Cambridge: 1971.

Rousiers, *Labour* – Paul de Rousiers, *The Labour Question in Britain*, London: 1896.

Timmins – Samuel Timmins (ed.), *The Industrial Resources of Birmingham and the Midland Hardware District*, London: 1866.

Ure, *Dictionary* – Andrew Ure (ed.), *Dictionary of Arts, Manufactures and Mines*, 3 vols, London: 1860.

1 Originally published in *History Workshop Journal*, 3:1, Spring 1977, pp. 6–72.

2 David Landes, *The Unbound Prometheus*, Cambridge: 1969, p. 41.

3 For an autobiographical account by one who traded in adulterated soot, see George Elson, *The Last of the Climbing Boys*, London: 1900, pp. 78–81. For complaints of the master chimney sweeps about 'pirate' soot merchants, see Booth MSS, B. 160, fol. 16, and for a soot merchant in Poplar, see B. 120, fol. 80. For the soot trade in Westminster, see Westminster Archives, St Martin's in the Fields Paving Commission MB, 24 April 1844. For fluctuations in the price of soot, see J. Thomson and Adolphe Smith, *Street Life in London*, London: 1877. For soot and manure, see *Liverpool Mercury*, 10 October 1845, p. 400 (I am grateful to Tim Mason for this reference). For haddock, see Mayhew, *London Labour*.

4 For the effect of heavy sizing on the health of those who had to work with it in the mills, see PP 1872 (203) LIV, PP 1884 (c.3861) LXXII. For a moving autobiographical account, Alice Foley, *A Bolton Childhood*, Manchester: 1973, p. 51.

5 Goldsmith's Coll.; Mayhew, *London Labour*, p. 40. Nicoll was under-sheriff of the City of London; he and his brother were said to be worth £80,000 apiece.

6 H. A. Shannon, 'Bricks, a Trade Index', *Economica*, 1934.

7 Hobsbawm, 'The Machine Breakers', in *Labouring Men*.

8 PRO, For. 3/559,3/263. The explosion, like others in the district,

seems to have been the work of Walter Virgo and the Blakeney gang.

9   Howell Coll., *The Moxon Loom Arbitration Proceedings*, Kidderminster: 1879. *Cf.* also J. N. Bartlett, 'The Mechanization of the Kidderminster Carpet Industry', *Business History*, 1967, IX.

10 J. Reynolds, *The Letterpress Printers of Bradford*, Bradford: 1971, pp. 5–6; Sid Wills, 'The Compositor's Frame', in *The Workshop Trades*.

11 John Ball, 'Account of the Northamptonshire Boot and Shoe Makers Strike in 1857/8/9', *Trade Societies and Strikes*, London: 1860. There are very full reports of these strikes in the *Northampton Mercury* and the *Northamptonshire Free Press*.

12 'Murderous Threats to Workmen m the Screw Bolt Trade', *The Ironmonger*, 30 December 1865, VII, pp. 180–1.

13 *Capital*, XV, pp. 464–96, and XVI, pp. 5–19.

14 Peel to Croker, 27 July 1842, in *Sir Robert Peel: From his Private Papers*, ed. C. S. Parker, London: 1899, II, p. 529. *Cf.* also G. Kitson Clark, 'Hunger and Politics IO 1842', *Journal of Modern History*, 1955.

15 *Capital*, XI, p. 297; *cf.* XV, p. 422.

16 Karl Marx and Friedrich Engels, *Selected Correspondence*, London: 1935, pp. 10–11.

17 The Patent Office Library is a useful resort for British Museum readers who find a title they are searching for has been consigned to that elastic category 'Destroyed by Bombing in the War'.

18 There is an account of the Tate and Lyle works in W. Glenny Crory, *East London Industries*, London: 1876. Booth MSS, A. 24 para. A, fols 17–23 for two usefully detailed biographies, and for some other back-street manufacturers see B. 10, fol. 125, and B. 16, fols 43, 91, and B. 44, fols 26, 41, and B. 45, fols 60, 147.

19 For the rolling mills, PP 1876 (c.1443–1), XXX, Rep... Fact. & Workshops Act, QQ. 12058–61; for a list of the 55 trades 'in union', see Frank Hill, 'Combinations in Sheffield', *Trade Societies and Strikes*, London: 1860, pp. 564–5.

20 PP 1876, XXX, Rep... Fact. & Workshops Act, QQ. 5529, 5644; Webb Coll., Sect. A, Vol. X, fol. 386; A. B. Searle, *Refractory Materials*, London 1917, p. 144.

21 *Morning Chronicle*, 23 December 1850, Birmingham.

22 Ellis A. Davidson, *Our Houses*, London: 1869, p. 96; Prof. Barff, 'Glass and Silicates', in Bevan, *Manufacturing Industries*, pp. 76–7.

23 Clapham, *Economic History*, II, p. 83; H. Heaton, *The Yorkshire Woollen and Worsted Industries*, Oxford: 1965, p. 358. For a wages agitation of the Pudsey handloom weavers, see *Beehive*, 11 November 1871; and for an attractive autobiographical account

from Colne Valley in the 1870s, see Ben Turner, *About Myself*, London: 1930, pp. 34–5. See also Mathew Blair, 'The Silk Trade', in Cox, *British Industries*, p. 65; PP 1861 (161), XVI, 3rd Rw; MO Privy Council, p. 159.

24 Sir R. Lloyd Patterson, 'The Linen Industry', in Cox, *British Industries*, p. 58. For some strike movements among the hand-loom linen weavers of Barnsley, *Beehive*, 10 February, and 10, 24, 31 March, and 10, 17, 24 November, and 8 December 1866.

25 PP 1861 (161), XVI, 3rd Rep. Med. Off. Privy C, p. 169. For the slow spread of steam in the industry, W. Felkin, 'The Lace and Hosiery Trades of Nottingham', *Stat Soc. J.*, XXIX, 1866; Roy Church, 'Technological Change and the Hosiery Board of Conciliation 1860–1884', *Yorkshire Bull. of Econ. and Soc. Research*, May 1963, XV:1, p. 53; Dodie Weppler, 'Seamers and Stitchers', unpublished paper given at Ruskin History Workshop 8, 'Women in History', May 1972.

26 The Bolton hand-mule spinners numbered 1,326 in their association in 1874, *Capital and Labour*, 16 September 1874. For their amalgamation with the self-actor minders, Bolton, Spinners' Hall MSS, Hand Mule Spinners Assocation Minutes, 21 February 1880. For an employer's view of the hand-mule spinners, 'The Bolton Strike' in *Capital and Labour*, 12 September 1877, IV, p. 466. Clapham, *Economic History*, II, p. 81, for a more detailed discussion of hand-mule spinning inside the factories, Harold Catling, *The Spinning Mule*, Newton Abbot: 1970, pp. 46, 51, 63, 119, 115–16, 118–19, 123. Readers might be interested in Marx's discussion of the survival of hand-mule spinning: *Capital*, pp. 376–7.

27 Andrew Wynter, *Curiosities of Civilization*, London: 1860, pp. 262–3; J. D. Goodman, 'On the Progress of the Small Arms Manufacture', *Stat. Soc. J.*, XXVIII, 1865, pp. 495–8.

28 Sid Wills, 'The Compositor's Frame', in *The Workshop Trades*.

29 For a good account of one of them, see George Dodd, *Days at Factories*, London: 1843, pp. 17–40.

30 John Lord, *Capital and Steam Power, 1750–1800*, London: 1923; for a very helpful general discussion of the diffusion of steam power, A. E. Musson, 'Industrial Motive Power in the United Kingdom, 1800–1870', *Econ. H. R.*, August 1976, 2nd series, XXIX:3.

31 Clapham, *Economic History*, II, p. 123. In the year ending 1 March 1873, 30,671 brewers took out licences in England: T. A. Pooley, 'Brewing', in Bevan, *Manufacturing Industries*, p. 202. London brewers recruited many of their workers from the small country brewers: Booth MSS, B. 122, fols 31, 81.

32 Nineteenth-century windmills seem to have been as much

subject to 'improvement' as any other species of capital equipment, among them Messrs J. Warner's patent annular sails. John Ashton, *The History of Bread*, London: 1904, p. 106. For some other nineteenth-century improvements in windmills, Rex Wales, 'Suffolk windmills', *Newcomen Soc.*, XXII, XXIII, 1941–3.

33 For silk, *Morning Chronicle*, 22 November 1849, Macclesfield; Sir Frank Warner, *The Silk Industry*, London: 1922, pp. 135, 319, 322; PP 1886 (c.4715), XXII, 2nd Rep. Depression of Trade, Q. 7454; for woollens, Rousiers, *Labour*, p. 306; J. H. Clapham, *The Woollen and Worsted Industries*, London: 1907, p. 58. For hand-looms in the Kidderminster carpet factories, W. J. Gordon, *Midland Sketches*, London: 1898, p. 104.

34 J. W. C. Haldane, *Steam Ships and their Machinery*, London: 1893.

35 Harry Brearley, *Steel-Makers*, London: 1933, pp. 26–8. For an earlier account, John Scoffern et al., *The Useful Metals and their Alloys*, London: 1857, p. 349. In the 1890s, Sheffield used 14,000 clay crucibles a week in which to fuse its steel. R. A. Hadfield, 'On the Early History of Crucible Steel', *Iron and Steel J.*, 1894, XLVI, p. 324.

36 A. B. Searle, *Refractory Materials*, London: 1917, pp. 308–9.

37 There is an account of the collier brigs by one who served with them in Walter Runciman, *Collier Brigs and their Sailors*, London: 1926.

38 F. M. L. Thompson, 'Nineteenth-Century Horse Sense', *Econ. H. R.*, February 1976, 2nd series, XXIX:I, for these and other useful horse statistics and an interesting discussion of them.

39 Mitchell and Deane, p. 60.

40 Samuel, 'Mineral Workers', in *Miners, Quarrymen and Saltworkers*, 1977, p, 9, for some details of the traffic.

41 *Morning Chronicle*, 23 December 1850.

42 Detailed discussion of tactics and the clothing trades is held over for a subsequent article.

43 C. W. Waring, 'On the Application of Machinery to Cutting Coal', *Transaction South Wales Institute of Engineers*, 1862–3, III, p. 95.

44 *Manchester Examiner*, 26 July 1865, p. 5, cols 2–3; cf. *Barnsley Chronicle*, 1 September 1866; *Capital and Labour*, 15 April 1874, *Iron and Coal Trades Review*, 15 May 1872, p. 386. For the 1901 figure, see J. E. Williams, *The Derbyshire Miners*, London: 1962, p. 174; for the 1913 figure, see H. J. Habakkuk, *American and British Technology in the Nineteenth Century*, Cambridge: 1962, p. 200. For some of the technical obstacles encountered by the coal cutter, PP 1873, X(313), SC on Coal, QQ. 2198–9; Rousiers, *Labour*, pp. 121–2; PP 1892, XXXVI (6795-VII), RC on Labour, Answers to Questions, Group 'A', p. 263; A. J. Taylor

'Labour Productivity and Technical Innovation in the British Coal Industry', *Econ. H. R.*, 2nd series, XIV, pp. 58–62.

45 In earlier years the hewers had been expected to do their own propping, but in the second half of the nineteenth century they were vigorously resisting this because it cut down their piece-rated earnings. *The Times*, 5 July 1873, p. 5; *Iron and Coal Trades R.*, 13 March 1872.

46 Mitchell and Deane, pp. 60, 119.

47 Thompson, 'Nineteenth-Century Horse Sense', Appendix, p. 80, from estimates supplied by Alan Griffin.

48 'Tools', *The Quarry*, April 1896, pp. 63–4; W. G. Renwick, *Marble and Marble Working*, London: 1909, p. 28; *Crossing's Dartmoor Worker*, Newton Abbot: 1966, pp. 70–1, J. A. Howe, *The Geology of Building Stones*, London: 1910, p. 99.

49 Interviews of the writer with David Powell, Ivor Probert, and Harry Powell, Clydach Vale, Monmouthshire, August 1974.

50 William Knight, 'Granite Quarries of Aberdeenshire', *Transactions of the Highland Agricultural Society*, 1835, 2nd series, IV. The 'Blondin' was invented by Fyfe of Kenmay, one of the chief granite-working centres of Aberdeenshire: William Diack, 'The Scottish Granite Industry', *The World's Work*, 1903, pp. 636–7. I am grateful to Bob Duncan for this reference.

51 Fred Bower, *Rolling Stonemason*, London: 1936, pp. 40–1.

52 Walter White, *A Londoner's Walk to Land's End*, London: 1861, pp. 126–30, for a vivid description.

53 Joseph H. Collins, *Principles of Metal Mining*, London: 1875, pp. 60, 63.

54 From an autobiographical account recorded in Kenneth Hudson, *The History of English China Clays*, Newton Abbot: 1969, p. 32.

55 This paragraph is based on L. T. C. Rolt, *The Potter's Field: A History of the South Devon Clay Industries*, Newton Abbot: 1974.

56 John Grey of Dilston, 'A View of the Present State of Agriculture in Northumberland', *Royal Ag. Soc. J.*, 1841, II, p. 165; *British Husbandry*, 1837, 11, p. 340.

57 John Algernon Clarke, 'On the Great Level of the Fens', *Royal. Ag. Soc. J.*, 1847, VIII, pp. 92, 101, 119, and also his *Fen Sketches*, London: 1852, p. 256.

58 E. J. T. Collins, 'Harvest Technology and Labour Supply in Britain, 1780–1870', *Econ. H. R.*, 1969, 2nd series, XXII:3; David Morgan, 'Harvesters', in *Village Life and Labour*. Collins's article is of first-class importance for the subject of this essay.

59 Charles Whitehead, 'Report on the Market Garden and the Market Garden Competition', *Royal Ag. Soc. J.*, 1879, 2nd series, XV, p. 842. For some estimates of labour costs on arable farms

see the very interesting article by Frederic Clifford, 'The Labour Bill in Farming', *Royal Ag. Soc. J.*, 1875, 2nd series, XV.

60   Charles Whitehead, 'Hops, Fruit, Vegetables', *Royal Ag. Soc. J.*, 2nd series, XIV, 1878, pp. 750, 850, 864. For potato planting near Gillingham, Trinity Coll., Cambridge, see MS Diary of A. J. Munby, XVIII, 9 March 1863 (I am grateful to Anna Davin for this and the other Munby market-gardening references).

61   C. W. Shaw, *The London Market Gardens*, London: 1879, p. 187.

62   Whitehead, *Royal Ag. Soc. J.*, 1879, p. 845.

63   Ibid., p. 846; Shaw, *London Market Gardens*, p. 191; PP 1868–9, (4202.I) XIII, 2nd Rep., Emp. in Agriculture, A, Pershore, Worcs.

64   Whitehead, *Royal Ag. Soc. J.*, 1879, p. 858; Munby Diaries, XII, 1 March 1862, and XXV, 16 May 1865.

65   For migrant pea-pickers and contract work in Essex, Glenny 'Market Gardening', *Victoria County History of Essex*, 1907, II, pp. 476–7; G. Cuttle, *The Legacy of the Rural Guardians*, Cambridge: 1934, pp. 267, 273. *Toilers in London by One of the Crowd*, London: 1883, p. 96, gives a description of the pea-pickers' living quarters. PP 1867–8, (4068.I), XVII, 1st Rep., Emp. in Agriculture, App. Pt II, p. 359, for itinerant Irish pea-pickers at Stoke Poges, Bucks.

66   Patrick MacGill, *Children of the Dead End*, London: 1914, p. 75. For Irish potato-pulling gangs in earlier times, Emp. in Agriculture, 1st Rep., PP 1867–8, (4068.I) XVII, c. 120, 272; d. 212, 260, 276, and pp. 385, 387, 388, 390; Emp. in Agriculture, 2nd Rep., PP 1868–9, (4202.I) XIII, App. II, A. 1, 130. For a more recent account of the Irish potato-picking gangs in Scotland, see *Observer*, 13 June 1971.

67   Whitehead, *Royal Ag. Soc. J.*, 1879, pp. 841, 848; Whitehead, *Market Gardening for Farmers*, London: 1880, p. 12; for a personal recollection of this kind of work at Tiptree, Essex Record Office, T/Z 25/378, Mrs Field, 'My First Job'.

68   Andrew Wynter, *Curiosities of Civilisation*, London: 1860, p. 235; Shaw, *London Market Gardens*, pp. 151–60.

69   Oral history: interviews of the writer with Mrs Anne McClough of Liverpool, April 1972–79.

70   Booth MSS, B. 117, p. 34.

71   Charles Booth, *Life and Labour*, 1st series, IV, pp. 288–9.

72   James Jefferys, *Retail Trading in Britain, 1850–1950*, Cambridge: 1954, p. 181; Janet Blackman, 'The Food Supply of an Industrial Town', *Business History*, 1962, V:I, pp. 86, 91; Robert Roberts, *The Classic Slum*, London and New York: 1973, pp. 88–9; J. B. Shon, *The Butcher's Shop*, Oxford: 1928, pp. 11, 13.

73   For the bad meat trade, see police court prosecutions in e.g. *The Times*, 5 February 18xx, 28 March 18xx, 8 April 18xx,

23 August 18xx, 28 September 18xx; and *Morning Chronicle*, 30 May 18xx. For the 'slink' butchers of Newton Heath, Manchester, see Rawlinson, *Rep. to the General Board of Health ... Newton Heath*, London: 1852, pp. 28, 29, 30, 45, 52–3; Holborn archives, Holborn Bd of Works, MB 6 January 1873, for Joseph Hen, a Leicestershire dealer who made a speciality of bad meat transactions; for dealings on Salisbury Plain, Alexander Somerville, *The Whistler at the Plough*, Manchester: 1885, pp. 1–3, and I, pp. 389–90.

74 J. Chalmers Morton, 'On Cheese-Making in Home Dairies or Factories', *Royal Ag. Soc. J.*, 2nd series, XI, 1875, p. 273; A. D. Hall, *A Pilgrimage of British Farming, 1910–1912*, London: 1913, p. 410; G. Gibbons, 'Cheddar Cheese Making', *Journal of the Bath and West of England Society*, 1890, 4th series, I, p. 102; G. E. Fussell, *The English Dairy Farmer, 1500–1900*, London: 1966, pp. 191, 229, 240, 242; T. D. Acland and W. Sturge, *Farming of Somerset*, London: 1851, p. 53.

75 PP 1864, (3381) XXI, Ann. Rep. on British Fisheries 1863, p. 14; Bob Gilding, 'Journeymen Coopers', in *The Workshop Trades*; *The Practical Fishmonger and Fruiterer*, London: 1914–17, I, p. 68, and IV, pp. 130–6; G. R. Sims, *Off the Track*, pp. 49–53; Booth MSS, B. 346, p. 113; Tony Watley, 'The Marsh Side Shrimpers', Ruskin College history thesis, 1974; PP 1898, (c.8753) XIV, Rep. on the Fish Curing Trade, p. 11.

76 PRO, H04s/9622/A 17459; William Jago, 'Modern Developments of Bread-Making', *Journ. Soc. Arts*, 27 December 1889, XXXVIII, p. 93; Andrew Low, 'Flour Milling under Free Trade', in Cox, *British Industries*, p. 256, G. J. S. Broomhall and J. H. Hubback, *Corn Trade Memories*, Liverpool: 1930, pp. 40, 42, 43, 189, 244; John Burnett, *Plenty and Want*, London: 1966, pp. 104–6; Marx, *Capital*, p. 232; PP 1862, (3027) XLVII, Rep. Journeymen Bakers, p. xiii; George Dodd, *The Food of London*, London: 1856, p. 197; John Burnell, 'The Baking Industry in the 19th Century', *Business History*, V:2; John Ashton, *The History of Bread from Pre-Historic to Modern Times*, London: 1904, p. 140; Ure, *Dictionary*, I, p. 408; *The Miller*, 1 March 1875, p. 4; *Bakers' Record*, 28 August 1869, p. 5, and 25 September 1869, p. 4, and 9 October 1869 p. 4 – for some representative complaints from the 'full-priced' end of the trade.

77 Eddie Dare, 'Thoughts of a Journeyman Baker', *History Workshop Journal*, 3:1, Spring 1977, p. 138 (the same issue as the present essay [ed.]).

78 John Burnett, *Useful Toil*, London: 1974, pp. 92–5; Banbury Ref. Lib. MSS, Arthur Jonas, 'A Cherwell Boy or Banbury in the 1900s'; Samuel, 'Quarry Roughs', in *Village Life and Labour*,

p. 202. For the increase of 'small makers' specialising in half-penny and farthing novelties, see A. E. Coombe, 'A General Chat on the Toffee Trade', *Confectionary*, 12 March 1896, p. 50, and 13 April 1896, and 12 May 1896; J. D. Burn, *Commercial Enterprise and Social Progress*, London: 1858, p. 130; Andrew Wynter, *Our Social Bus*, 2nd series, London: 1866, pp. 204–5. Goldsmiths Coll., 'The Working Classes of Edinburgh, 1853; Confectioners'. So late as the 1890s G. H. Duckworth, visiting an East London sweet factory, noted that 'the steam process used in jam-making is not powerful enough for sweets', Booth MSS, B. 11736.

79 R. A. Church, *The Great Victorian Boom, 1850–1873*, London: 1975, p. 34.

80 E. Dobson, *Rudiments of the Art of Building*, London: 1849, pp. 25, 42–3, 261. For the extraordinary elaboration expected in high-class painter's work, J. W. Facey, *Elementary Decoration*, London: 1882; Adam Hammond, *Rudiments of Practical Bricklaying*, London: 1874, pp. 1, 25, 42–3, 44; Dobson, *Rudiments of the Art*, pp. 119–23. For a vivid illustration, 'The Staircase Hand of the Old School', *The Builder*, 6 July 1878, XXXVI, pp. 693–4; F. Walker, *Brickwork*, London: 1885, pp. 58–87.

81 Sidney and Beatrice Webb, *The Story of the King's Highway*, London: 1963, p. 200.

82 Telford's specification for the London and Holyhead road, quoted by Thomas Hughes, *The Practice of Making and Repairing Roads*, London: 1838, p. 28.

83 Andrew Wynter, *Peeps into the Human Heart*, London: 1874, II, pp. 187–8; Samuel, 'Mineral Workers', p. 83, for the competition between asphalt and granite.

84 Booth MSS, B. 149, fols 2, 3, 7.

85 Ronald Clark, *The Development of the English Traction Engine*, Norwich: 1960, p. 167; *cf.* also *The Builder*, 19 October 1867, XXV, p. 767, and 14 December 1867, XXV, p. 915.

86 Quoted in *Report of the Highway and Sanitary Joint Committee of the Paddington Vestry on Wood and Other Pavements*, London: 1878, p. 51.

87 *The Quarry*, May 1896; Knight, 'Aberdeenshire Granite', pp. 66–8; PP 1912–13, (Cd 6390) XLI, RC Metalliferous Mmes, QQ. 8593–4; M. Powis Bale, *Stoneworking Machinery*, London: 1884, p. 75.

88 For some examples, *The Builder*, 11 May 1867, 6 July 1867, 21 September 1878, XXXVl, p. 997. 'Church Building News', together with its appendage, 'Dissenting Church Building News' is a regular column in *The Builder* of the 1860s and 1870s, and 'Town Halls and Exchanges' became a regular heading in 1865.

For the employment this gave Jude Fawley, see Thomas Hardy, *Jude the Obscure*, New York: 1977, Ch. VII.

89 Henry Broadhurst, *The Story of His Life Told by Himself*, London: 1901, pp. 28–9; *Reminiscences of a Stonemason*, pp. 89–90, 105. So late as the 1890s stone-working machinery seems to have made little impact on the industry, so far as stonemasons themselves were concerned: *cf.* Booth MSS, A. 3 fol. 279 (interview with Hancock, secretary of the Operative Stonemasons); Congress House records, *United Builders and Labourers, Trade Circular and Monthly Report*, September 1895, pp. 8–9. For an early strike against machinery, interestingly by masons' labourers, *Beehive*, 25 August 1866, p. 6, col. 3. For patents and experiments, Powis Bale, *Stoneworking Machinery*; *Building News*, 6 January 1865, XII:17, *Capital and Labour*, 1875, II:722, 14 November 1877, IV:605. For the eventual impact of machinery on workers in the trade, *Reminiscences of a Stonemason*, p. 255.

90 Thomas Brassey, the contractor, quoted in Coleman, *Railway Navvies*, p. 39.

91 *Personal Recollections of English Engineers, by a Civil Engineer*, London: 1868, p. 42; Coleman, *Railway Navvies*, p. 48.

92 When a moving platform was invented by the engineer to 'supersede the necessity of thus perilling life and limb', the navvies, 'considering it to diminish their labour and wages', broke it. Williams, *Our Iron Roads*, p. 72.

93 PP 1867, (3873) XXXII, RC Trade Unions, Q. 2546; *Free Lance*, 27 February 1869, IV, p. 66.

94 *Reminiscences of a Stonemason*.

95 Carpenters claimed 'grinding money' when they were sacked from a job – i.e. a monetary equivalent for the time it took them to make their tools ship-shape. For the one-hour claim, see *North Yorks. Bldg. Trades Review*, 22 January 1876, p. 7; *Brick, Tile and Bldrs Gaz.*, 8 May 1888, III, p. 336; for the two-hours claim, see *Builders Weekly Reporter*, 26 February 1875, p. 209; *Capital and Labour*, 5 March 1875, 8 March 1876.

96 Davidson, *Houses*, p. 59; John Black, *Gas Fitting, A Practical Handbook*, London: 1886, pp. 17–18; W. E. J. Crane, *The Sheet-Metal Worker's Guide*, London: 1883.

97 For the small builder, A. Howarth and Mona Wilson, *West Ham*, London: 1907, pp. 10–12; *Brick, Tile and Bldrs Gaz*, 19 April 1888, III, p. 298; H. J. Dyos, 'The Speculative Builders and Developers of Victorian London', *Victorian Studies*, Summer 1968; for the Manchester outrages, PRO, H.O. 45/8428; *Building Trade Circular*, 5, 12, 19 May 1870; Richard Price, 'The Other Face of Respectability', *Past and Present*, February 1975.

98 *Brick, Tile and Bldrs Gaz*, 19 April 1888.

99 Kenney, *Westering*, pp. 80–1.
100 George R. Burnell, *Rudimentary Treatise on Limes, Cements, Mortars, Concretes, Plastering, etc.*, London: 1850, for contemporary uses of lime.
101 *Morning Chronicle*, 29 December 1849.
102 Dobson, *Building*, p. 109; Davidson, *Houses*, p. 46.
103 C. le Neve Foster, *A Text-Book of Ore and Stone Mining*, London: 1894, p. 546.
104 For an excellent account of the Purbeck industry by a stone-worker, see Eric Benfield, *Purbeck Shop*, Cambridge: 1948. For contemporary accounts, *Morning Chronicle*, 23 January 1850; C. E. Robinson, *Rambles in the Isle of Purbeck*, London: 1882; Dorset County Mus., O. W. Farrer, 'The Marblers of Purbeck', *Purbeck Soc. Papers*, 1859–60, pp. 191–204.
105 Merfyn Jones, 'Y Chwarelwyr: The Slate Quarrymen of North Wales', in *Miners, Quarrymen and Saltworkers*, p. 121.
106 *The British Clayworker*, October 1898.
107 Charles Tomlinson, *Illustrations of the Useful Arts and Manufactures*, London: 1859, pp. 26, 25; Dobson, *Rudimentary Treatise on Bricks*, London: 1850, p. 22; J. Geraint Jenkins, *Traditional Country Craftsmen*, London: 1965, p. 149. According to Ure, clay was tempered 'by the treading of men or oxen', and in the London district mainly by horseginned pug-mills: Ure, *Dictionary*, I, p. 443.
108 Arthur Aiken, *Illustrations of Useful Arts and Manufactures*, London: 1841, pp. 19–20, 70; H. Chamberlain, 'The Manufacture of Bricks by Machinery', *Soc. of Arts J.*, 6 June 1856, IV, pp. 491–2. For an account based on oral history, Donald Young, 'Brickmaking at Broadmayne', *Proc. Dorset Natural Hist. Soc.*, 1967, LXXXIX; Dobson, *Bricks*, p. 81. Percy Dell of Cholesbury Common, Chesham, letter to Bill Keal of Princes Risborough, 29 April 1873 (I am grateful to Bill Keal for collecting this account by one who worked as a hand-brickmaker in the 1920s).
109 Chamberlain, 'Manufacture of Bricks', pp. 491–500; *Brick, Tile and Blders Gazette*, 12 April 1887, II, p. 295, William Johnson, *Lecture on Brick-Making Machinery and Bricks*, Leeds: 1886, pp. 3, 14; *The British Clayworker*, 1893, III, p. 214; A. Searle, *Modern Brickmaking*, London: 1911, pp. 39, 424–5. For the predominance of hand brickmaking in 1870s Birmingham, see A. H. Stephenson, *The Trade Associations of Birmingham Brick Masters, 1864–1933*, privately printed: 1933, pp. 83, 84, 90, 96. For the transition from hand to machine in the Nottingham district, Webb Coll., Sect. A. Vol. X, fols 82–8.
110 PP 1873, (C. 745) XIX, Fact. Inspectors Reps, p. 19.

111 Thomas Allen, *A History of Surrey*, London: 1831, I, p. 35; K. W. Gravett and E. S. Wood, 'Merstham Limeworks', *Surrey Arch. Colls*, 1967, LXIX; Surrey Record Office, Merstham Limeworks, accounts and papers (I am grateful to Miss Gollancz, the county archivist, for bringing these papers to my notice).

112 Dobson, *Bricks*, p. 122.

113 Ibid., and Chamberlain, 'Manufacture of Bricks', p. 500.

114 James Greenwood, 'Mr. Dodd's Dust-Yard', in *Unsentimental Journeys*, London: 1867, pp. 64ff for a description, and engraving, of one of them. The most famous metropolitan dust heap was the one at the King's Cross end of what is today Gray's Inn Road. It was sold by an enterprising London capitalist to the Tsarist government for the rebuilding of Moscow after the great burning of 1812. G. M. L. Strauss et al., *England's Workshops*, London: 1864, p. 161; *London City Mission Magazine*, 1 November 1860, XXV, pp. 318–19; *Good Words*, 1 September 1866, p. 645, and 1879, pp. 739–42; Thomson and Smith, *Street Life*, pp. 94–5, 'Our Dust-Bins', *Leisure Hour*, 2 November 1968; Uncle Jonathan, *Walks in and Around London*, London: 1889, p. 150.

115 PP 1883, (c.3516) XVIII, Rep. White Lead Poisoning.

116 PP 1893–4, (c.7239) XVII, White Lead Committee, pp. 7–8; QQ. 245, 250, 2527–9, 220, 3008.

117 Brian Didsbury, 'Cheshire Saltworkers', in *Miners, Quarrymen and Saltworkers*, pp. 155–7; *Pottery Gazette*, 1 July 1880, IV, p. 432; *Iron and Steel J.*, 1895, LVIII, p. 327; Apsley Pellatt, *Curiosities of Glass Making*, London: 1849, pp. 61, 82; Percival Marson, *Glass and Glass Manufactures*, London: 1932, p. 81; Walter Rosenheim, *Glass Manufacturing*, London: 1919, pp. 107, 133.

118 Robert Swinburne, 'The Manufacture of Glass', in W. G. Armstrong (ed.), *The Industrial Resources of the Tyne, Wear & Tees*, Newcastle upon Tyne: 1864, pp. 195–6; Theodore Barker, *Pilkington Brothers and the Glass Industry*, London: 1900, p. 87.

119 'Glass and Silicates', in Bevan, *Manufacturing Industries*, pp. 79, 80–1.

120 George Dodd, *Where Do We Get It*, London: 1862, p. 248; cf. George Dodd, 'Glass and its Manufacture', in *Curiosities of Industry*, London: 1852, p. 20. For other description of sheet glass-making at Messrs Chance's Smethwick works, see *Morning Chronicle*, 23 December 1850; 'Birmingham and her Manufactures IV', in *The Leisure Hour*, 20 January 1853.

121 PP 1865 (3548) XX, 4th Rep. Children's Emp. Com., Q.14; *Leisure Hour*, 2 November 1868; G. L. M. Strauss et al., *England's Workshops*, pp. 16–17; 4th Rep. Children's Emp.

Com. QQ. 82–3, *Morning Chronicle*, 23 December 1850; PP 1899, (c.9073) XII, 3rd Rep. on Dangerous Trades, pp. 16–17.

122 4th Rep. Children's Emp. Com., QQ. 15018–20.

123 'Birmingham Flint Glass Manufacture', in Timmins, p. 430; Rosenheim, *Glass*, p. 78. *Cf.* Webb Coll., N. of England Glass Bottlemaking, Half-Yearly Rep., December 1890, p. 31: 'Under the Gas Tank system work is a lot more severe. The heat is 50 degrees hotter.'

124 'Birmingham Flint Glass Manufacture', in Timmins, p. 531; Children's Emp. Com. Q. 12–13, 86; George Dodd, *British Manufactures*, London: 1844–6, IV, pp. 61–5; Pellatt, *Curiosities*, pp. 125ff; George Dodd, *Curiosities of Industry*, London: 1852, pp. 13, 15 (I am grateful to Toshio Kusanutsu for helpful discussion on this point).

125 W. C. Scoville, *Revolution in Glassmaking*, Cambridge, MB55, 1948, p. 175; Charles J. Phillips, *Glass, The Miracle Worker*, New York: 1941, pp. 19, 155, 191, 199. *Cf.* PP 1913, (6711) XXIII, Rep. Night Work, QQ. 842–5. The persistence of handicraft methods no doubt owed a good deal to the glassworkers' trades unions, which were quite exceptionally strong in all the main centres of the trade – the glass bottlemakers of Castleford no less than the flint glassmakers of Stourbridge. They maintained strict production quotas or 'tantums', controlled worker hiring and firing, and operated their own work sharing systems when employment in the trade was slack. 'The relation of master and man in the blown flint and bottle trades amount to a chronic strike', a Tyneside manufacturer wrote in 1864, complaining of the 'insensate' worker opposition to improvements: 'Large orders have been transferred from the Tyne to Belgium, and the manufacturers here purchase foreign glass, for the production of which they have every appliance at home, except labour at a reasonable cost.'

126 Neil McKendrick, 'Josiah Wedgwood and Factory Discipline', *Historical Journal*, 1961, IV; Walter White, *All Round the Wrekin*, London: 1860, p. 297; *Pottery Gazette*, 2 July 1883; *The Builder*, 19 October 1878; PP 1863, (3170) XVIII, 1st Rep. Children's Emp. Com, pp. 33–4; PP 1889, (5697) XVIII, p. 90.

127 Old Potter, *When I was a Child*, London: 1903, p. 46. The fitting of handles was at one time even more physical, as 'Old Potter' recalls in his account of childhood work in the 1840s: '(Handles) were made by two half moulds made to fit into one another by niches on one side and holes on the other. The piece of clay to form the handle was placed in the bottom half of the

mould, then the top half was put on and pressed down by the boy's stomach, with a sort of wriggle.'

128 PP 1889, (c.5697) XVIII, p. 90; *Morning Chronicle*, 24 January 1850; 'Through the Potteries', *Industrial World*, 2 December 1892.

129 PP 1861, (161) XVI, 3rd Rep. Med. Off. Privy Council, App. VI, Dr. Greenhow Rep on Lung OLSCBSCS, p. 108; PP 1863, (3170) XVIII, 1st Rep. Children's Emp. Com App. p. 2.

130 PP 1893–4, (C.6894-XXIII) XXVII–I, RC Labour, Collet, pp. 61, 62.

131 Arlidge, loc cit.; PP 1910, (cd 5278) XXIX, Rep... Lead in Potteries, App. XXVII, pp. 64, 144.

132 PP 1863, (3170) XVIII, 1st Rep. Children's Emp. Com., App. pp. 3, 7, 8, 17, 18, 21, 23.

133 Collet, p. 62.

134 J. R. McCulloch, *A Statistical Account of the British Empire*, London: 1837, II, p. 118; PP 1892, (c.6795–VI) XXXXVI, RC Labour, Group C. II, Q. 15,038; *Morning Chronicle*, 15 November 1850; Ure, *Dictionary*, II, pp. 676–95, and III, pp. 848–9; *The Manufacturer*, 25 April 1868, p. 27; Nuffield Coll., *Work in Bristol*, Bristol: 1883, pp. 116–25; W. G. Rimmer, 'Leeds Leather Industry in the Nineteenth Century', *Thoresby Soc. Pubs*, 1960, XLVl:2; *Boot and Shoe Trade Journal*, 15 January 1887; PP 1883, (c.3778-I), XXVIII, Local Government Bd Rep., App. 13, 'London Hide and Skin Trades'.

135 Alexander Japp, *Industrial Curiosities*, London: 1880, pp. 48–50, G. Philips Bevan, *Industrial Classes and Industrial Statistics*, London: 1876, p. 147, *Hatters Gazette*, 30 April 1877; *The Hosier and Glovers' Gazette*, 1 February and 1 June 1884; PP 1868–9, (4202.I) XIII: Women and Children in Agriculture, 2nd Rep., K. 44–54, k. 135–85; PP 1865, (3483) XXVI, 7th Rep. MO Pnvy C., App. 6, Dr Hunter's Rep. on Rural Labs, pp. 198, 253; 'The Leather Trades of Birmingham', *Saddlers, Harness Makers and Carriage Builders Gazette*, December 1873–January 1874; Thomas Middlemore, 'The Birmingham' Saddlery Trade' in Timmins, pp. 474–5; W. J. Gordon, *Midland Sketches*, London: 1898, p. 120.

136 Japp, *Industrial Curiosities*, pp. 146–7.

137 PP 1890, (169) XVII, SC Sweating, 5th Rep., p. xxxvl; *Morning Chronicle*, 23 and 30 January 1851. R. L. Greenall, 'The History of Boot and Shoemaking at Long Buckby', *Northamptonshire Past and Present*, V:5, pp. 437–45 is a welcome study of one of the new Northamptonshire outworking villages – one which remained a centre of the band-sewn trade down to the

end of the nineteenth century. Oddly it omits to mention Long Buckby's peculiar political complexion; in the 1840s it was a kind of Chartist commune, whose activities can be followed in the *Northern Star*.

138 Walter Rose, *Fifty Years Ago*, Haddenham: 1920s, p. 27; Joseph Severn, *The Life Story of a Phrenologist*, Hove: 1929, p. 58; George Sturt, *The Wheelwright's Shop*, Cambridge: 1963, p. 57.

139 *Morning Chronicle*, 4 July and 8 August 1850; Christopher Thomson, *The Autobiography of an Artisan*, London: 1847, pp. 166–7, 171.

140 *Morning Chronicle*, 29 August 1850.

141 Alfred Williams, *Life in a Railway Factory*, London: 1915, p. 56; W. Mosses, *The History of the United Patternmakers Association, 1872–1922*, n.p.: 1922; J. W. F. Rowe, *Wages in Theory and Practice*, London: 1928, p. 93; 'Pattern Making and Capitalism', *The Socialist*, November 1904 (this last is an exceedingly interesting article, written by a patternmaker and describing the way his fellows were being robbed of their skill; I am grateful to Anna Davin for the reference); Strauss et al., *England's Workshops*, pp. 217, 243; Wynter, *Our Social Bees*, 1st series, p. 220. For the new classes of coopers' industrial ware, see Gilding, 'Journeymen Coopers'.

142 T. A. Welton, 'Forty Years of Industrial Changes', *Trans. Manchester Stat. Soc.*, 1897, p. 168; Sir Westcott Abell, *The Shipwright's Trade*, Cambridge: 1948, pp. 108–11.

143 Charles Knight, 'Localised Handicrafts in South Midlands Agricultural Districts', *British Almanac Companion*, London: 1861, p. 27. There is a good general account of the industry in L. J. Mayes, *The History of Chairmaking in High Wycombe*, London: 1960.

144 *Morning Chronicle*, 12 September 1850.

145 Oral History: conversation of the writer with Charles Connor, 10 December 1972; Mr Connor started work as a cooper in the London docks in 1912.

146 Goldsmith's Coll., Condition of the Working Classes of Edinburgh and Leith, 1853.

147 *Morning Chronicle*, 8 and 22 August 1850; for difficulties in assembling a kit of cabinet-making tools, see *The Life and Struggles of William Lovett*, London: 1876, pp. 28–30. 'A workman was not thought much of without a good chest of tools', Islington Ref. Lib., MS Diary of Henry Price, 1824–1905, p. 12 (Price was a cabinet-maker who worked in the London piano industry).

148 When the premises of Messrs Holland and Hannen, the Bloomsbury builders, were destroyed by fire in 1866, joiners' tools were

valued from £4 and £5 to as much as £50 or £60 a man. *Annual Register*, August 1866, II, p. 124. Darlington joiners in the same year estimated the average value of their tools at £20, with 'not less than 1s. 6d. a week' for replenishment and repair, *Darlington and Stockton Times*, 23 June 1866; *Morning Chronicle*, 11 July 1850; 'Labour and the Poor, Met. Dists LIX, Carpenters & Joiners', p. 5 is full of valuable details about tool insurance.

149 Levi, *Wages and Earnings*, pp. 146–7.

150 Mosses, *History of the United Patternmakers*, p. 9; J. W. C. Haldane, *Life as an Engineer*, London: 1904, p. 76; *The Autobiography of Peter Taylor*, Paisley: 1903, p. 90; Webb Coll., UK Pattern Makers Assoc., Monthly Reports, May 1886.

151 *The Cabinet and Upholstery Advertiser,* 14 December 1878.

152 H. J. Fryth and Henry Collins, *The Foundry Workers*, Manchester: 1959, p. 44; Ure, *Dictionary*, II, p. 203.

153 *Personal Recollections of English Engineers*, p. 218; Ure, *Dictorionary*, II, p. 203.

154 For the trade union, H. J. Fyrth and Henry Collins, *The Foundry Workers, a Trade Union History*, Manchester: 1958. For the restrictive practices, see *Capital and Labour*, 22 April 1874; W. G. Riddell, *Adventures of an Obscure Victorian*, London: 1932, pp. 33–6, Booth MSS, 8.89, fol. 55'; PP 1867–8, (3980-1) XXXIX, RC Trade Unions, QQ. 13, 176–13, 211. Ure decsribes the moulders as 'a very numerous class of mechanics demanding and receiving high wages': Ure, *Dictorionary*, II, p. 203.

155 S. F. Walker, 'Starting an Engineering Business II', *Practical Engineer*, 1907, XXV, quoted in Roderick Floud, *The British Machine-Tool Industry, 1850–1914*, Cambridge: 1976, p. 50; Baines, *Industrial North*, pp. 50–1; Edward Cressy, *A Hundred Years of Mechanical Engineering*, London: 1937, p. 208; Floud, *British Machine-Tool Industry*, pp. 42, 51, 53, 55–8, 60, 65, 67. For a helpful discussion of this point, Goldsmith's Coll., Condition of the Working Class of Edinburgh Smiths; H. W. Strong, *Industries of North Devon*, Rep. Newton Abbot 1971, p. xiii; J. E. Bellis, 'A History of G. E. Bellis & Co.', *Newcomen Soc.*, 1965, XXXVII; L. N. Bun, 'Watford & Papermaking', *Newcomen Soc.*, 1945–7, XXV, p. 105; A. Hawkes, 'Intensified Production', *Trans. Birmingham Assoc. of Engineers*, 1907, p. 9 for some contemporary examples. 'Speciality of Manufacture is a Peculiarity of All the Great Iron Establishments in England and in Many in Scotland', Goldsmiths Coll., Samuel Kydd, 'The Condition of the People', fol. 86.

156 Wal Hannington, *Never on Our Knees*, London: 1967, pp. 28–9. This book should be warmly commended to anyone who cares about London history or who would like to read

the autobiography of a fine agitator. There are brief references to the St Pancras Ironworks in the *Architects and Contractors Handbook*, London: 1883, pp. 32, 39, 112, which has some drawings of its products, and Ronald H. Clark, *The Development of the English Steam Wagon*, Norwich: 1963, p. 58.

157 W. F. Watson, *Machines and Men: An Autobiography of an Itinerant Mechanic*, London: 1935, p. 21; Wal Hannington, *The Rights of Engineers*, London: 1944, p. 13; Rowe, *Wages in Theory*, pp. 106–7. For the use of grindstone as an unofficial meeting place, *Autobiography of Peter Taylor*, p. 55.

158 For a brief description of a workshop in 1870s Shoreditch, see George Barnes, *From Workshop to War Cabinet*, London: 1924, pp. 26–7.

159 Rowe, *Wages in Theory*, pp. 106–7; R. B. Hodgson, *Machines and Tools Employed in the Working of Sheet Metals*, Manchester: 1903, p. 217; *Autobiography of Peter Taylor*, pp. 80–2; Haldane, *Life as an Engineer*, p. 69.

160 James Jefferys, *The Story of the Engineers, 1800–1945*, London: 1945, pp. 24, 55–6; Rowe, *Wages in Theory*, pp. 90–2, 263–6.

161 Jefferys, *Story of the Engineers*, pp. 59, 101, 123; Rowe, *Wages in Theory*, pp. 90–2, 101–2; Cressy, *Mechanical Engineering*, p. 208.

162 For some examples, *Autobiography of Peter Taylor*, pp. 127, 137, 145, 166; W. G. Riddell, *The Thankless Years*, London: 1948, p. 146; David Kirkwood, *My Life of Revolt*, London: 1935, pp. 53, 60.

163 For the relationship of boy to adult-male labour at two leading machine-builders, PP 1864, (3414-I) XXII, 3rd Rep. Children's Emp. Com., c.22–6.

164 Rousiers, *Labour*, pp. 254–5.

165 Williams, *Our Iron Roads*, p. 250.

166 *Autobiography of Peter Taylor*, p. 105; Kenneth Hudson, *Working to Rule*, Bath: 1970, pp. 38–9, 50–1, 52–3.

167 Williams, *Our Iron Roads*, p. 190; for a splendid description of the smith's work at Swindon in later times, see Alfred Williams, *Life in a Railway Factory*, London: 1920, pp. 82–8.

168 *Hugh Stowell Brown, His Autobiography*, ed. W. S. Came, London: 1887.

169 Eric N. Simons, *Lockwood & Carlisle Ltd: A Chapter of Marine History*, Sheffield: 1962, pp. 10, 11.

170 Riddell, *The Thankless Years*, p. 22.

171 Robert Armstrong, *Rudimentary Treatise on Steam Boilers*, London: 1850, p. 98; George Piggott, 'Boiler Plate Working', in Timmins, p. 97. At Laird's Birkenhead, in the early 1890s, the larger boiler plates were bent by machinery, the smaller ones by

hand: James Samuelson, *Labour Saving Machinery*, London: 1893, p. 26.

172 Williams, *Our Iron Roads*, p. 230; Richard Peroni, *Industrial Lancashire*, Hendon Mill: 1976, p. 128; Robert Armstrong, *Steam Boilers*, London: 1865, pp. 141–2; Goldsmith's Coll., Kydd, 'Condition of the People', fol. 88.

173 Williams, *Life in a Railway Factory*, p. 113.

174 David Pollock, *Modern Shipbuilding*, London: 1884, p. 136; David Pollock, *The Shipbuilding Industry: Its History, Practice, Science and Finance*, London: 1905, p. 122, For the hand-riveting of gun-carriages, J. S. Jeans, *Notes on Northern Industries*, London: 1878, p. 117; for its use in galvanised iron, PP 1864, (3414–1) XXII, 3rd Rep. Children's Emp. Com. b. 166. For the relationship of boys to men in the riveting gangs, PP 1864, (3414–1) XXII, 3rd Rep. Children's Emp. Com. c. 64–73; *Illustrated Exhibitor*, 30 August 1851, p. 233; Williams, *Our Iron Roads*, p. 181.

175 Bell, *At the Works*, pp. 68–70.

176 Ure, *Dictionary*, II, pp. 579–80; *The Engineer*, 19 and 26 May 1865; Baines, *Industrial North*, p. 25, *Ironworkers Journal*, 15 April 1872, pp. 2–3; Williams, *Life in a Railway Factory*, p. 17.

177 Sir George Head, A *Home Tour of the Manufacturing Districts*, London: 1835, pp. 130–1.

178 Haldane, *Steam Ships*; 'Rolling Armour Plates', *The Builder*, 21 September 1867.

179 W. Graham, 'Tin and Tinplate', in Bevan, *Manufacturing Industries*, p. 168; Henry Loveridge, 'Wolverhampton Trades', in Timmins, p. 118; see also Timmins, p. 639.

180 Ure, *Dictionary*, I, pp. 904–5; James Wilson, 'On the Manufacture of Articles from Steel, Particularly Cutlery', *Soc. of Arts J.*, 11 April 1856, IV, pp. 357–61, G. I. H. Lloyd, *The Cutlery Trades*, London: 1913, p. 37.

181 Robert K. Dent, *Old and New Birmingham: A History of the Town and Its People*, Birmingham: 1880; PP 1880, (c. 6330) XIX, Fact Insp. Reps pp. 27–8; W. Graham, 'Brass Founding', Bevan, *Manufacturing Industries*, p. 146; Edward Peyton, 'The Manufacture of Iron and Brass Bedsteads', in Timmins, p. 627; PRO HO 45/00115/B 12393/K; HO 45/8124/28; PP 1862, (179) XXII, 4th Rep. Med. Off. Privy Council, App. IV, p. 144; W. Graham, *The Brassfounders Manual*, London: 1868, pp. 8, 10–16, 20–21, 28. 'Brassfounding is not a round of ... mechanical operations ... it is a "craft and mystery" of the utmost variety, and of ever-increasing novelty and improvement': Goldsmith's Coll., Thomas Cooper, 'Pictures of the People', fol. 4.

182 Marx, *Capital*.

183 For woad workers, see Norman T. Willis, *Woad in the Fens*, Lincoln: 1970; H. O. Clerk and Rex Wailes, 'The Preparation of Woad in England', *Newcomen Soc.*, XVI, 1935–6; J. B. Hurry, *The Woad Plant and its Dye*, Oxford: 1930 (I am grateful to Eve Hostettler for these references). For tin miners, see PP 1861, (161) XVI, 3rd Rep. MO Privy C., pp. 130–1; PP 1864, (3389) XXIV, Comm. on Non-Inspected Mines, pp. VIII, XIV–XV. For boilermakers, see Williams, *Railway Factory*, p. 115.

184 J. S. Wright, 'On the Employment of Women in Factories in Birmingham', *Trans. Nat Ass. Soc. Science*, 1857, pp. 539–40.

185 George Smith, *The Cry of the Children, from the Brickyards of England*, Leicester: 1871, p. 11; PP 1873, (c.745) XIX, Fact. Insp. Reps, pp. 14–15; PP 1866, (c.3675) XXIV, 5th Rep. Ch. Emp. Com., K. 55–9. At a Tipton yard it was estimated that the girl clay-earners, who brought clay to the moulder's table made 300 journeys a day, travelling 17 miles and carrying an average weight of 8 tons each. They earned the clay in their arms or on the head. PP 1865, (3473) XX, Fact. Insp. Reps, p. 22.

186 *Autobiography of Peter Taylor*, p. 76.

187 PP 1865, (3548) XX, 4th Rep. Ch. Emp. Com., Q. 68, and generally QQ. 64–79 and pp. xlii–xlv.

188 Booth, *Life and Labour*, 2nd series, II, p. 136.

189 Dodd, *Days at the Factories*.

190 PP 1912–13, (Cd 6184) XXVI, Rep. Shuttle-Kissing.

191 *Morning Chronicle*, 4 March 1850.

192 William Felkin, 'The Lace & Hosiery Trades of Nottingham', *Stat. Soc. J.*, 1866, XXIX, pp. 536–8.

193 E. J. Hobsbawm, 'The Tramping Artisan' in his *Labouring Men* is the fundamental article on this subject.

194 Goldsmith's Coll., Kydd, 'Condition of the People', fol. 88. 'As to the boilermakers, the number, vary with the work. We have never less than forty or fifty, and at present we have 100': Captain Watson, Gen. Supt. Cunard Co., Rep., *Unemployed in Liverpool*, Liverpool: 1894. For the still greater irregularity of employment in the ship repair yards, Howell Coll., Am. Soc. of Shipwrights, 60th Q. Rep January–March 1897, p. 17, and January–March 1899, p. 1.

195 Fyrth and Collins, *The Foundry Workers*, p. 4411. For the remarkable turnover in TU membership, partly reflecting this high level of unemployment, Howell Coll., Friendly Soc. of Iron Founders, Ann. Rep. 1887, p. 10; see also Fyrth and Collins, *The Foundry Workers*, p. 57.

196 Webb Coll., Glass Bottle Makers of Yorkshire, Q. Reps, 12 June 1909, XXII, p. 76. For fluctuations of employment in the flint glass trade, see Rousiers, *Labour*, pp. 52–3.

197 For a valuable and extended discussion of the theme, see Habakkuk, *American and British Technology*. Habakkuk's study had provoked an extensive critical literature. Among the more accessible studies are those reprinted in S. B. Saul (ed.), *Technological Change, the United States and Britain in the 19th Century*, London: 1970; and D. H. Aldcroft (ed.), *The Development of British Industry and Foreign Competition, 1875–1914*, London: 1968.

198 *The Builder*, 28 September 1878, XXXVI, pp. 1010–11, for an early account of it. Coleman, *Railway Navvies*, p. 50; Sir Bosdin Leech, *History of The Manchester Ship Canal*, Manchester: 1907, II, p. 22; Samuelson, *Labour Saving Machinery*, pp. 76–7; J. Swift, 'Engineering', in Galton, *Workers*, p. 103.

199 *Ironmonger*, 18 January 1879, XXI, p. 69. For the extensive controversy on the comparative merits of English and American locks, see *Ironmonger*, 18 January 1879, XXI, pp. 35, 43, 52–3, 74–9, 106, 133, 199, 172–4, 251, 323, 338; for an anticipation of it, Elihu Burritt, *Walks in the Black Country and its Green Borderland*, London: 1868, p. 213.

200 PP 1854–5, (o.11)L, Committee on Machinery, p. 69; Ure, *Dictionary*, II, p. 216.

201 John T. Day, 'The Boot and Shoe Trade', in Cox, *British Industries*, p. 239.

202 Reference temporarily mislaid. For transatlantic contrasts of the same kind in tinplate working: J. H. Jones, *The Tinplate Industry*, London: 1914, pp. 130–1.

203 Great Exhibition of 1851, *Juries Report*, I, p. 428; PP 1854–5, (o.11)L, Committee on Machinery, p. 52.

204 Marx, *Capital*, pp. 390–1; S. J. Chapman, *The Cotton Industry and Trade*, London: 1905, p. 30; L. G. Sandberg, 'American Rings and English Mules: The Role of Economic Rationality', in S. B. Saul, *Technological Change: The U.S. and Britain in the Nineteenth Century*, London: 1970.

205 Church, *Great Victorian Boom*, p. 44; A. J. Taylor, 'Labour Productivity and Technical Innovation in the Coal Industry 1859–1914', *Econ. H. R.*, 1961, 2nd series, XIV. For the apparent slowing down of mining productivity, whether because of worker resistance or a declining proportion of face workers: R. Walters, 'Labour Productivity in the South Wales Steel Industry, 1870–1914', *Econ. H. R.*, May 1975, 2nd series, XXVIII:2.

206 Hobsbawm, 'British Gas Workers', in *Labouring Men*, pp. 160–1, Webb Coll., E, A:XLI, fol. 298; Will Thorne, *My Life's Battles*, London: 1925, pp. 64–5.

207 Clara Lowe, *God's Answers: A Record of Miss Macpherson's Work at Spitalfields*, London: 1882, p. 25.

208 Church, 'The British Leather Industry and Foreign Competition 1870–1894', *Econ. H. R.*, 2nd series, XXIV, 1971, pp. 549–50.

209 W. Turner Berry, 'Printing', in C. Singer et al. (eds), A *History of Technology*, Oxford: 1958, V, p. 713.

210 For the workers' opposition, *cf.* Jaffray papers, British Museum Add. MSS 57576, 57623.

211 Bill Benfield, 'Women Bookbinders and the Bible Strike of 1849', in *The Workshop Trades*.

212 Alan Fox, A *History of the National Union of Boot and Shoe Trade Operatives, 1874–1957*, Oxford: 1958, pp. 14–15.

213 C. P. R. Mountfield, 'The Footwear Industry of the East Midlands', *East Midlands Geographer*, June 1966, IV:1. In Leeds and Bristol, riveting marked the beginning of wholesale manufacture: *Boot and Shoe Trade Journal*, 24 October, I, p. 885, and XVI, p. 3, and 26 January 1884, XIII, pp. 56–7.

214 *Boot and Shoe Trade Journal*, 23 April 1892, XXVII, p. 535.

215 *Oliver's, 1869–1950*, Leicester: 1950, p. 8; Northampton Ref. Lib., *Recollections of William Arnold*, pp. 20–3; for another description of the process, *Boot and Shoe Trade Journal*, 12 February 1881, VII, p. 77.

216 Alan Fox, A *History of the National Union Boot and Shoe Operatives, 1874–1957*, Oxford: 1958, p. 15; for some contemporary references to outworking riveters, *Boot and Shoe Trades Chronicle*, I, August 1879 (Daventry), and p. 22 (Leicester).

217 *Ironmonger*, 30 November 1870, XII, pp. 1010–11, and 31 October 1871, XIII, p. 912.

218 *Ironmonger*, 3 May 1879, XXI, p. 541.

219 Reference temporarily mislaid.

220 Andrew Wynter, *Our Social Bees*, London: 1861, p. 189. The description of earlier stages of the needle-making process is taken from Ure and from W. C. Alken, 'Needles', in Bevan, *Manufacturing Industries*, pp. 106–7.

221 *Pottery Gazette*, 1 April 1882, VI, p. 343.

222 Thomas Phipson, 'The Pin Trade', in Timmins, p. 601; S. R. H. Jones, 'Price Associations and Competition in the British Pin Industry', *Econ. H. R.*, May 1973, 2nd series, XXVI:2; Ure, *Dictionary*, III, pp. 458–9; C. Violet Butler, 'Pins', in *Victoria County History of Gloucestershire*, London: 1907, II, p. 207.

223 *Pottery Gazette*, 1 April 1882, VI, p. 343; Harold Owen, *The Staffordshire Potter*, London: 1901, p. 311.

224 For accessible accounts, see Owen, pp. 63–71; An Old Potter, *When I Was a Child*, London: 1903, pp. 186–7. Quote from S. J. Thomas, 'Pottery', in F. Gaitan (ed.), *Workers on their Industries*, London: 1895, p. 191.

225 *Pottery Gazette*, 1 November 1879, p. 428; *Pottery and Glass Trades Gazette*, April 1881, V, p. 305.

226 James Caird, *English Farming in 1851*, London: 1851, pp. 21, 84; Isaac Mead, *The Life Story of an Essex Lad*, Chelmsford: 1923, pp. 32–4, for a good description of threshing barley by hand in the 1880s.

227 Fussell, *Dairy Farming*, pp. 198–9; David Taylor, 'The English Dairy Industry, 1860–1930', *Econ. H. R.*, 2nd series, 1976, XXIX:4.

228 Kenneth Hudson, *Towards Precision Shoemaking*, Newton Abbot: 1968, p. 10; Clapham, *Economic History*, II, p. 79, quoting an article by G. Richards in *Trans. Inst. of Mechanical Engineers*, 1885.

229 S. and B. Webb, *Industrial Democracy*, London: 1920, p. 395; PP 1864, (3414-I) XXII, 3rd Rep. Children's Emp. Com. p. 392.

230 'The Cutlery Trade of Sheffield', in Cox, *British Industries*, p. 47.

231 *Ironmonger*, 31 October 1871, p. 913; *Illustrated Exhibitor*, 23 August 1851. When Messrs Wheatman and Smith of Sheffield tried to introduce machinery into saw grinding, the men's trade union attempted to blow the works up. Frank Hill, 'Combinations in Sheffield', *Trades Societies and Strikes*, 1860, p. 582.

232 PP 1863, (3170) XVIII, Children's Emp., 1st Rep. App., pp. 267, 289.

233 William Charley, 'Flax in Ireland', *Journ. Soc. Arts*, 10 February 1860, VII, p. 202. The finer classes of Irish linen were still being made by hand in the 1870s. *The Textile Manufacturer*, 15 March 1875, p. 104.

234 'The Miscellaneous Trades', in Timmins, pp. 641–2. Charles Tomlinson, *Cyclopedia of the Useful Arts*, London: 1866, III, p. 190.

235 For some examples, see *The British Clayworker*, August 1897, VI, p. 112, and April 1893, VII, p. 33.

236 Prof. Wrightson, 'Agricultural Machinery', p. 137 in Bevan, *Manufacturing Industries*.

237 William Fairbairn, 'On the Durability and Preservation of Iron Ships and on Riveted Joints', *Proceedings of the Royal Society*, 1872–3, XXI, pp. 260–3.

238 Ure, *Dictionary*, II, p. 480. 'Three essential things were necessary in the manufacture of good chain cables, neither of which is cheap, viz. the best of iron, the best workmanship and the best coal': *Mechanics Magazine*, 30 March 1860, III, p. 209.

239 C. S. Orwin and E. H. Whetham, *British Agriculture, 1846–1914*, London: 1964, p. 348; *cf.* F. Clifford, 'The Labour Bill in

Farming', *Royal Ag. Soc. J.*, 1875, 2nd series, XI p. 87; Fussell, *Dairy Farming*, pp. 198–9.

240 Hackney Ref. Lib., *The Life Story of T. J. Hunt.*

241 'Steam power or gas power cannot be used – heavy machinery must be tabooed, for the house would not bear its vibrations, were the landlord willing to allow it to be introduced – and he generally stipulates that it may not': 'London Shoe Factories', *Boot and Shoe Trade Journal*, 18 November 1882, X, p. 257.

242 *The Builder*, 19 October 1878.

243 *Iron and Steel J.*, 1895, XLVIII, pp. 326–7.

244 *Morning Chronicle*, 4 July 1850.

245 PP 1871, (440) LXII, Census of Production.

246 For the 'bull' week in the Sheffield trades (and the 'calf' and 'cow' weeks preceding it): PRO, HO 45/9833/B 9744/2, *Labour News*, 28 November 1874, and 2 January 1875; *Ironmonger*, 31 December 1860, II, p. 209, and 31 December 1863, V, p. 353.

247 W. E. Minchinton, *The British Tinplate Industry, a History*, Oxford: 1957, pp. 35, 40: 'As the demand did not yet exist for a standardized product there were no economic advantages to be secured by building larger works.'

248 'On Rolling Heavy Iron', *Trans. S. Wales Insc. of Engineers*, 1860–61, II, p. 78.

249 Floud, *British Machine-Tool Industry*, pp. 51, 55–8.

250 Museum of Eng. Rural Life, Reading, Ransome Collection (I am grateful to Alun Howkins for this reference).

251 Floud, *British Machine-Tool Industry*, pp. 51, 55–6, 67.

252 *Ironmonger*, 30 September 1865, VII, p. 136.

253 *Ironmonger*, March 1873, XV, p. 291; 10 August 1878, XX, p. 799.

254 Samuel Sidney, *Rides on Railways*, London: 1851, p. 96. Marx, *Capital*, vol. 1, p. 337.

255 *Ironmonger*, 28 February 1880, XXIII, pp. 298–9; W. K. V. Gale, 'Notes on the Black Country Iron Trade', *Newcomen Soc.* 1943–5, XXIV, pp. 2–4.

256 J. D. Marshall and M. Davies-Shiel, *The Industrial Archaeology of the Lake Counties*, Newton Abbot: 1969, pp. 174–7; *Stephenson's New Guide to Southport*, Southport: 1885, p. 92; J. M. H. Hunter, 'The Location of Industry in Greater Nottingham', *East Mids Geographer*, December 1964, III, p. 341.

257 For country coopers, see Bob Gilding, 'The Journeymen Coopers of East London', *History Workshop*, 1971; M. E. Bulkley, *Minimum Rates in the Boxmaking Indusctry*, London: 1915, p. 4. For handmade work in paper bag making, mainly for local orders, H. L. Williams, *The Workers Industrial Index*

to London, London: 1881, pp. 10–11; Booth MSS A. 17, Part A, fol. 79, B. 02, fol. 53.

258 J. T. Sampson, 'Paper Staining', *Artisans' Reports on the Paris Exhibition of 1889*, p. 517.

259 Gervase Wheeler, *The Choice of a Dwelling*, London: 1872, p. 260. *Cf.* also Great Exhibition of 1851, *Juries Reports*, II, p. 1204.

260 Timmins, p. 66.

261 For some early attempts, *Patent Journal*, 1847–8, IV, p. 266; *Journ. Soc. Arts*, 30 September 1859, p. 707; Ure, *Dictionary*, II, pp. 202–3. For the very well-sustained workers' opposition to file-cutting machinery, see *Ironmonger*, 30 August 1862, IV, p. 234, and 30 May 1863, V, p. 147, and 1 October 1874, XVI, p. 1233, and numerous reports during the big file-cutters strike of 1866. For workers' opposition in later years, see Webb, *Industrial Democracy*, p. 395n; Talbot Baines, *The Industrial North in the Last Decade of the Nineteenth Century*, Leeds: 1928, p. 63; PP 1886, (C.4715) XXI, RC Depression of Trade, QQ. 1150, 1184–1209.

262 *Ironmonger*, 10 August 1878, XX, p. 792.

263 For examples in copper braziery, see *Ironmonger*, 15 November 1879, XXII, p. 625, and 25 September 1880, XXIV, p. 338.

264 Arthur Shadwell, *Industrial Efficiency*, London: 1906, I, p. 150.

265 *Ironmonger*, October 1877, XIX, p. 388.

266 S. C. L. Fuller, 'Machinery in the Carriage Manufactory', *Papers Read before the Institute of British Carriage Manufacturers, 1883–1901*, p. 361.

267 [Reference missing in MS]

268 Frank Klingender, *Art and the Industrial Revolution*, London: 1975, p. 14: Klingender uses this excellently apposite phrase to describe Sir Matthew Digby Wyatt's official catalogue of the Exhibition.

269 'Wood', in Dodd, *Curiosities of Industry*, p. 18.

270 Strauss, *England's Workshops*, p. 186; *Illustrated Exhibitor*, 7 June 1851.

271 *Illustrated Exhibitor*, 23 August 1851.

272 *Morning Chronicle*, 4 July 1850.

273 Floud, *British Machine-Tool Industry*, p. 49.

A Spiritual Elect? Robert Tressell and the Early Socialists

1 Originally published in *The Robert Tressell Lectures 1981–88*, Workers' Education Association South Eastern District, Rochester, Kent: 1988, pp. 55–69. The essay is based on the transcript of

a lecture, originally given as the annual Robert Tressell Lecture, Falaise Hall, Hastings, on 16 March 1985. Several changes from the originally published version have been made based on annotations made by Raphael Samuel to his edition of the published text.

2 Raymond Williams, 'The Ragged-Arse Philanthropists', *The Robert Tressell Lectures 1981–88*. Essay also included in Raymond Williams, *Writing in Society*, London: 1983 [ed.].

3 Ball worked painstakingly on Tressell's life and manuscripts, publishing *Tressell of Mugsborough* in 1951 and *One of the Damned* in 1973.

4 In 1905, the firm that Tressell worked for, Bruce and Burton's, was commissioned to redecorate St Andrew's church, Hastings. The church was demolished in 1970, but a small section of a mural painted by Tressell was saved and later restored, with the surviving panel put on display in the Hastings Museum and Art Gallery in 1982. The panel shows evident skill in design and execution, as well as the clear influence of William Morris and the Arts and Crafts movement [ed.].

5 The 'Finsbury Park Impossibilist' was Alex Anderson, one of the founders of the Socialist Party of Great Britain – 'impossibilists' because of their rejection of immediate social or economic reform under capitalism, after it split from the SDF in 1904 [ed.]

6 Samuel is here referring to the pamphlet by Marion Phillips and Averill D. Sanderson Furniss, *The Working Woman's House* [ed.]

7 Samuel is here referring to the case of Alan Thornett, who ran a branch of the Workers' Revolutionary Party (not the RWP) at the Cowley car plant, Oxford, before his expulsion in 1974, after which he went on to set up the even smaller Trotskyist group the Workers Socialist League. The incident is referred to, also, in *The Lost World of British Communism*, p. 94. [ed.].

The Roman Catholic Church and the Irish Poor

1 Originally published in Roger Swift and Sheridan Gilley (eds), *The Irish in the Victorian City*, London: 1985, pp. 267–301.

2 'New Convent and School, Newport Market, Soho', bound with *St. Patrick's, Soho, Reports and Guides*, 1870–78.

3 St Patrick's, Soho MSS, 'About St. Bridget's Confraternity'. The register is initialled 'N.T.S.' and the writer identified from the *Catholic Directory*, 1881.

4 A. M. Sullivan was a moderate nationalist and editor of *The Nation*; Father Theobald Mathew was the celebrated Irish temperance advocate.

5 'St Patrick's, Soho MSS, 'About St. Bridget's Confraternity', 28 February 1881, and 20 April 1881.

6 The title 'pleasant', however, was sometimes looked on with dismay. K. S. Inglis, *Churches and the Working Classes in Victorian England*, London: 1963, pp. 79–85.

7 In a report on the Blackburn sewing schools during the cotton famine, there is a striking contrast between the picture given of the factory girls gathered together under the aegis of the Bible women ('hoarse with reading for many hours'), at whose direction they rise from their seats to sing, 'after one or two failures in starting' –

> Come let us Join our cheerful song
> With angels round the throne

– and those in the Roman Catholic sewing school, where the singing under the direction of a priest, was by no means confined to sacred hymns: 'Whenever they sing ... as they are often asked to do, the mournful song of "Hard Time", he has it followed by "There's a Good Time coming, Girls", as a corrective.' Wigan Ref. lib., 'Y.B.'. *The Blackburn Sewing Schools*, 1863, bound with Wigan Typographical Pamphlets, VII, pp. 344, 346–7.

8 Newman to Bowden, 21 September 1849, in C. S. Dessain (ed.), *The Letters and Diaries of John Henry Newman*, London and Edinburgh: 1963, XIII, pp. 260–1. See also A. Chapman, *Father Faber*, London: 1961, p. 234, and the printed and MS volume in the Brampton Oratory archives, *The Oratory in London*, pp. 94–5. Forty-six patients were anointed, of whom thirty-four died.

9 Other songs included 'The Jolly Miller', the duet 'All's Well', and a rendering of 'An Old English Gentleman' which followed the address of thanks to the clergy of the district. Dom O. F. Blundell, *O.S.B. Broughton Catholic Charitable Society*, Preston: 1923. The society, 'a native growth of Lancashire piety and good fellowship', had been established in May 1786, 'to assist the living, who were in distress, and to have masses and prayers said for the dead'. Blundell, *O.S.B. Broughton*, pp. vii, 1. *British Catholicity, Its Position and Wants. Addressed to His Eminence Cardinal Acton*, Edinburgh: 1844, p. 16; *Oratory in London*, pp. 109–10.

10 On the agitation to protect the religious status of Catholic pauper children, see PAO HO 45/7646, HO 45/6840; Ed. 9/31; T. Burke, *Catholic History of Liverpool*, Liverpool: 1910, pp. 120–1, 130–34, 141–2, 165; Canon E. St John, *Manning's Work for Children*, London: 1929. The important question, for this subject, of soldiers is one I have not yet begun to explore. In 1861,

out of an army of 205,829 men, 58,630 were Roman Catholics. W. G. Lumley, 'The Statistics of the Roman Catholics in England and Wales', *Journ. Stat. Soc.*, London: 1864, XXVLL, p. 322. At Millbank, where the letters 'A.C.' were appended to the name of the Catholic inmate on his cell-door, there was a small room reserved for the Catholic clergyman, 'where the prisoners of that faith confess'. H. Mayhew and J. Binney, *The Criminal Prisons of London and Scenes of Prison Life*, London: 1862, p. 257, and *cf*. pp. 266, 525–7, 530, 564, 568, 569, 617, for the treatment of Catholics in London prisons.

11 *Franciscan Missions among the Colliers and Ironworkers of Monmouthshire*, London: 1876, is an admirable memoir, whose writing takes on something of the dramatic character of the countryside it describes. It is not listed in the recent bibliography of Welsh history. Lanes, CRO Archdiocese of Liverpool MSS (RCLv), Visitation Returns, 1865, Holy Cross.

12 Charles Burke, *History of the Camberwell Catholic Mission, 1860–1910*, London: n.d., p. 7.

13 Booth speaks of a 'citadel of poverty' of which Sultan Street was 'the centre' and described it as 'a strange group of streets, hemmed in on one side by the railway and entered only here and there on the other three sides like a fortress through its gates'. 'Many of the inhabitants', he writes, 'are said to be Cockney Irish and, whether Irish or not, mostly general labourers'; and he quotes with evident agreement the 'forcible language used by one of his witnesses: "a collection of streets where beastly men and women live bestially"'. Booth, *Life and Labour*, 3rd series, VI, pp. 15–19. See also H. J. Dyos, *Victorian Suburb, a Study of the Growth of Camberwell*, Leicester: 1961, p. 111.

14 D. Attwater, *The Catholic Church in Modern Wales*, London: 1935, pp. 72, 137; *Franciscan Missions*, pp. 22, 35. On Welsh hostility to Roman Catholics generally, see Attwater, *Catholic Church*, pp. 33, 38–9, 68–9, 71–2, 91, 101, 115–19, 122, 129–30, 135, 207, 223–4, 275. See also Attwater, *Catholic Church*, p. 91. On the opposition at Wednesbury, where, to undermine the foundations, a Protestant party threatened to purchase the mines and minerals beneath the chapel, see J. F. Ede, *The History of Wednesbury*, Wednesbury: 1950, p. 318; and J. F. Bromfield, *St. Mary's Parish Centenary*, Wednesbury: 1950.

15 *Franciscan Missions*, pp. 16–17.

16 R. Smith, *Ye Chronicles 306–1910 of Blackburnshire*, Nelson: 1910, p. 195. At Burnley itself, the opening of St Mary's in 1849 provoked an outburst of Protestant hostility, 'the walls of the town were flooded with no popery placards, the exterior carvings round the church were gravely damaged and the statue of Our

Lady within the church ... shot at'. Odo Blundell, *Old Catholic Lancashire*, London: 1925, I, p. 30.

17 T. Burke, *Catholic History of Liverpool*, Liverpool: 1910, p. 45.

18 *Franciscan Missions*, p. 38–9.

19 'Caswall's brother was followed by the rabble the other day in London, having a long cloke, which they took for an Oratorian. He faced round, pulled aside the cloke, and showed his trousers – When they saw him all sound below, they gave him a cheer and left him.' See Newman to Faber, 4 November 1850, in *Letters of Newman*, XIV, pp. 117–28.

20 J. F. Cassidy, *The Great Father Tom Burke*, Dublin: 1947, p. 31; W. J. Fitzpatrick, *The Life of the Very Rev. T. N. Burke*, London: 1885, I, pp. 149–52.

21 Lanes, RO DDX.177/5, 'Letters and Pictures: Liverpool'; U. Young, *Life of Father Ignatius Spencer*, London: 1933, pp. 137, 141, 143, 175, 178, 184.

22 Young, *Father Ignatius Spencer*, pp. 178, 180, 182, 197, 203; Birm. Dioc. MSS, Shrewsbury to Ullathorne, 29 June 1852.

23 Lady A. Kerr (ed.), *Sister Chatelain: or, Forty Years Work in Westminster*, London: 1900, pp. 26–7.

24 Rev. F. J. Kirk, *Reminiscences of an Oblate of St. Charles*, London: 1905, p. 99.

25 Kerr, pp. 32–3.

26 St Chad's Cath. MSS, 'Catholic Poor Schools', 21 August, 11 September, 30 November 1849. Willam Dallman, 'a very powerful, ill-looking man, lodging in London Prentice Street, was alleged to have struck the fatal blow in the Painter murder'. Joseph Allday, Full and Correct Reports of the Trials ... for the Murder of Mr. Painter, etc., Birmingham: 1835, p. 30.

27 *Rep ... St. Peter's District Visiting Society for 1844*, Birmingham: 1845, p. 3. Twenty years later the street was described of as containing 'a mixture of the worst class of Irish and of regular thieves': 'The Night Side of Birmingham', Osborne Newspaper Cuttings, II, p. 184, Birm. Ref. Lib. London Prentice Street was the scene of a famous Protestant scandal in 1848 when Father Molloy, a local Catholic priest, was accused of having seized a New Testament from one of his parishioners, and publicly burnt it in the street. For the indignant sermons, see Rev. J. C. Miller, *Bible Burning, the Substance of a Sermon*, Birmingham: 1848; Rev. I. C. Barrett, *The Protestant Bible Burnt, a Sermon*, London: 1848. 'My scripture reader was actually kicked by an Irishman, as he went out of the court, who used the strongest language and exclaimed "Break his neck!" "IT WOULD LEAD TO THE BIBLE!"', Miller, *Bible Burning*, pp. 7–8.

28 A. H. Kiernan, *The Story of the Archdiocese of Birmingham*,

Birmingham: n.d, p. 33; Carr's Lane MSS, 'Mr Clay's Journal', esp. 20 February 1839, on the difficulties among them of a town missionary.

29 Letter signed by 'an English Catholic', in *Birmingham Daily Gazette*, 1 July 1867; James Murphy, *The Religious Problem in English Education: The Crucial Experiment*, Liverpool: 1959, p. 17; Burke, *Catholic History*, p. 73.

30 *Report of the Catholic Poor School Committee*, London: 1847, pp. 65, 69.

31 Joseph O'Connor, *Hostage to Fortune*, Dublin: 1951, p. 11.

32 PRO Ed. 3:19.

33 Kirk, *Reminiscences of an Oblate*, p. 90.

34 L. G. Vere, *Random Recollections of Old Soho*, Barnet: 1912, p. 28.

35 Rev. T. Livius, *Father Furniss and His Work for Children*, London and Leamington: 1899, pp. 45, 49–50, 143; PRO Ed. 3:26, St Leonard's Bromley, Ed. 3:6, St Francis Xavier's, Seven Dials; St Peter's Reg., Birmingham, 19, 26 July 1863, 27 March, 3 April, 7 August 1864; Lancs RO RCLv Sch. Exam. & lnsp. Ret., 1858 St Pat., Wigan; Visit. Ret., 1858, The Willows; PRO Ed. 9:14, Alderson to Sandford, 28 April 1875.

36 Booth, *Life and Labour*, 3rd series, VI, p. 105; Vere, p. 248.

37 L. G. Vere, *Random Recollections of Homerton Circuit*, Barnet: 1912, p. 199. Fr Vere returned to St Patrick's, Soho, after a period of service at Homerton.

38 PRO Ed. 3:13.

39 S. J. Lond, Foley MSS, III, series 1 and 2; Burke, *Catholic History*, p. 151.

40 Vere, *Old Soho Days*, pp. 31–2.

41 St Pat., Soho, MS., 'St. Joseph's School'. In all, 71 of the 135 whose addresses are recorded came from Princes Row itself, and the remainder were drawn almost entirely from the immediately surrounding neighbourhood. In 1875 the Puseyites left, and their school in Princes Row was taken over on behalf of St Patrick's by the Poor Servants of the Mother of God: Vere, *Old Soho Days*, pp. 21–2, 31.

42 PRO Ed. 3:19, St Joseph's, Fitzroy Court.

43 The words are those of Father Barge, Missionary Rector of St Patrick's, Soho. Vere, *Old Soho Days*, p. 72.

44 Mayhew, *London Labour*, I, p. 114.

45 Father Caroll at Merthyr, an Irish priest who covered the district of Merthyr, Dowlais, Rhymney and Tredegar in the 1830s and 1840s (he died of the fever in 1847) lived in a poor workman's cottage in Dowlais, the entrance to which 'was almost blocked up by two or three sacks of meal or potatoes, which he retailed

under market price for the benefit of the poor, yet eking out thereby his own maintenance'. Attwater, *Catholic Church*, p. 74.

46 Vere, *Old Soho Days*, p. 87.

47 St Pet. Reg., Birm., 18 January, 26 April 1863, 31 January 1864. In December 1862, Fr Patrick McLaughlin, Catholic priest at Eastmuir, a village on the outskirts of Glasgow, was committed to prison for contempt of court. He had addressed an envelope for a member of his flock who was making restitution to a fellow-worker in Ireland, the letter containing money he had embezzled. Fr McLaughlin refused to disclose the name of the addressee, and served fourteen days of a thirty-day sentence to prison. J. E. Handley, *The Irish in Modern Scotland*, Cork: 1947, pp. 66–7.

48 Vere, *Old Soho Days*, pp. 54, 113. Rev. E. Price, *Sick Calls, from the Diary of a Missionary Priest*, London: 1850, pp. 423, 318–9. Price was minister at the Sardinian Chapel, Lincoln's Inn Fields.

49 St Pet. Reg. Birm., 23 November 1862, 11 January 1863. At St Oswald's Ashton-in-Makerfield, Wigan, it was requested that sick-calls 'Should be sent by some responsible person – not by children', St Osw. Reg., Ashton-in-Makerfield, 25 February 1879.

50 E. M. Sneyd-Kynnersley, *HMI: Some Passages in the Life of one of HM Inspectorate of Schools*, London: 1908, pp. 233–4.

51 Lanes, RO RCLv, Bp. Goss Visit, Diary, Great Crosby, 7–8 April 1867; J. A. M. Brennan, *Memories of an old Catholic Doctor*, London: 1937, p. 11. On early communion, Livius, *Father Furniss*, p. 116–17.

52 Booth, *Life and Labour*, 3rd series, II, p. 79. (St James the Great, on Bethnal Green Road, a church that Booth describes, at the time of his inquiry, as a 'disgrace', even amidst the 'laxity and unworthiness of the Church in this parish' [ed.].)

53 Booth, *Life and Labour*, 3rd series, VII, p. 244. In the doorways of Drury Lane, noted Fr Edward Price, even the prostitutes – 'groups of girls whose looks and attire betrayed their infamous calling' – curtseyed as he passed. Price, *Sick Calls*, pp. 396, 398. 'They are all convinced at heart', a priest remarked to Booth of the Catholic London poor, and emphasised his opinion by adding that those accounted lapsed 'were the worst of all in sending for the priest at "untimely hours"': Booth, *Life and Labour*, 3rd series, VII, p. 255.

54 Pat O'Mara, *The Autobiography of a Liverpool Irish Slummy*, London: 1934, p. 18. Cf. the description of one of his successors at St Vincent's, 'that natural fighter' and 'bitter Fenian' Father Toomer, in O'Mara, *Autobiography*, p. 69. Carr's Lane MSS, Joseph Frye's Journ., 19 March, 9 May, 4 October 1850.

55 Booth, *Life and Labour*, 3rd series, VII, p. 255. Vere, *Old Soho Days*, pp. 16–17, 43; St Mary's Wednesbury, p. 8; Ede,

Wednesbury, p. 318; PP 1836, Report on the Irish Poor in Great Britain, p. 18; Burke, *Catholic History*, p. 128.

56 O'Mara, *Autobiography*, p. 69; Booth, *Life and Labour*, 3rd series, VII, p. 246.

57 J. Denvir, *The Brandons: A Story of Irish Life in England*, London: 1903, pp. 45–6.

58 L. Faucher, *Manchester in 1844*.

59 St Pet. Birm., 'Subjects for Sermons', 28 June, 4 October 1857, 15 April 1869.

60 *The Times*, 21 August 1843. 'Amongst those who took the pledge was a man in such a drunken state that he could hardly stand, and it having been intimated to Father Mathew that it would be prudent to allow him to take the pledge while under the influence of liquor. He (Father Mathew) said, that he had had many drunken men come to him to take the pledge white under the influence of liquor, and in no one instance did he know of their breaking the promise. The man was therefore allowed to remain': *The Times*, 10 August 1843. St Pat. Soho, Rep. of 1876. For a vivid description of this kind of relationship between his mother and Father Ryan, see O'Mara, *Autobiography*, p. 123. Mayhew, *London Labour*, I, pp. 116–17.

61 Booth, *Life and Labour*, 3rd series, VII, pp. 243–4.

62 Ibid., p. 246.

63 See also Fr Daniel Hearne in the *Tablet*, 29 July 1843.

64 At their Mission Room in Haggerston, the Sisters of St Saviour's held for the children of the neighbourhood what was actually called 'Heathen Teas': Warburton, p. 137; PP 1852–3, *Rept rel. Census*, p. civiii.

65 *The Oratory in London*, I, p. 86.

66 Attwater, *Catholic Church*, p. 70.

67 PRO HO 45/6840, St Pat., Soho, Dioc. Visit, 1869, Q. 9/13; Percy Fitzgerald, *Fifty Years of Catholic Life and Social Progress*, London: 1901, II, p. 453.

68 'A London Rambler', *The Romance of the Streets*, London: 1872, p. 298.

69 Handley, *The Irish*, p. 116; Mayhew, *London Labour*, ii, p. 251.

70 Even Pagan O'Leary the Fenian, a 'fiery, truculent man', who 'delighted' in the religious implication of his soubriquet, was ready to respect the association. Questioned by prison officials after arrest, and ordered to classify himself under the heading of 'Religion' he attempted at first to claim he was a Pagan. No, they said, they could not accept that – they had headings in their books, 'Roman Catholic', 'Protestant', and 'Presbyterian', but not 'Pagan'. 'Well', he said, 'you have two kinds, "the Robbers" (meaning Protestants) and the "Beggars" (Catholics), and if I

must choose, put me down as a "Beggar".' Denvir, *Old Rebel*, p. 87.

71 Rylands lib., R.62533, Manch. News. cutt., 'The Census in the Slums, No. 2'.

72 S. Bamford, *Passages in the Life of a Radical*, London: 1905, II, p. 153.

73 'Wigan Examiner', *Local Notes and Queries*, Wigan, 1883, XI:198.

74 Mayhew, *London Labour*, I, p. 110.

75 Ibid., p. 111. Some of the English stood in fear of them. A street-patterer who had not hesitated, in quest of newsworthy sensation, to kill off the Duke of Wellington on two separate occasions – 'once by a fall from his horse, and the other time by "a sudden and mysterious death"' – felt it prudent to abstain from exercising his talents upon a comparably prominent Catholic subject: 'He once thought of poisoning the Pope, but was afraid of the street Irish', Ibid., pp. 240, 244.

76 Booth, *Life and Labour*, 3rd series, VII, p. 255; Vere, *Old Soho*, p. 27.

77 PRO Ed. 9/14, Sandford to Sandford. Matthew Arnold referred to them as 'trying material': PRO Ed. 9/14, Arnold to Sandford, 29 April 1875. Livius, *Father Furniss*, pp. 65, 160; St Chad's Cath. Reg. Birm., III, 22 November 1881; St Pet. Reg. Birm., 29 March 1863, Holy Week 1864.

78 *Wigan Observer*, 1 July 1859; *Preston Guardian*, 30 May 1868; Denvir, *Irish in Britain*, pp. 306–7.

79 Cf. e.g. Rev. P. Rogers, *Father Theobald Mathew, Apostle of Temperance*, Dublin: 1943, p. 86, for the Irishwomen at Deptford 'with shillelaghs inside their umbrellas who formed part of a selfappointed bodyguard for Father Mathew; *Aris's Birmingham Gazette*, 28 September 1867, for Mary Ann Gilmour, a rag sorter of 'Little Ireland', Dudley, who disturbed the service at the Wesleyan Free Chapel as the officiating preacher was praying for the conversion of Papists; *Ashton Reporter*, 23 May 1868, for the poor washerwoman of Flag Alley, Bridget Cullen; PRO HO 45/36331/2 for the Regent's Park disturbances of 1884, some of the Irishwomen 'having their sleeves tucked up and declaring they were going to "walk in heretic's blood"'. C. Aspin, *Haslingden*, Haslingden: 1962, p. 133, for an Irishwoman taken in charge with a rolling pin.

80 'A stick with a cog-wheel at the end', 'short sticks loaded with lead and iron', and 'portions of scythe-blades' were among the weapons recovered from the Ashton-under-Lyne Irish during the Murphy riots, LRO CPR/1. T. M. Healy, *Letters and Leaders of My Day*, London: 1928, I, pp. 24–5. During the Ashton rioting

William Ibbetson was shot in the bowels from St Mary's Roman Catholic church, while at St Peter's, Stalybridge, the parish priest himself, the Rev. Joseph Daley, was charged with wounding a man with a gun: LRO CPR/1.

81 Carr's Lane MSS, Mr Jackson's Journ., 20 July 1842, 11 August 1843; Carr's Lane MSS, Joseph Frye's Journ., 19 March, 15 May, 4 October 1850.

82 'We were once Catholics and carried Saint Colman of Cloyne about wid us in a box; but after hearing a sermon at a church about images, we went home, took the saint out of his box, and cast him into a river.' G. Borrow, *Wild Wales*, London: 1927, quote from p. 610.

83 Carr's Lane MSS, Mr Sibree's Journal, 28 February 1839.

84 A. Burton, *Rushbearing*, Manchester: 1891, p. 64.

85 M. Trench, *Life of Charles Lowder*, London: 1881, p. 80; *Preston Guardian*, 27 November 1867; *Oldham Chronicle*, 11 July 1863, in LRO QEV 18/4; Birm. Ref. Lib., Miss Journ. of R. A. Finnigan, pp. 44–5: 'abuse from a poor drunken Irishman who laid hold of me, and wanted me to fight him – it was a matter of sport to many persons, and though he tore part of my waistcoat I took it all in good part and quietly got out of his clutches'.

86 *The Christian Mission*, II:9, September 1870.

87 Ibid., II:3, March 1870, II:7, July 1870, II:4, May 1870.

88 O'Mara, *Autobiography*, p. 82; Gipsy Smith, *His Life and Work, by Himself*, London: 1901, pp. 102, 105–6. The rioting, which went on for two successive nights, was provoked by the 'several converts' Gipsy Smith had been able to record ('two young women brought their beads and rosary ... and gave them up').

89 Mayhew, *London Labour*, II, pp. 503–4.

90 J. Toole, *Fighting Through Life*, London: 1935.

91 Denvir, *Old Rebel*, p. 244.

92 Booth, *Life and Labour*, 3rd series, IV, p. 197.

93 Sexton, *Agitator*, pp. 18–19.

94 T. Barclay, *Memoirs and Medleys, the Autobiography of a Bottle-washer*, Leicester: 1934, pp. 5–8, 19.

95 George Lansbury, *My Life*, London: 1928, pp. 26–7.

96 T. A. Jackson, *Solo Trumpet*, London: 1953, referring to the time of his father's childhood.

97 *The Times*, 21 August 1843, 19 August 1843.

98 J. F. Maguire, *Father Mathew, a Biography*, London: 1863, pp. 140–1, 151–2; Rogers, *Father Theobald Mathew*, pp. 44–5, 56, 60.

99 Birm. Ref. Lib., p. 419 (IR 533), 'Father Mathew in Birmingham'.

100 Maguire, *Father Mathew*, p. 48 (I am very grateful to Mr Brian Harrison for this reference).

101 *The Times*, 9 August 1843. During the demonstration at Westminster 'the notorious captain Acherley, who professes to cure all manner of diseases by the aid of a wonderful lamp, made his appearance, and for a time divided the attention of those present', *The Times*, 25 August 1843.

102 Denvir, *Old Rebel*, pp. 13–15.

103 Livius, *Father Furniss*, p. 90; St Pet. Reg. Birm., 5 June 1964; O'Mara, *Autobiography*, pp. 143, 153, 218. Sneering at the scapular and Agnus Dei which they wore, and in one case destroying them, was one of the humiliations alleged to have been imposed upon the Fenian prisoners in Portland prison: PRO HO 45/19461. When the Manchester Martyrs, Larkin, Gould, and Allen, were executed, 'each of the men bore a cross upon his breast': *Preston Guardian*, 27 November 1867. Carr's Lane MSS, Mr Jackson's Journ., 11 August 1843; Mayhew, *London Labour*, I, p. 111.

104 Price, *Sick Calls*, p. 82; Mayhew, *London Labour*, II, p. 504, and I, p. 116; *Cf.* also Mayhew, *London Labour*, I, pp. 111, 114; E. Waugh, *Home-Life of the Lancashire Factory Folk During the Cotton Famine*, London: 1867, pp. 76, 77, 85; Denvir, *Irish in Britain*, pp. 442–3.

105 Barclay, *Memoirs and Medleys*, p. 7.

106 Mayhew, *London Labour*, I, p. 114; *Franciscan Missions*, p. 69. 'His parents, who died when he was quite young, were Irish and Catholic, and he had, of course, been baptised ... but he knew nothing himself'; occasionally he attended Mass on Sundays 'because he saw that other Catholics did so', but 'he had not the faintest notion what it meant'.

107 Barclay, *Memoirs and Medleys*, pp. 26–7.

108 'The Irish in England', *Dublin Review*, 1856, p. 504.

109 Price, *Sick Calls*, pp. 241–5; Denvir, *Old Rebel*, p. 15; *The Nation*, 7 June 1856.

110 Kirk, *Reminiscences of an Oblate*.

111 *Reminiscences of a Stonemason*, pp. 16–17; *cf.* LRO QJD 1/197 for the use of Irish during a riot against the police; *Preston Guardian*, 25 March 1868, for the use of Irish during a neighbourhood row; Borrow, *Wild Wales*, pp. 609–11, for the use of Irish in moments of embarrassment; *The Nation*, 7 June 1856, for the prevalence of Irish among the colony at Wednesbury; Birm. Ref. Lib. Journ., of T. A. Finnigan, Birmingham Town Mission, 1837–1838 and F. W. Hackwood, *Religious Wednesbury*, Wednesbury, 1902, p. 117 for the use of Irish-speaking Scripture readers.

112 Barclay, *Memoirs and Medleys*, pp. 3, 10, 23.

113 Denvir, *Irish in Britain*, pp. 259–60; St Vincent's, Sheffield,

Centenary, p. 19; Attwater, *Catholic Church*, pp. 70–1. Father Sherlock, one of the finest specimens of the good old 'soggarth aroon', presided over the first Home Rule Convention in 1873: Denvir, *Old Rebel*, pp. 176–7.

114 Mayhew, *London Labour*, I, p. 514, and *cf.* I, pp. 123, 151, 515.

115 Sunday evenings appear to have been the only time of the week when Irish servant girls were allowed by their mistresses to attend their chapels. Vincent Smith MSS, 'Catholic Tyneside', pp. 27–8; Price, *Sick Calls*, p. 324; *Birmingham Daily Gazette*, 22 May 1879. For a similar situation at the Brownlow Hill workhouse, Liverpool, see Burke, *Catholic History*, p. 133; *cf.* Birm. Dioc. MSS, 'Catholic Chapel in the Birmingham Union Workhouse', 24 February 1858; *Birmingham Daily Post*, 8 and 21 May 1879, *Birmingham Daily Gazette*, 18 November 1880. At St Patrick's, Soho, the fourth confessional in the church, 'a temporary arrangement erected by the side of the Altar of the Seven Dolours', was occasionally used 'for the deaf old people of the Workhouse during Sunday Mass': Vere, *Old Soho*, pp. 86–7.

116 Denvir, *Irish in Britain*, pp. 408, 410–12; Birm. Dioc. MSS, Lempfreed to Ullathorne, 25 December 1848: Foley MSS, IV, p. 345; Rev. B. Kelly, 'Bollington Catholicism', MS hist., 1930–40.

117 *Franciscan Missions*, p. 61. For the same complaint about the congregation at Abersychan, *Franciscan Missions*, p. 26; for a memoir of the congregation at Abertillery, M. F. Ryan, *Fenian Memories*, Dublin: 1945, p. 49.

118 *The Nation*, 7 June 1856.

119 Sneyd-Kynnersley, *HMI: Some Passages*, p. 231.

120 The Meaneys, 'a family which ... sent out many priests from Ireland to labour among the Irish poor abroad', provided two as missionary priests at Blackburn, and one at St Mary's Levenshulme. A nephew of the Blackburn Meaneys, Fr Patrick O'Connor, also worked for a time at Blackburn. Fr Denis Byrne, the first Rector at St Patrick's, Bolton, was a brother of Fr Michael Byrne, of St Marie's, Bury, and Fr Thomas Byrne of St Michael's, Manchester, Bolton. Sneyd-Kynnersley, *HMI: Some Passages*, pp. 80, 107, 109, 120–1, 143, 145, 174, 190, 212. Father Tracy of Heaton Norris, Stockport, who seems himself to have been a Nationalist sympathiser, had a brother, Mat, a reporter on the *Cork Examiner*, who was able for carrying a musket during the Fenian rising of 1867, but was able to extract compensation from the British Government for wrongful arrest. 'Friends gathered round him night after night, to enjoy his compensation and hospitality. At the end of his ... evenings he would raise his glass

in pathetic self-pity, crying, "Ah, boys! the British Government has been the ruin of me".' Healey, I, p. 25.

121 *Franciscan Missions*, p. 27; Bolton, pp. 184, 192. When the foundation stone was laid at St Vincent's, Liverpool (a ceremony observed on St Patrick's Day, 1856): 'The Irish ship carpenters of the parish passed in single file, each faying one day's wages on the newly blessed stone. Then followed the dock labourers with their offerings, the total amounting to one hundred pounds, nine shillings': Burke, *Catholic History*, p. 126. *Franciscan Missions*, pp. 39–40, 59; Foley, MSS, III, series 1, II, p. 579; P. Alden, 'The Problem of East London', in R. Mudie-Smith (ed.), *The Religious Life of London*, London: 1904, p. 38; Denvir, *Irish in Britain*, p. 303; Booth, *Life and Labour*, 3rd series, I, pp. 83, 88, 233, and II, pp. 38–9, and IV, p. 127, and V, p. 68, and VII, pp. 243, 265.

122 Birm. Dioc. MSS, Phillips to Walsh, 12 September 1836. RCLv, Visit. Rets, 1855–8.

123 George Eliot, *Adam Bede*, Edinburgh and London: 1878, I, p. 52.

124 W. Bowman, *England in Aston-under-Lyne*, Ashton-under-Lyne: 1963, p. 23; RCLv, 'Notes on Diocesan History'; Bolton, p. 150.

125 Burke, *Catholic History*, p. 123.

126 Ed. W. Astle, 'Stockport Advertiser', *Centenary History of Stockport*, Stockport, 1922, p. 141; Bolton, p. 177; Kirk, *Reminiscences of an Oblate*, p. 32.